The Atlas of
LOST CULTS
and mystery religions

The Atlas of LOST CULTS

and mystery religions

Rediscover extraordinary traditions from the dawn of time

DAVID DOUGLAS

A GODSFIELD BOOK

An Hachette Livre UK Company
www.hachettelivre.co.uk

First published in Great Britain in 2009 by
Godsfield Press, a division of Octopus Publishing Group Ltd
2–4 Heron Quays, London E14 4JP
www.octopusbooks.co.uk
www.octopusbooksusa.com

Distributed in the United States and Canada by
Hachette Book Group USA,
237 Park Avenue, New York, NY 10017 USA

ISBN 978-1-84181-334-9

A CIP catalogue record for this book is available from the British Library

Printed and bound in China

2 4 6 8 10 9 7 5 3 1

CONTENTS

Introduction

What names shall we give belief? Or faith? Or religion? Humankind has found a huge wealth of ways to seek the Divine, worship the sacred and understand the powers that govern life. Many movements have come and gone, unable to survive the rigours of opposition that they have faced. Others have lost their way and foundered in a desert of their own making. Some have lost their leaders, their high priests and priestesses and have let their people down.

Great flowerings of spiritual knowledge have taken place, only to be cut down by authorities that refused to countenance their existence. Others have gone underground, some so deep that questions over their continued existence are still debated by the general populace – even though their initiates know the truth. Other movements have sustained themselves over thousands of years. Some have simply disappeared and are truly lost for ever.

In an age when questions about faith and religion are becoming more important, it seems only wise to ask where, as a people, we have travelled in the many lands of the Divine? What are the strands of belief that have influenced our current world, and from where do they originate? Are there aspects of the world's major religions that we simply don't understand? Are there philosophical and religious systems that the world has rejected, unaware that a spiritual pearl of great value had been neglected or destroyed?

ENDURING FAITH

Lost cults they may be, but what is often remarkable about the religious movements that have disappeared is their ability to live on in subtle, symbolic and sometimes metaphorical ways. To the trained eye and the open heart, the cults of gods and goddesses from ancient Greece, Rome, Egypt or Sumeria, for instance, will suddenly make themselves visible in modern life. Myths and legends that informed worship are found to have deep resonance today in new forms: the Goddess can be found in modern towns and villages; the influence of the stars is still present in the pages of newspapers; and nature still tells us when to celebrate and when to rest, when to dance and when to die. Spiritual meaning is everywhere and the profound influence of spiritual traditions pervades our landscape, whether we see it or not.

It is also worth remembering that one person's cult is another person's mainstream: where belief and faith are concerned, it is all too easy to accept political ideas of democracy: that the largest religion must be the best, or at least the one that should be accepted by the people. The separation of religion and state is one of the gifts of the modern world, and the ability to pursue one's own individual spiritual path without fear of persecution or death is a relatively recent advance in some countries. We all know of places where such freedom does not yet exist, or where it is under threat.

SECRET AND MYSTERY RELIGIONS

The history of religion is also a history of abuses of power. Many 'cults' have disappeared through persecution, while others have become too dominant and have overwhelmed those who would prefer to think other thoughts and worship other gods. The middle ground of tolerance and freedom has sometimes been a small, or even non-existent, area. With this landscape, it comes as no surprise that some religious and spiritual traditions have decided to remain secret: even though they may wish to transform the world, they will achieve this slowly, one heart at a time. Many are still engaged in the struggle.

Mystery religions have a habit of flowering and dying, only to be resurrected in another historical cycle. Gnosticism, for example, is a strand of worship that has existed in many cultures at different times – in the early centuries of the Christian Era as Hermeticism (which underwent a revival during the Renaissance), and in the faith of the medieval French Cathars during the 11th to 13th centuries CE. Just when the religious authorities believe they have stamped out heresy, it rears its head, phoenix-like, to let the faithful know that while people may be persecuted, tortured and executed for their beliefs, the truth cannot be killed. Truth, if it is real, will return and find new forms. This is one of the triumphs of ideas. In the modern day, Tibetan Buddhism has provided an example: while the Chinese People's Liberation Army may have been the cause of hundreds of thousands of deaths among Tibetan Buddhists following their invasion of Tibet in 1950, the faith only seems to have become stronger as a result. Its new journey around the world has seen it attract many new adherents.

Left *Simon de Montfort died while fighting in the Albigensian Crusade against Catharism, a Christian sect. While cults such as this have been actively destroyed, many develop into others or seemingly disappear, only to re-emerge centuries later.*

Right *Siva is one of the main tenets of Hinduism, as is Sakta, or goddess worship. Religions based upon the worship of goddesses have often adapted certain characteristics and traits of previous goddesses.*

ESOTERIC TRADITIONS

It is also important to realize that for every outer form of major religion – Christian, Jewish, Islamic, Buddhist, Shinto – there is a corresponding inner form or esoteric tradition that has been kept for the initiated. Many spiritual traditions are like reinforced fortresses, with their citadels hiding behind multiple layers of protective shields. Spiritual treasures, their adherents say, should not be given away lightly to those who would not value them. For those who seek a way to their centre, these traditions can be forbidding, challenging, frightening. The way will not be made easy for the seeker – this is one of the marks of the esoteric traditions. In contrast to

widely available, exoteric faiths, which tend to proselytize and attempt to convert the outsider, welcoming all-comers to swell their numbers, the inner traditions make a different demand: seek God in your heart, negotiate the traps that your psyche lays and find the truth in your own inner temple.

Perhaps the big difference between exoteric religions and esoteric cults is the contrast between, on the one hand, morality – a set of beliefs and acceptable behaviours, moderated by intellectually inspired self-control – and, on the other, a way of life inspired by a direct connection to and experience of the Divine, which activates the conscience to increasing levels of love and forgiveness.

'KNOW THYSELF'

Anthropologists of religion, such as the American professor Joseph Campbell, have done much to show us the links and similarities between different religious and spiritual traditions, and have been influential in helping people see the communality in the human search for truth. Psychologists have similarly taught us that, fundamentally, we seek the same experiences – we simply differ in the ways we use to get there. They also tell us that without a framework for understanding ourselves, religion alone may not be sufficient to lead us to the truth that we seek. From contemporary events we know that the giant, but subtle traps that the

Left *The Temple of Apollo at Delphi is one of many examples of remarkable religious buildings around the world. As places of homage and worship, they were often built to be impressive and awe-inspiring.*

human ego sets mean that the most innocent people can use religious beliefs to justify the most terrible and destructive acts. The Delphic Oracle, a cult of its own, taught humankind to 'Know thyself', and that the secret knowledge of our own psyches may be more important than all the ornate religious ideas that are on offer.

In a secular world, a world of science and ultra-rationalism, atheism can appear to be the dominant norm. For those who have no faith, who see a monochrome landscape of religious disagreement and conflict, it may come as a surprise that spirituality contains myriad fascinating shades of grey – subtle differentiations of ideas that transcend conventional boundaries. In this book, many different ideas about life appear, and the thoughts that our ancestors carried to sustain them can be beautiful and nourishing just as much to the believer as to the unbeliever.

Above *The Greek philosopher Plato described the culture of Atlantis as spiritually advanced and sophisticated. The idea of this lost continent captured many imaginations and formed the basis of the belief systems of numerous spiritual movements.*

PART 1

CULTS OF FERTILITY, NATURE WORSHIP AND SACRIFICIAL RITES

I call upon loud-roaring and revelling Dionysus,
*   primeval, double natured, thrice-born, Bacchic lord,*
wild, ineffable, secretive, two-horned and two-shaped.
Ivy-covered, bull-faced, war-like, howling, pure,
You take raw flesh, you have feasts, wrapt in foliage,
*   decked with grape clusters.*
Resourceful Euboleus, immortal god sired by Zeus
When he mated with Persephone in unspeakable union.
Harken to my voice, O blessed one,
And with your fair-girdled nymphs breathe on me in a
*   spirit of perfect agape.*

INVOCATION TO DIONYSUS, *ORPHIC HYMNS*

Connecting with elemental forces

Earlier civilizations with less access to nature-controlling technologies than ourselves felt themselves more vulnerable to the uncertainties of life and responded to this with various forms of worship and story-making. Creation myths and stories of warring gods fed into cultural and religious practices, which it is believed would increase the blessings that fertility could bring them.

Fertility was important in all its meanings. Once human civilization moved from hunter-gathering to agricultural practice, fertility was both organized and almost automatically ritualized simply by virtue of the need for optimum timings of planting and harvesting. Everyone knew that without food the people would die; an appeal to the gods for their blessings was a natural impulse and could never do any harm. For the tribe or social grouping to survive and flourish, it had two essential requirements: food and sex. If they could feed themselves and reproduce, and then feed their offspring, life could go on for ever – barring natural accidents, illness and the attacks of enemies. Numbers, though, were a solution to those problems. If the tribe was large enough, it could overcome these other vagaries – but only with the help of the larger forces of a spiritual world, a divine universe. Without the help of those forces, success could not be assured. And one of the ways to demonstrate respect for those supernatural forces was through sacrifice – a word meaning 'to make sacred'.

HUMAN AND ANIMAL SACRIFICE

Many forms of worship involve material sacrifice, whether of grain, fruit, animals or even human beings. Most sceptics claim that such practices are a superstitious type of life (or death-delaying) insurance, but worshippers appeal to a causal logic based on circumstantial connections or a faith in the real and tangible power of terrestrial and celestial forces. Sacrifice, and the failure to observe the correct rules of sacrifice, lies at the heart of the Minoan myth (see pages 14–17). When King Minos failed to kill the beautiful white bull sent to him by Poseidon for ritual sacrifice, he set in motion a terrible chain of events that led to a series of tragic losses. The fact that his wife was impregnated by the bull, and subsequently gave birth to the terrible Minotaur, led to the need for the further sacrifice of seven men and seven women every eight years to placate the beast. The story is clearly a warning to those who would abuse the sacred process.

The Mithraic cult (see pages 22–25) also features a bull that is ritually killed, but in this case the symbolism is different. Mithras' dominance over the bull puts humankind at the centre of a universe of celestial forces. The bull – *taurus* – is only one of many constellations that feature in the cult's imagery. For adherents of the Dionysian cult (see pages 18–21), sacrifice was something that might occur during their wine-fed excesses. It was said that some people grew so wild in the woods that they would tear animals apart with their bare hands, and it is reputed that human deaths also sometimes occurred.

The Druids (see pages 26–31), whose modern image is of a peaceful, nature-loving movement, were also practitioners of sacrifice. Their rituals frequently involved animal sacrifice, and Julius Caesar, writing in his record of the Gallic Wars, mentioned accounts of human sacrifice for the purposes of divination, although these are still disputed.

In all of human history, the masters of human sacrifice were the Aztecs (see pages 32–35). Capable of killing tens of thousands of victims in a single event, they eventually saw the precious rituals become the engine of their own self-destructive implosion. When the Spanish conquistadors discovered the depths of their depravity (and the size of their treasuries), the Aztecs were demonized and regarded as deserving of their own deaths. Little was understood of the fearsome logic or of the creation myths that drove their mayhem onward.

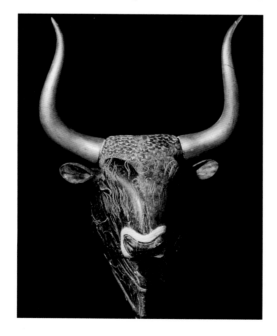

Left *Ritual killing plays a significant role in many forms of worship, with animals often being slain for symbolic purposes. The Mithraic cult is based around Mithras killing the bull and demonstrates Man's dominance in the world.*

MEXICO.

MEXICO. REGIA ET CELEBRIS HISPANIÆ NOVAE CIVITAS.

Fortunately, very few religious views lead to such blood-letting. Japanese Shintoism (see pages 36–39) and its predecessor 'kami worship' demonstrate how a nature-loving faith can sustain its people and itself over thousands of years of development. It begs the question: how can one set of beliefs lead people to a harmonious relationship with nature, while another leads them to a form of hell?

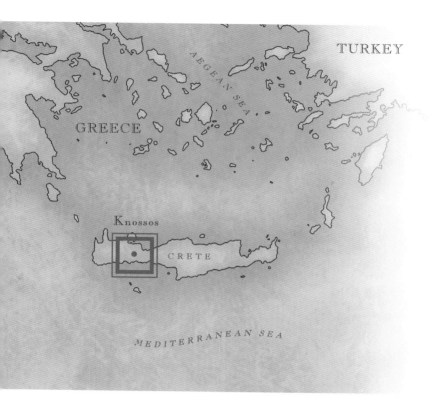

Beliefs of the Minoan cult

One of the most intriguing of the ancient spiritual traditions is that of the Minoans – a bronze age civilization that arose and flourished on the island of Crete (in the 3rd and 2nd century BCE). The discovery of extraordinary architecture and artefacts in the early 20th century and the evidence of profound mythic traditions have combined to reveal a people who were focused on the worship of nature and generative forces.

In Minoan myth, King Minos, one of the sons of the Greek god Zeus, claimed the throne of Crete under dubious circumstances. In a story that echoes Shakespeare's *King Lear*, Sarpedon (one of Minos' two brothers) claimed that their step-father Asterius, the King of Crete, had wished that the island be divided equally between the three men. Seeking to validate his claim to sole kingship, Minos boasted that the gods would answer

any request he made of them. He dedicated an altar to Poseidon, god of the sea that surrounded Crete, and prayed that a bull might come from the waters to be sacrificed. As if to vindicate Minos' claim to power, a beautiful white bull emerged immediately from the waves. But Minos, stunned by the animal's fabulous appearance decided that he would keep Poseidon's bull and sacrifice another, lesser beast.

THE BUILDING OF THE LABYRINTH

Poseidon was so upset by this abuse of his blessing that he caused Minos' wife Pasiphaë to fall in love with the bull. With the help of the craftsman Daedalus (more famous for his later aerial flight from Crete with his doomed son Icarus), Pasiphaë hid herself in a hollow model cow and allowed the white beast to impregnate her. From this coupling was born

SERPENT-GODDESS FORMS

Of the sculpture that has been uncovered at Knossos, the female figures (often bare-breasted) appear to have some fertility value and are evidence of a moon-goddess or matrilineal cult. These serpent-goddess figures hold snakes in their hands, demonstrating both their power over evil (possibly male) forces and their grasp of esoteric knowledge.

While it may be King Minos who is dominant in the mythology, the word *Minos* actually means 'moon being' and the word Crete is derived from the Greek word *crateia*, meaning 'strong or ruling goddess'. Many small metal and clay figures and objects have been found throughout Crete: models of animals including bulls, human figures

(predominantly women), solar discs, miniature vessels and the double-headed axe (see page 16) have all come to light. These objects indicate that a Minoan cult was active in many forms, and that worship of family and archetypal forces – in the hope of gaining protection and the blessings of providence – was prevalent throughout Crete.

Below *Dating from around 1,600 BCE, this snake-goddess figurine was found at Knossos, Crete. The snakes symbolize power over evil forces while the female form represents fertility.*

the Minotaur, a creature with the head of a bull and the body of a man. Such was the disgrace that Minos had brought upon himself and his family that, on consulting an oracle, he was told to ask Daedalus to build him a retreat at Knossos – this was the Cretan Labyrinth to which the shamed king retired with his wife and the Minotaur.

As with a great number of Greek myths, there are many different versions of each tale. In some tellings there is no Minotaur; instead it is simply the white Cretan bull that sits at the centre of the Labyrinth. For Minos and his people to continue to flourish, though, it seems there had to be continual sacrifice to the gods. To fulfil this observance, seven young men and seven young damsels, sent every eight years from a subservient Athens, would enter the Labyrinth, only to be lost and devoured by the beast at its centre.

THE OCTENNIAL CYCLE

The eight-year cycle is significant because it represents the period that links the sun and the moon in their astronomical positions: only once every eight years does the full moon coincide with the longest or shortest day. This octennial cycle of sacrifice by Athens continued until its third repetition, when Theseus (son of the King of the Athenians) arrived determined to kill the Minotaur. With the secret help of Ariadne, King Minos' daughter, Theseus entered the labyrinth trailing a piece of string behind him. When he reached the Minotaur, he killed it and – using Ariadne's thread – managed to trace his way back out of the maze.

The bull was important to this early culture because it represented the solar principle. The idea behind this was that the Minos king retired at the end of each eight-year period to an oracular cave on Mount Ida, where he would commune with his metaphysical father Zeus to assess the previous eight years and re-empower his wise rulership. Without this form of sacred renewal, the king would not be worthy of the throne for the next eight-year period.

The Palace of Knossos

Now the largest Bronze Age archeological site on Crete, the Palace of Knossos was once the ceremonial and political heart of the Minoan's vanished sea empire. It is also believed to be the Labyrinth of Greek mythology. The vivid wall art and startling goddess iconography unearthed at Knossos give a rare insight into the religious practices of the Minoans.

Several archeologists had begun to excavate Knossos in the late 19th century, but it was the arrival of the visionary (although unorthodox) amateur archeologist Arthur Evans in March 1900 that really began the serious work of unveiling Knossos.

Evans uncovered a significant number of buildings that he called the Palace of Minos. Although the term 'palace' has remained attached to the buildings at Knossos, it is clear that their function was much more than simply a home for a king. Knossos was a 2.4 ha (6 acre) complex of around 1,300 linked rooms, which encompassed such diverse functions as administration rooms, ceremonial and religious spaces, theatrical performance, wine-pressing, grain-milling, craftspeople's workshops and housing.

The greatest flourishing of the Bronze Age Minoan civilization at Knossos seems to have occurred between the 19th and 15th centuries BCE in what is now called the 'Old Palace' period, when it may have been the centre of a community with a population of around 8,000 people.

ART REVELATIONS

As with many archaeological sites, it is often the art that reveals most about the culture and religion of a civilization. At Knossos fine examples have been found of pottery, sculpture, ritual weaponry and frescoes.

In the frescoes that adorn the walls in the palace a cult of youth, aesthetics and athleticism emerges: the great majority of individuals featured are young, beautiful adults of both sexes. Perhaps the most striking and mysterious of all the artworks at Knossos – and the piece that has garnered most attention – is the large 'Toreador' fresco, apparently depicting bull-jumping. In the image, an athletic young man appears to have literally 'grabbed the bull by the horns' and is somersaulting over the huge white animal's back, while the scene is witnessed by two women.

Whether this was a sport or had a more ritual or initiatory value is not absolutely clear, but the appearance of the bull in Minoan art is significant in itself and provides a connection with the bull-headed Minotaur of Greek mythology that dwelt within the Cretan Labyrinth. Moreover, there are those who believe that the Labyrinth was not a separate structure nearby, but was in fact the Palace of Knossos itself, with its maze of rooms, courtyards and steps: an apparently impossible place to escape from.

One piece of bronze work that seems to have carried much meaning for the Minoans was the double-headed axe known as the *labrys*, a word etymologically related to 'labyrinth'. There is little evidence for the warring aspirations of the Minoans, and the bronze *labrys*, although it was a weapon, seems to have held a more symbolic significance. Some theories interpret the axe as representing thunder, lightning or storm. Others, including the poet and great student of Greek myth, Robert Graves, have interpreted the axe head as representing the crescent shape of the moon. Archeologists believe the evidence from Knossos indicates that such axes were wielded only by female divinities and priestesses, not male.

① CENTRAL COURT

The central courtyard was the major organizing principle of the palace complex. At the middle archeologists have discovered the base of what is believed to be an altar.

② MAGAZINES

On the outer western edge of the palace were magazines where wine, grain, oil and honey were stored in large jars called *pithoi*. In holes beneath the *pithoi* it is believed that valuables such as gold and jewellery would once have been hidden.

③ LIGHT WELLS

The palace was multi-storeyed with interior staircases built around light- and air-wells. Roof edges may have been decorated with a stylized bull's-horn icon.

④ COLUMNS

Minoan columns were made of wood and tapered towards the base. It is thought that the columns had some religious significance, as the base of the column of one of the lower storeys of the palace is surrounded by a trough for libations.

⑤ THRONE ROOM

The throne room was located on the north-western side of the central court. To its south, facing the central court, was a smaller room where a statue of a snake goddess was discovered. These statuettes, holding snakes aloft in each hand, are one of Knossos' most striking finds.

⑥ QUEEN'S *MEGARON*

Here were found elaborate frescoes depicting bullfights, processions and images of nature, including birds, flowers and frolicking dolphins.

The rites of Dionysus

The Greek god Dionysus is popularly known as the personification of the vine, of the wine obtained from its fruit and its intoxicating effects. His origins are somewhat obscure, but his worship is complex and wide-ranging. Some believe that worship of Dionysus emerged from the tribes of Thrace, while others see the Dionysian cult emerging from Minoan Crete from as early as 3000 BCE right up to 1000 BCE.

Wherever the Dionysian cult took root, it seems to have involved wild dances, trance-inducing music and drinking to excess – a practice that has survived in various secular forms right up to the present day. Fire-walking, drumming and animal sacrifice also formed part of the rituals at different times.

EVOLUTION OF THE DIONYSIAN MYSTERIES

Wherever the Dionysian rites first sprang from, their presence in Greece is almost always attributed to a 'wine cult'. It is probable that the actual vine plant, its annual and whole-life cycle, its harvest and fermentation were seen as an expression of the living god. The Dionysian cult, in all its forms, contains the theme of death and rebirth, a characteristic of all cults that draw on vegetative nature worship.

It is important to distinguish between two distinct sets of rites that developed in Greece as the worship of Dionysus. The more public, 'outer' or exoteric rites – known as the Dionysia – are generally agreed to have developed before the inner, esoteric and more secret rites of initiation.

The earlier rural Dionysia would have taken place at 'the clearing of the wine', a stage in wine's fermentation that generally happened just after the winter solstice, when it was considered that Dionysus was born again from the death of cold and winter. There would also have been celebrations around the time of the grape harvest and at the taking of the grapes to the wine press.

Dionysus was revered at Delphi, home of the Oracle, where he was the patron god for November, December and January. The dark months were always associated with the rule of the Underworld and the appropriation of souls into the world of death. This is reflected in modern times in Hallowe'en and All Souls' Day (nominally on 2 November). In classical Greece, the main Athenian Dionysia developed into a festival of drama, music, poetry and performance. The city festivities took place around the time of the spring equinox when the first leaves started to appear on the vines.

As well as the Athenian Dionysia, which took place in daylight, there were biennial nocturnal winter rites known as the Tristeria. These were held on Mount Parnassus, home

Above *The vines on this Greek vase painting of the god Dionysus show the centrality of wine in the Dionysian cult. Every aspect of the production and consumption of wine was celebrated.*

of the nine Muses, and involved wild orgies over two days. The first day was overseen by the Maenads, women followers of Dionysus in an altered state of madness or possession, who would hunt animals and rip them apart with their bare hands; some stories even tell of humans who became victims of these ravages. The second day was given over to the nymphs and satyrs in a more sensual and less violent bacchanal (see page 20).

THE SECRETS OF INITIATION

The Dionysia and the Tristeria were the more public aspects of the Dionysian rites; behind these lay the hidden mysteries of initiation, to which only some people were given access. In the Dionysian Mysteries there was a deep understanding and wisdom about the place

in human life for the more primal (or even bestial) side of our natures. The purpose of the mystery initiations was to promote the integration – rather than the repression – of this primal nature into the human psyche. Whereas some cults stressed the need for self-control and self-domination as a way to achieve a form of inner, psychic power, the Dionysian Mysteries aimed at the mastery of this shadow self through acceptance of its place in life's whole.

The ritual that developed in relation to this idea was more about the enactment of the process of death and rebirth than about excesses of a sexual kind. In this event, which echoed the descent of Dionysus into the Underworld, the male initiate would go on a journey through a frightening cave or

subterranean temple in order to find some particular object, the essence of which could be brought back to the surface. On completion of this task, he would be presented with a *thyrsus* wand (see page 20) – his reward and a symbol of his initiation. For women, the experience was different, for they represented Ariadne waiting in the Underworld as the potential bride of Dionysus. Whether they experienced sexual union with a male representative of Dionysus, or were penetrated by a wooden (or animal) penis, might depend on the particular version of the rites in which they were involved. Whatever the reality of the sexual experiences that were part of the Dionysian cult, sexual union was often followed by some form of feast or communion.

For the Greeks of the first millennium BCE, the extravagant practices of Dionysian worship were in strict opposition to the clear thinking and general sobriety of Greek culture. And yet Dionysus' popularity spread quickly through the Greek population, appealing directly to an untamed wildness that could not be suppressed simply by an encouragement of the love of aesthetics and intellectual truth that characterized Classical Greece.

BACCHUS AND THE 'BACCHANALIA'

The Greek tragedian Euripides wrote of the ancient rites that took place in rural Greece in his play, *The Bacchae*. He describes feast-day processions held high in the mountains:

Following the torches as they dipped and swayed in the darkness, they climbed mountain paths with head thrown back and eyes glazed, dancing to the beat of the drum which stirred their blood … In this state of ekstasis or enthusiasmos, they abandoned themselves, dancing wildly and shouting 'Euoi!' (the name of the god) and at that moment of intense rapture became identified with the god himself. They became filled with his spirit and acquired divine powers.

In Rome, Dionysus was known as Bacchus and he appeared through the introduction of the 'Bacchanalia' – secret rites attended by women only on 16 and 17 March; these took place in the grove of Simila, close to the Aventine Hill. From their first appearance in around 200 BCE, the rituals developed to include men and increased in frequency, eventually taking place as often as five times a month. It appears that these festivals became a breeding ground for the planning of crime and political manoeuvring. As a result, the rites were banned under a Senate decree in 186 BCE and could only be performed with special permission from the Senate. So the Bacchanalia went underground and the rites continued to be performed in secret. It is believed that they took place up until the time of St Augustine in the 4th century CE.

REPRESENTATION AND ACCOMPANIMENT

Typically the figure of the Greek god Dionysus is represented with a particular group of animals and plants: the serpent and bull are often present, and he sometimes rides a leopard or is in a chariot pulled by panthers. In the plant world, the vine is nearly always with him, as are the toxic ivy and the fertile fig. And Dionysus is frequently seen carrying the *thyrsus* – a staff made of a dried fennel stem, wrapped in ivy leaves. This phallic symbol with its seed-tipped pinecone was another indication of his link to the sexual aspect of the life-force.

Dionysus is also strongly associated with specific creatures of myth: the satyrs, the centaurs and the sileni. The satyrs were a group of male companions for both Pan and Dionysus. With a tail and sometimes with horses' hooves, their natural habitats were woods and mountainous regions. They represent an expression of male wildness and unbridled sexual drive. In sculpture and on ceramics they are usually shown with prominent erections, always ready for the sexual act. Centaurs – half-men, half-horses – are often portrayed with similar endowments, while the sileni (whose chief was a minor deity called Silenus) were a collection of drunkards, often fat-lipped and bald. Silenus himself, who was one of Dionysus' closest companions and his teacher, was the oldest and wisest of the wine god's companions. When drunk, he was believed to possess supernatural knowledge and the gift of prophecy. As the Latin saying goes: *in vino veritas*, 'In wine, truth!'.

PLATO AND THE *ORPHIC HYMNS*

The great Greek philosopher Plato was intimately knowledgeable about the Dionysian Mysteries and saw them as important initiations on the road of life that led to the certainty of death:

And I conceive that the founders of the mysteries had a real meaning and were not mere triflers when they intimated in a figure long ago that he who passes unsanctified and uninitiated into the world below will live in a slough, but that he who arrives there after initiation and purification will dwell with the gods. For 'many', as they say in the mysteries, 'are the thyrsus *bearers, but few are the mystics' – meaning, as I interpret the words, the true philosophers.*

Some scholars have compared the Dionysian Mysteries to the Orphic Mysteries. In the *Orphic Hymns* we find an Invocation of Dionysus that expresses much about the relationship of the devotee to God:

I call upon loud-roaring and revelling Dionysus, primeval, double natured, thrice-born, Bacchic lord, wild, ineffable, secretive, two-horned and two-shaped.
Ivy-covered, bull-faced, war-like, howling, pure, You take raw flesh, you have feasts, wrapt in foliage, decked with grape clusters.
Resourceful Euboleus, immortal god sired by Zeus
When he mated with Persephone in unspeakable union.
Harken to my voice, O blessed one,
And with your fair-girdled nymphs breathe on me in a spirit of perfect agape.

Left *Anselm Feuerback's painting 'Plato's Symposium' shows the Greek philosopher's support for the Dionysian Mysteries. Links have also been made between the Dionysian and the Orphic mysteries.*

Right *Dionysus was often depicted holding a* thyrsus *staff. Made from a fennel stem wrapped in ivy leaves, it is a phallic symbol representing the god's association with sexual elements of the life force.*

The Cult
of Mithras

The meaning of the Roman cult of Mithras appears to be as mysterious to modern seekers as it was to outside observers in their own day. Fiercely protected by initiates of the cult, the Mithraic Mysteries were never written down in scriptures or texts. Instead they were transmitted orally, in initiatory rituals, and in the artworks and iconography that enshrined the symbolic teachings of Mithras within their temples.

Right *Remains of a Mithraeum Temple in Rome. These subterranean temples were dominated by a focal point at one end: the Tauroctony. This was a representation of Mithras killing the bull.*

The origins of Mithraism, as it is known today, are obscure, but many scholars hold to the belief that the cult of Mithras developed out of a Zoroastrian cult of Mithra, which was itself based on an Indo-Iranian cult of *mitra*. Other theories suggest connections with Greek/Hellenic cults that included worship of the sun god Helios. A Manichean deity named Mithra is also known to have existed and may have played a part in the cult's origins. In a similar way to Christianity's focus on the miracle of the resurrection, Mithraic iconography is focused on the Tauroctony or bull-slaying.

What is known about Mithraism as a Roman cult, however, is that it was only available to men, and that many of its members were soldiers and those of higher rank in society, although some freed slaves (*libertas*) may also have joined the ranks of initiates. As well as occurring in Rome and Ostia, Mithraic temples have been discovered in places where the Roman army was active, such as present-day Germany, Bosnia and at Hadrian's Wall in northern England. The many inscriptions found within Mithraic temples point to the identity of those who

were committed to the cult and felt they owed a debt of gratitude to Mithras' protection and inspiration. As with many cults, though, there is a question as to whether it was a source of spiritual nourishment for this life or the next.

THE TAUROCTONY

Worship took place in the Mithraeum, a small subterranean temple, typically no bigger than 23 m (75 ft) by 9 m (30 ft) with a central aisle. Some 20–30 participants would sit along the sides of the aisle beneath a vaulted roof. At one end of every Mithraeum was the focus of worship, the Tauroctony – a two- or three-dimensional portrayal of Mithras on the back of a bull, killing the animal by stabbing it in the neck or throat. Indeed, there are even more common features that mark out the typical Tauroctony: the young Mithras sits astride the bull with his left knee thrust into the animal's back, while his right leg trails along the flank. His dress is generally consistent, too: trousers, a tunic, his trademark 'Phrygian cap' and a cape that billows behind him like the ark of a night-time sky. Sometimes this cape contains a map of the stars, indicating Mithras' ability to contain and possibly overpower the Universe.

As Mithras kills the bull, he pulls its head back and inserts the blade of his dagger or short sword into the beast's neck. At the same time he turns away from the action – either towards us, the viewers, or looking back over his shoulder towards a raven that is flying. A dog jumps forward to drink blood from the fresh wound, and a scorpion is on hand to cut into the bull's testicles, or possibly to inject them with poison. A snake arrives, slithering; it is unclear whether the reptile wants to attack the dog or the bull. Two young men are present as witnesses: Cautes and Cautopates. Each carries a torch, one of which points up, the other down. Other deities are sometimes present at the dynamic rite, and an archway of astronomical or astrological signs often surrounds the event.

CELESTIAL CORRESPONDENCES

What is interesting in the common portrayal of Mithras (as above) – apart from the stunning drama of the action – is that each of the characters appears to have a corresponding relationship with a celestial object or constellation. While the two young men may be seen to the modern eye as the Gemini twins, they are more likely to portray the setting and rising of the sun. The scorpion is clearly Scorpio. The bull is, naturally enough, Taurus, Scorpio's opposite in the Heavens. The dog is either Canis Major or Canis Minor. The snake is Hydra. As for Mithras himself, in his previous appearances within cult worship he often represented the sun, but there is evidence that he is a power beyond even that – that he is, in some sense, the centre of the Universe, around which all other objects make their long sojourn. For those whose lives were fragile and quickly ended, the knowledge that they were aligned with celestial powers was more than a comfort.

Whether or not the Tauroctony represented the essential core of the Mithraic Mysteries, as many have suggested, or whether there were further levels of initiation beyond is unclear. As a powerful cult, however, Mithraism seems to have offered its members a glimpse of their place in the Universe and of their link to the Divine.

MITHRAIC TEMPLES

Mithraic temples have been discovered across the mainland of Europe in modern Italy, Germany, Switzerland and Slovenia. In Ostia Antica, Rome's port, the remains of 17 Mithraea have been found, demonstrating the importance of the cult to the city. In the UK three Mithraic sites have been discovered close to Hadrian's Wall. But the most significant discovery in England occurred in 1954 during building works that were being carried out in the City of London. After the initial find, the director of the Museum of London, W.F. Grimes, excavated the site, initially believing that it was an early Christian church. As the temple was uncovered, however, evidence soon revealed that the builders had discovered the most important Roman Mithraic temple in England.

LONDON'S MITHRAIC TEMPLE

The temple, dated to the mid-3rd century CE, was originally built on the eastern bank of the now covered-over River Walbrook. At the time of the Roman occupation this river was an important source of fresh water for Londinium (as London was known). When the find was made, however, it was necessary to move the Mithraeum to another site in Temple Court, London, although now there are plans to reinstate the temple in its original location. In its current location, the temple's foundations are visible above ground, although in its original position the Mithraeum would have followed the pattern of all temples to Mithras and would have been located partially or wholly underground. This placing was intended to represent the original cave in which Mithras was believed to have slain the bull and released primordial powers of creativity and life-force into this world.

Among the artefacts unearthed in the digs was a head of Mithras – wearing his distinctive Phrygian cap (Phrygia being an ancient region of Asia Minor) – shaped to fit an absent torso. A marble relief, 0.5 m (1½ ft) across, depicts Mithras killing the bull – the telltale Tauroctony that is the signature of a Mithraeum. In the image, which shows the annual wheel of the Cosmos, Mithras is accompanied by the two figures of the celestial twins: Cautes, signifying light, and Cautopates, the dark twin. Outside the wheel, in the top left, the Roman sun god Sol rides through the Heavens, while at the top right the moon goddess Luna descends in her chariot. In the bottom corners the wind gods Aquilo and Favonius (known to the Greeks as Boreas and Zephyrus) show their faces. The panel carries an inscription: *VLPIUS SILVANUS FACTUS ARAVISIONE EMERITUS LEG II AVG VOTUM SOLVIT.* Most translations from the Latin give this as 'Ulpius Silvanus, veteran soldier of the Second Augustinian Legion, in fulfilment of a vow, makes this altar (as a result of) a vision.' This demonstrates once again the involvement of the Roman military and their willingness to reveal their allegiance to the Mithraic cult.

Also found close by the temple ruins were heads of the Roman goddess Minerva and the Greek-Egyptian god Serapis, with his distinctive beard and carrying a small grain basket or *modius* on his head – the Romans absorbed beliefs from different religions as they expanded their empire, often identifying other cultures' gods with their own. A likeness of Mercury, the Roman shepherd of dead souls, was also found, as well as clay figurines of the goddess Venus.

Mithraic temples have been discovered across the mainland of Europe in modern Italy, Germany, Switzerland and Slovenia.

A Latin inscription at the site reads: *PRO SALVTE D N CCCC ET NOB CAES MITHRAE ET SOLI INVICTO AB ORIENTE AD OCCIDENTEM.* This translates as 'For the salvation of our lords, the four emperors, the Noble Caesar, the god Mithras and the invincible sun'. The inscription has been dated to sometime between 307 and 310 CE and is another clear indication of the temple's dedicated purpose.

The initial confusion that made archeologists believe they had unearthed an early Christian church was understandable.

The form of the temple was indeed similar to Christian churches, with aisles either side of a long nave, leading to an altar and an apse. Followers would have sat on benches on either side of the nave. For some scholars this is another indication of the theory that Christianity borrowed heavily from the ideas and rituals of the Mithraic cult. Despite this borrowing, and after Constantine the Great (ruled 306–337 CE) legitimized Christianity in 312 CE, a process of destruction was unleashed on Mithraic worship and its temples – a process that would erase all but a few Mithraea.

Below *This Mithraic temple is one of a number found in Rome. Temples were subterranean in order to represent the original cave in which Mithras was believed to have killed the bull.*

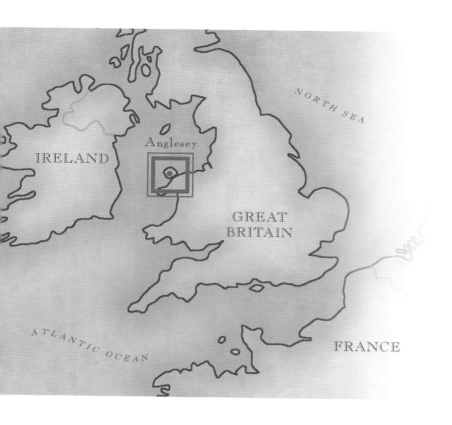

Druidry and Celtic polytheism

The roots of Druidry lie deep within British, Celtic and European culture. At the same time they are difficult to trace historically, and the earliest-known records of Druids date only as far back as the 3rd century BCE. Many scholars believe that their presence is much older, but unfortunately evidence to support this is scant.

Above *Much knowledge of the Druidic tradition comes from Julius Caesar. His writings show that their sacred beliefs were passed on orally for secrecy.*

This is partly because of the Druidic preference for the oral transmission of its lore and wisdom, and partly because of post-Christian attempts to erase or cover up the importance of Druidic culture throughout Europe. Druidry is part of the religion now known as 'Celtic polytheism', and within this overall belief system the Druids were the priestly class, revered by the followers of this widespread religious movement. Druids were also healers, scholars and lawyers, often responsible for the moral life of their cultures. They stood alongside the other two professional classes: bards, the keepers of poetry and song; and *vates* – seers or soothsayers who were responsible, under the guidance of Druids, for performing sacrifices and other rituals.

DRUIDIC PRACTICE AND PHILOSOPHY

Religious rites were almost exclusively held outdoors, often in woods or specific sacred groves. Many of the ceremonies are likely to have had sacrificial elements. These would have involved animals, but a number of Roman writers claim that the Celts also carried out human sacrifice. There is little archeological evidence that this was true, and it is possible the Romans used these claims to justify their domination of a 'more primitive' culture. When they conquered lands occupied by Druids, they often destroyed the sacred groves in an effort to crush Druidic worship.

It is known that the island of Anglesey off the coast of Wales played host to a centre for advanced Druidic learning. Students of Druidry would travel there from many European countries to learn the esoteric secrets of the cult. These are likely to have included the study of divination, prayers, poetry and songs as well as an understanding of nature and its symbolism. Druidry also stressed the importance of life beyond death, and in some interpretations the philosophy seems to have followed Pythagorean ideas of reincarnation or metempsychosis – the transmigration, or journeying, of the soul in a series of different bodies.

ORAL TRADITION AND LANGUAGE

A significant part of modern knowledge about the Druidic tradition comes from the writings

Above *An ancient burial mound on the island of Anglesey, Wales, demonstrates the Druidic belief in the reality of the afterlife. Anglesey was an important Druidic centre and one of the last Celtic strongholds.*

of the Roman leader Julius Caesar (ruled 49–44 BCE), in his *Commentaries on the Gallic War*. Here he reports that what written material the Druids did create – for public records and private correspondence – utilized 'Greek letters'. According to Caesar, the Druids did not put their sacred doctrines into written form, 'lest it should become vulgarized and lest, also, the memory of the scholars should become impaired'. There is evidence, though, that the Druids and Celts used another alphabet known as Ogham. A variety of Ogham forms existed throughout pre-Greek and pre-Roman times, although the alphabet system used by the Druids seems also to have been a hand- or finger-signing system – much like the modern communication methods used by deaf and mute people.

In Gaul (present-day France) Julius Caesar says the Druids were the priests who, along with noblemen, represented the classes of highest rank. Druids were exempt from service in the military and were not required to pay taxes. As the scholars and guardians of ancient unwritten law, they also held the power of legal judgement over the populace. The most severe punishment meted out by them seems to have been exclusion from society – a form of shunning.

With the arrival of the Romans in Gaul and their insistence on use of the Latin alphabet, other forms of writing rapidly disappeared. Although there are some examples of marks on various artefacts that could equate to Ogham-type letterings, there would appear to be no examples of any written sacred Druidic texts. When people were trained in the ways of the Druids – philosophy, poetry, law, and so on – this was achieved through oral transmission.

Caesar grew close enough to the Druids to understand their educational system:

With regard to their actual course of studies, the main object of all education is, in their opinion, to imbue their scholars with a firm belief in the indestructibility of the human soul, which, according to their belief, merely passes at death from one tenement to another, for by such doctrine alone, they say, which robs death of all its terrors, can the highest form of human courage be developed. Subsidiary to the teachings of this main principle, they hold various lectures and discussions on astronomy, on the extent and geographical distribution of the globe, on the different branches of natural philosophy, and on many problems connected with religion.
Commentaries on the Gallic War, Julius Caesar

While Caesar was bent on subsuming the Druid culture, it appears that he was not without some respect for its learning and its values.

FESTIVALS

Natural and astronomical events in the Druidic year were marked by a cycle of annual festivals. The four main events were: Imbolc, the holiday that denotes the first signs of spring; Beltane, showing the full growth of nature; Lughnasadh, a celebration of the first harvests; and Samhain, marking the end of harvest and the descent into the darkness of winter.

It is an example of the modern revival and reinvention of Druidry that these festivals are now often placed at key moments in the Gregorian calendar. In the original Druid timings, they were determined more by the lunar calendar and by seasonal changes than by specific fixed dates. So Imbolc would have occurred on a full moon between the winter solstice and the vernal equinox; Beltane between the vernal equinox and summer solstice; Lughnasadh between the summer solstice and autumn equinox; and Samhain between the autumnal equinox and winter solstice. In modern society some of these events have been absorbed into Christian and other secular festivals: Groundhog Day and Candlemas occupy the place of Imbolc; Easter occurs around Beltane; Lughnasadh compares with harvest festivals; and Samhain is replaced by Hallowe'en and All Saints' Day.

A FORM OF NATURE WORSHIP

Festivals would often have taken place in sacred groves or close to sacred wells and other natural phenomena. In Druidic polytheism (worship of many gods) or pantheism (the belief that the Divine is in all things), the gods were multiple and everywhere. Flora and fauna were expressions of the gods or different aspects of them. They could provide messages or omens of the gods' intentions or wishes.

Left *This stone in County Waterford, Ireland, is covered with Ogham carvings. The Ogham alphabet was used by Druids in pre-Greek and pre-Roman times to maintain administrative records.*

Right *Druidic festivals were often held in sacred groves. Expressions of the gods could be found among flora and fauna, following the pantheistic belief that the Divine is present in all things.*

The Greek historian Diodorus Siculus reported on the prophetic work of the Druids: 'These men predict the future by observing the flight and calls of birds and by the sacrifice of holy animals: all orders of society are in their power ...' He also pointed to the idea that human sacrifice was involved in the process of prophecy: '... in very important matters they prepare a human victim, plunging a dagger into his chest; by observing the way his limbs convulse as he falls and the gushing of his blood, they are able to read the future.' Whether this kind of report was intended to give a negative or barbaric portrait of the Druids' practices, and thus justify the Romans' oppression of Celtic culture, is still a matter of debate. It was perhaps easier to concentrate on the more sensational aspects of Celtic ritual than to delve into their relationship with nature. Julius Caesar's successor, the Emperor Augustus (ruled 27 BCE–14 CE), issued an order forbidding Roman citizens throughout the empire from practising Druidic rites. Later, under the Emperor Tiberius (ruled 14–37 CE), a decree was issued by the Senate with the express intention of suppressing the Druids. Not wholly successful, it was renewed by the Emperor Claudius in 54 CE.

THE CULTS AND GODS

Within the Celtic polytheistic worship that the Druids oversaw, there were a number of different cults based on specific gods, as well as phenomena both astronomical and natural. Caesar recognized the five main gods worshipped by the Gauls in France, but identified them with their Roman equivalents.

Mercury, the most important, was referred to by various extra names, such as Visucius, Cissonius and Gebrinius, but was clearly aligned with Lugh, the originator of the Lughnasadh festival. He seems to have been a god of kingship, and French depictions often show him with wings or horns emerging from his head. Often accompanied by a ram or a cockerel, he carries his *caduceus*, a herald's staff or wand wrapped with snakes, implying wisdom. The other planetary gods that the Celtic Gauls worshipped were: Jupiter, often shown with a thunderbolt; Minerva, the blesser of handcrafts; Apollo, healer of disease; and Mars, associated with war. In each case an individual cult grew up around the god's supposed power or domain and the need to invoke that god's blessing on the cult's followers.

Healing cults were also popular and – as in modern Christian experience – were often focused on particular locations. For the Druids, however, the reason was not an 'appearance' by a particular spiritual personage; rather, they were associated with the power of natural phenomena. Springs and wells that gave life in the form of water were attributed with additional powers; some of these were linked to deities such as Brighid, the goddess of healing, poetry and smithing, and the Irish goddess Airmed, who was linked to a sacred well. The groves and woods where particular sacred plants grew in abundance were already important for the energies of their trees. Yew trees and particularly oaks were held in reverence, although each of the main native species – hawthorn, hazel, elm, beech, and so on – had an importance and could be called upon for their blessings in times of need.

Healing cults were also popular and – as in modern Chrstian experience – were often focused on particular locations.

Left *This engraving
of an Arch Druid in
his Habit represents
the magical powers
that the Druids were
believed to possess.
Many Druidic stories
talk of magic, spells
and supernatural
connections.*

THE PERSISTENCE OF THE DRUIDS

When the Romans expanded their empire and suppressed the native religions of continental Europe and Britain, it might have been expected that the Druid influence would disappear for good. Nevertheless there are many examples of ways in which Druid culture survived in both explicit and implicit forms, despite its repression.

Often the spiritual functions of the Druids were taken over directly by bishops and abbots. In Ireland, however, the Celtic impulse survived for longer. Irish manuscripts dating from the 12th century CE – but based on texts from as far back as the 8th century CE – contain numerous stories of Druids acting as important advisers and mentors to kings. The Druids in these stories are often attributed with powers that we might call supernatural. They can foretell future events: the Druid Bec mac De predicted the death of Diarmait mac Cerbaill, the High King of Ireland, with more accuracy than the combined wisdom of three Christian saints; in the Ulster cycle of stories, Cathbad, chief Druid at the court of Conchobar, the King of Ulster, was present at the birth of the tragic heroine Deirdre, predicted her tragic life and her fate, but his words of warning were ignored by King Conchobar; and in the story known as *Tain Bo Cuailnge*, Medb, the Queen of Connacht, called on the knowledge of her Druids in the face of oncoming war and they suggested delaying the march on the enemy until an auspicious omen prompted action.

In these stories Druids are also called on for their magical powers: when Cuchulainn is tempted into the world of the fairies by a beautiful fairy goddess Fand, he falls in love with her; when he returns to his wife Emer, he is unable to forget Fand until he is given a potion by the Druids and the memory of his love is wiped from his mind and he is able to love his wife again. The story of Etain contains more Druid magic: Etain is loved by Eochaid Airem, the High King of Ireland; but Etain was also once loved by a god named Midir, who comes to her and declares his continuing love for her. He takes her away, leaving Eochaid Airem devastated. But the High King has the sense to consult his Druid Dalgn, who – using four wands made from yew wood and inscribed with Ogham characters – is able to divine the location of the couple and rescue Etain for the King.

While the powers of the Druids may be exaggerated in these stories – which also include control of the weather and the ability to fly – they show the respect and even awe in which the wizard-like Druids were held by those who were the keepers of the culture.

MODERN DRUIDRY

There seems to be confusion about the modern face of Druidry and the extent to which it is, or is not, based on its original roots. The world of Neo-Pagans, Neo-Druids and New Age nature worshippers seems to have borrowed from original Celtic sources of wisdom and practice, without necessarily understanding the true purposes of Druidic ritual and how they fitted in with their original societies. It is in some ways inevitable that a culture that survived for many hundreds of years, using an almost exclusively oral tradition, could fail to maintain its identity after long periods of suppression and apparent disappearance. The English scholar Robert Graves, author of a famous book on Celtic culture entitled *The White Goddess*, described the role of the Druid thus: 'The ancient Celts carefully distinguished the poet, who was originally a priest and judge as well and whose person was sacrosanct, from the mere gleeman. He was in Irish called "fili", a seer; in Welsh "derwydd", or oak-seer, which is the probable derivation of "Druid".'

Modern movements such as Celtic Reconstructionist Paganism attempt to recreate the original practices of Celtic Druidry using archaeological records and written sources, while applying them to a modern context. New Age Druidry is often more casual in its borrowings from the Celtic past, and events at Stonehenge and other stone circles in England at key times of the year do not necessarily reflect the ancient rites that would once have taken place at these important sites.

Druidic influence is unlikely to disappear completely, however, as it is almost sewn into the weft of Western culture, whether through recognition of the seasons, superstitions about animals or understandings about the value of trees and other natural features. The true Druids may be gone, but their work is not forgotten.

Right *Worshippers celebrate the Summer Solstice at Stonehenge. Modern Druidry is often only distantly based on original practices and some scholars argue that its mainly oral tradition has led to a distortion of its essence.*

UNITED STATES OF AMERICA

MEXICO

GULF OF MEXICO

Tenochtitlan

PACIFIC OCEAN

Aztec sacrificial rites

More commonly known as the Mexicas, the Aztecs rose to prominence in around 1325 CE and went on to become the dominant culture in central Mexico and beyond until the arrival of Hernando Cortés and the Spanish conquistadors ended their rule in around 1521 CE. As the largest pre-Hispanic culture on the entire North American continent, the Aztecs had a profound influence culturally, politically and spiritually.

When the Spanish first arrived in present-day Mexico on 8 November 1519, Tenochtitlan, the lake-island city that would later become Mexico City, was already home to around 250,000 people and was one of the largest centres of civilized habitation in the world. While the Spanish may have been shocked by the human sacrifices carried out in the name of Aztec gods, they were also impressed by the lavish wealth that the Aztecs had accumulated. How could this primitive society, which carried out such savage and demonic practices, have developed such a rich and complex culture? Since the following years would see the wholesale destruction of Aztec life and history, many of the answers to these important questions about their culture and spirituality would be buried – only to be rediscovered much later.

THE ROOTS OF AZTEC IDENTITY

The Aztecs' own story of their development started in the early 12th century BCE on an island called Aztlan, which has never been properly located. Some people believe it was in the Valley of Mexico, while others have placed it as far north as the south-western United States. This uncertainty has led to a belief that Aztlan, 'the place of the herons', is simply a place of myth. Some scholars also see further back, to the civilization of Teotihuacan, which had flourished between 1 and 750 CE; and to Tula, which had risen and fallen between 900 and 1200 CE; as well as to other contemporary cultures, such as the Toltecs and the Olmecs, for the roots of Aztec identity.

Their own story, though, is founded in the myths of their gods who gave them life and had the power to take it away. Under the protection of their god Huitzilpochtli – 'Hummingbird on the Left' – the Aztecs appear to have wandered for some two hundred years before they arrived at Chapultepec in the Mexican Basin in around 1248 CE. The Tepanecs, who lived at Azcapotzalco, soon expelled these Mexicas, but in 1299 the Culhuacan ruler Cocoxtli allowed them to settle in the barren lands at Tizapan. This was not to last, however, and they were forced to leave Culhuacan in around 1323. The Aztecs' wanderings, and their limited sense of a permanent home within the many city states, would suddenly change when many of them collectively witnessed an event that had been predicted by their patron god Huitzilpochtli and was the fulfilment of his guidance. Together, a large group of them saw an eagle with a serpent in its mouth, perched on a *nopal* or prickly-pear cactus that was growing out of a stone. This vision was the sign that they had finally found the site of their capital city – the god's blessings had finally paid off. From this point on, the Aztecs gained a fresh and expanded sense of their identity; as a culture fit and ready to dominate (and rule) its neighbours.

BIRTH OF THE AZTEC EMPIRE

Tenochtitlan – the place of the stone cactus – was founded in 1325 (the Aztec year known as '2-House'), and the building of the first Templo Mayor (Grand Temple) was initiated on the large island in Lake Texcoco. The Aztecs were on their way to becoming one of the city states in the Valley of Mexico. Their path to domination would not be smooth, however, and much blood would be shed as the city states became

Left *The vision of an eagle perched on a prickly pear catctus was interpreted by the Aztecs as a sign that they had finally found their homeland. This illustration charts the history of founding the city of Tenochtitlan in 1325.*

embroiled in power struggles, before the Aztecs defeated the Tepanecs. In the early 15th century the Aztec Triple Alliance was formed by Tenochtitlan, Texcoco and Tlacopan – the Aztec empire was finally born and, over the next one hundred years,

their way of life, culture and spirituality would come to dominate the whole region. The vision predicted by Huitzilpochtli had inspired the Mexicas to this triumph, but who was this god and how did he fit into the Aztec pantheon?

While there are many gods whom the Aztecs respected and worshipped as part of their creation myths, it is the story of Huitzilpochtli that dominates Aztec identity and contains the seeds of the human sacrifice that came to typify their rituals.

HUITZILPOCHTLI'S STORY

This story is recorded in the Florentine Codex, a record taken by the Catholic priest Fray Bernardino de Sahagun from a group of Aztec scholars following the arrival of the conquistadors. In the story, before Huitzilpochtli is even born, his mother Coatlicue has had many children, including a multitude of boy children known as the Four Hundred Southerners (*Centzon Huitznahua*).

When the chaste Coatlicue finds a ball of feathers one day, she places them in her waistband, unaware that they contain the seeds of a new child, Huitzilpochtli. But when Coatlicue starts to swell with pregnancy, her children wonder who is the man who has caused this and start to pour shame on their mother goddess. The eldest daughter Coyolxauhqui is so enraged she decides that together they must slay their faithless mother.

But the child within Coatlicue's womb starts to console her and tell her that he is ready to defend her honour.

When Coatlicue goes to give birth on Mount Coatepec, she is pursued by her many children, who are intent on killing her. However, when Huitzilpochtli is born, fully armed and equipped with a weapon known as the *Xiuhcoatl* or Turquoise Serpent, vengeance is swift. Huitzilpochtli decapitates his half-

GIVING LIFE BACK TO THE GODS

The notion of sacrifice is more broadly sourced in the creation myths of the Aztecs and other Meso-American peoples. The gods had been involved in every aspect of creation: of humans, of the land, of food, of rain and of celestial phenomena. This creation had not been made without sacrifice by the gods –

often of their very lives. In return it was only respectful to offer the same; and so to give life back to the gods through human sacrifice had its own logic (however repellent to the modern world). The continued support and intervention of the gods required that they understood the Aztecs' gratitude

for the fullness of life they had already received. As Montezuma II (ruled 1502–1520) pointed out to his Spanish conquerors, Europeans also killed each other in battle; the Aztecs simply waited until the battles had finished to carry out the killings under more ritualized conditions.

sister Coyolxauhqui, before allowing her body to tumble down Mount Coatepec, breaking into pieces as it falls. In one image of the story, only brought to light in a recent excavation, the Turquoise Serpent pierces her chest, foreshadowing a later sacrifice technique. The newly born god then pursues the *Centzon Huitznahua* across the mountain, killing most of them, with just a few managing to escape to the south. In this way Huitzilpochtli becomes the dominant god in the pantheon.

RITUAL REMOVAL OF THE HEART

The imagery and symbolism in this story lie at the heart – quite literally – of the Aztecs' cult practice of human sacrifice. Cosmologically, Huitzilpochtli represents the newly risen sun chasing away the light of the stars, represented by the *Centzon Huitznahua*. But the story has another power: it tells of the ascendancy of the Aztec people and of their superiority over the other city states and tribes of central Mexico. For the Aztecs, it gave them unfettered permission to subdue their enemies, in the knowledge they were fulfilling the destiny of their patron god.

When the Aztecs founded their capital city at Tenochtitlan, their first act was to build the Templo Mayor, the pyramid temple surmounted by two shrines – each with its own stairway. One shrine was dedicated to Tlaloc, the god of rain, and the other to Huitzilpochtli, the god of sun and fire. The Huitzilpochtli side of the pyramid symbolized the mythic mountain Coatepec, birthplace of Huitzilpochtli. It was here that the first human sacrifices took place. In the Aztec system of 'flower wars', of ritualized war with the forces of other city states, the captured soldiers of the opposing side were taken to the top of the pyramid, where they were stretched across the sacrificial stone, their chests opened with a obsidian ritual knife and their hearts removed.

Their bodies – like that of Coyolxauhqui – were tossed down the mountain, reinforcing the myth of Huitzilpochtli's superiority.

Evidence for this connection was shown most clearly when artefacts were accidentally unearthed in Mexico City by electricity-company workers on 21 February 1978. At the place where the foot of the Templo Mayor would once have stood, a circular sculpture was discovered, depicting the dismembered figure of Coyolxauhqui. This marked the precise spot where the dismembered bodies of the Aztecs' sacrificial victims would have come to rest. Further excavations on the site revealed more than a hundred examples of sacrificial deposits and offerings, containing a total of some six thousand objects within stone boxes or 'cists'. Objects brought from Teotihuacan and other pre-Aztec centres have also been found here.

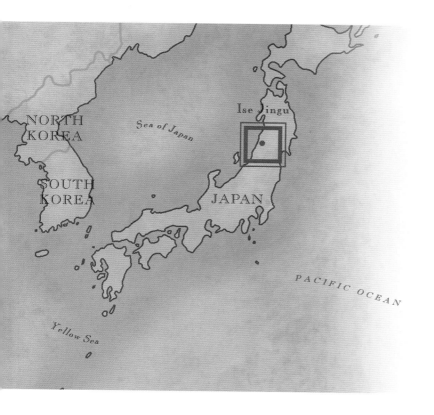

Shinto and kami worship

Shinto is the name for the native religion of Japan which was also, until the end of the Second World War, the state religion of the country – a patriotic force that was used to justify an extreme and militaristic form of nationalism. At the heart of Shinto, however, lies a reverence for nature and a worship of kami or spirits. Indeed, for many scholars there is little distinction between kami worship and Shinto as a formalized religion.

Like many religions, Shinto has evolved over hundreds of years and now takes many forms, each with a different stress or theme. Many Japanese practices – from garden design and architecture to sumo wrestling and flower-arranging – are rooted in the Shinto religion and show its influences in subtle ways.

Left Kami *shrines are located outdoors where the* kami *spirits are believed to live; reverence of nature is fundamental to the religion. The arrival of Buddhism led to* kami *cults being renamed 'Shinto'.*

EARLY KAMI WORSHIP

It seems that *kami* worship predated the origins of Shinto. For most historians, there has been at least one major migration to the Japanese islands, and some experts believe that what we now know as Shinto was brought to Japan during these cultural landings from China or even Korea during the Yayoi period (c.300 BCE–250 CE). Others think that some form of *kami* worship was indigenously present in Japan as far back as the Jomon period (c.13 000 BCE).

The main achievement of early Shinto was to unite a disparate set of *kami*-worshipping tribes under one principle. This was achieved as a result of the Yamato Kingdom's rise to prominence between the 3rd and 5th centuries CE. The Emperor of Japan and his family had their own deities and these were promoted to the populace as the pre-eminent spiritual forces. The mythologizing process involved the claim that the Emperor was a direct descendant of the great sun goddess Amaterasu.

Early worship is generally believed to have taken place outdoors, as a veneration of the dwelling place of the *kami*. These might have been places of particular beauty such as waterfalls, mountains, or even rice paddies. Sacred copses (*Iwakura*), or altars formed by natural collections of rocks (*himorogi*), played host to adherents. Following the arrival of Buddhism in 538 CE, all this changed with the idea that the *kami* could be housed in shrines. The first of these shrines is believed to have been at Izumo in 659 CE, while the next (and still the most important) was at Ise, where the first of the Ise Jingu shrines (see pages 38–39) was created in 690 CE.

THE UNION OF BUDDHISM AND SHINTO

The arrival of Buddhism in Japan prompted the naming of the *kami* cults as 'Shinto'. As the royal court adopted Buddhism, there was a need to bring together the mythologies of Buddhism and those of *kami* worship. The *kami*, said one explanation, were supernatural beings caught on the wheel of birth and rebirth. And the *kami* played an important role in the protection of Buddhism. This explanation was later challenged by the important spiritual teacher Kukai, who looked for actual correspondences between the *kami* gods and the manifestations of the Buddha. Hence the sun goddess Amaterasu (ancestor of the royal family) was, in Kukai's philosophy, *Dainichi Nyorai*, the Great Sun Buddha. In other words, the *kami* were simply emanations of the Buddhahood.

The bringing together of Buddhism and Shinto, the *shinbutso shugo*, as well as the encompassing of Confucianism and Taoism, were parts of the long process of cementing the central myth of the divinity of the imperial family. It was this idea that would maintain Japanese society for many hundreds of years. In 1868, however, after the Meiji Restoration, Shinto was made the official state religion of Japan and the idea of syncretism between Buddhism and Shinto was outlawed. State Shinto became a powerful force in all aspects of Japanese life, with politics and education following its ideological lead: the identity of the country was bound up with Emperor worship and a sense of the nation's destiny. This would be shattered at the end of the Second World War when Emperor Hirohito's role as a living god was exposed and he renounced his divinity, in the wake of the nuclear attacks on Hiroshima and Nagasaki.

MODERN SHINTO VARIATIONS

However, there are still many strands of Shinto that both predate State Shinto and continue to exist today. Sect Shinto (*shuha-shinto*) is made up of 13 groupings that formed during the 19th century and have individual focuses. They include faith-healing sects, Confucian sects and even sects that focus on the worship of mountains, such as Mount Fuji. Adherents do not generally worship in shrines. Folk Shinto (*minzoku-shinto*) encompasses various folk beliefs in the world of spirits and deities. While some of its practices are based on Taoist, Buddhist or Confucian traditions, many can be traced to ancient *kami* worship. Within Folk Shinto can be found practitioners of shamanic healing and exorcism, as well as those providing many forms of divination.

Perhaps the foremost of the surviving forms of Shinto, however, is Shrine Shinto (*jinja-shinto*), which still represents the major current of religious worship in Japan and is most clearly expressed at the Ise Jingu shrines in the Mie prefecture in Japan.

Above *The sun goddess, Amaterasu, played an important role in uniting the Buddhist and Shinto religions. Some scholars looked to establish links between* kami *gods and manifestations of the Buddha.*

Ise Jingu

The Naiku is not the only part of the shrine complex that is renewed every 20 years. A number of other buildings are literally 're-placed', including the Uji bridge, which links the shrine to the opposite bank of the Isuzu River and provides access for pilgrims. Although many thousands of rituals are performed at the Ise Jingu every year, entrance to the Kotaijingu within the Naiku is

Ise Jingu holds a special place in the spiritual life of Japan and the Japanese people. It was the first great Shinto shrine, founded more than two thousand years ago by Yamatohime-no-mikoto, daughter of the Emperor Suinin, after a 20-year search for a permanent place of worship for the goddess Amaterasu Omikami. In Shinto history, Yamatohime's journey came to an end in the Mie Prefecture when she heard the goddess's voice telling her that she wished to be venerated in Ise, close to the beauty of both mountains and sea.

The Ise Jingu (sometimes just called the Jingu) is actually a shrine complex made up of well over a hundred separate shrines. It is divided into two distinct parts by a pilgrimage road some 4.8 km (3 miles) long. The inner shrine, called the Naiku, is in the town of Uji, and it is this part of the shrine that is dedicated to Amaterasu Omikami. The outer shrine, or Geku, is dedicated to a different Shinto deity named Toyouke no Omikami and is located in the town of Yamada.

TRANSFERRING THE SHRINE

Although historians place the origins of the older Naiku as far back as the year 4 CE, evidence of the shrine's construction in its current form was first recorded in 690 CE. This is also the first recognized date of a remarkable ritual process known as *Shinkinen Sengu* – or transferring the shrine – which takes place on a regular timescale. Every 20 years (except for the period of the warring states in the 15th and 16th centuries CE) the main part of the central shrine, the Kotaijingu, has been replaced by another identical building on an adjacent plot. During the climactic ritual of *Shinkinen Sengu*, before the redundant shrine is taken down,

sacred objects (including vestments and tools) are transferred from the old shrine to the new. The most important of these is the sacred eight-sided mirror, or *yatakagami*, of the sun goddess Amaterasu Omikami. Twenty years later the shrine returns to the previous plot, because it perpetually alternates between east and west.

The process of building the new shrine reveals much about Shinto's reverence for the natural world. In an interesting paradox, the new building requires the cutting and fashioning of a huge amount of fresh wood. The process of selecting the timber is long and painstaking, and requires the advance identification of trees likely to provide the highest quality and greatest size of cedar wood for the demanding designs of the shrine. The great doors, for instance, require planks of cedar that are 1.2 m (4 ft) wide and completely without blemish or imperfection. Some trees have been identified for use as far as two hundred years ahead. The cutting of the trees is performed by three specially trained craftsmen, who work with axes to carry out the ritual felling. At the end of the process the top of the tree is placed in the stump, as a symbol of reverence for the tree's gift to the people.

restricted, with followers only being allowed to approach the four rows of tall wooden fences that protect the inner sanctum from being overlooked.

CONNECTION WITH THE NATURAL WORLD

Shinto is essentially an animistic religion which focuses on the everyday elements of life, the present moment and the quality of people's connections with each other and with the natural world. For their purity and focus, the Ise Jingu shrines are the highest and most important expression of Shinto in Japanese culture. Here, reverence for the mysteries of the shrines' cycles and the natural beauty of the place is still very powerful and likely to remain so.

① *TORII*

Toriis, or gates, are a very important part of the shrine complex. Formed of either straight or curved beams, they mark the entrance to the sacred area inside shrines, and may be decorated with plaited rope or with strips of white paper to indicate the presence of the *kami* or spirit.

② **FOREST SETTING**

Although the Ise Jingu shrines are surrounded by 5,500 ha (13,600 acres) of sacred Kumano forest, timber was only ever cut from the special 'shrine forest' or *misomayama*. Since 1391 CE, however, no timber for the new shrines has come from this forest, having been sourced elsewhere. But for the next *Sengu* ceremony in 2013, 20 per cent of the timber for the building will once again come from the 'shrine forest' – for the first time in more than six hundred years.

③ *HAIDEN*

The *haiden*, or oratory, is where worshippers say prayers to the spirit, and is a part of the shrine that is open to the laiety.

④ *HONDEN*

The *honden*, or inner sanctum, is only open to priests. It is the main dwelling place of the deity and contains the symbolic objects of Shinto worship – the sacred mirror, sword and jewels.

⑤ *CHIGI* AND *KATSUOGI*

Shinto architecture has great purity and simplicity. The crossed beams extending from each end of the roof gable are known as *chigi*, while the log-shaped sections set horizontally are called *katsuogi*.

⑥ *OI-YA*

The *oi-ya* is a small wooden hut or shed that contains the sacred central post of the previous shrine. The new shrine is erected over and around this post, so that the sacred post is never actually seen by worshippers.

PART 2

CULTS OF THE GODDESS

Bigger than the mountains am I,
The Empress of the gods am I,
The Queen of heaven am I
The earth's mistress am I.

<small>DESCRIPTION OF ISHTAR, BABYLONIAN SCRIPTURE</small>

Listen to the words of the Great Mother, she who of old
was also called among men Artemis, Astarte, Athene,
Dione, Melusine, Aphrodite, Cerridwen, Dana,
Arianrhod, Isis, Bride, and by many other names.

<small>DOREEN VALIENTE, CHARGE OF THE GODDESS</small>

Rediscovering the Goddess

There is no doubt that women have been neglected in the spiritual history of at least the last two millennia. The modern rise of feminist thought that began in the West in the 1960s has done much to start the recovery process, but there is still a great deal of work to be done. Enlightened psychologists and spiritual counsellors tell us that both men and women are grieving the loss of the empowered feminine aspect of the soul – the anima, as the famous Swiss psychiatrist Carl Jung named her. And yet it seems so long since she has been witnessed in her full glory that we appear to have forgotten who she really is.

Below *The goddess Astarte, as depicted in this terracotta relief, was revered in various forms and under different names by a number of goddess cults.*

From the violence of the Hindu goddess Kali (see pages 64–67) and the active feminine principle of Shakti, the Hindu expression of the Divine Mother (see pages 60–63), through the lustful Greek Aphrodite (see pages 56–59) to the purity of the Christian Mary (see pages 72–75), the role of the feminine in the life of the spiritual psyche is much richer and more multi-dimensional than we might imagine. As we look at the ways that goddess cults have developed over long periods of time, we can see how smaller cults that have worshipped particular female aspects are often absorbed into larger goddess cults. The Sumerian goddess Ishtar (see pages 44–47) appropriated many of the qualities of the earlier goddess Inanna in her rise to supremacy, and gathered myriad names to denote her different functions for certain sub-cultures on specific occasions or in particular cult worship. Venus, the Roman version of Aphrodite, similarly had many names to display her multiple blessings, depending on whether she was appearing as a goddess of war, of love, of healing or of sex.

COMPASSION AMID VIOLENCE

This ability to contain paradox is often witnessed within goddess cult worship. Even Kali, drenched with blood from the battlefield and wearing a necklace of severed heads, is worshipped as a kind maternal presence in some places. Similarly Tara (see pages 68–71) and Ishtar are worshipped for their compassionate aspects even in the face of their demon-slaying and apparently bloodthirsty actions. Worshippers may challenge the paradox, though: when the Goddess displays violence, it is targeted at demons or evil-doers and, more metaphorically, at untruth, ignorance and the traps of mortal life. These terrifying, dynamic forces are here to create liberation. They offer a pattern for those who need to cut through the obstacles on the path to enlightenment.

Another interesting feature of some goddess cultures is the interchangeability of roles within goddess myths. Queen Isis of Egypt (see pages 48–51) is both the sister of Osiris and his wife, and following Osiris' death and temporary resurrection she is able to give birth to their son Horus. Then, as the myth develops over time, Horus and Isis are seen to be married: Horus has become his own father and has taken his place. This apparently incestuous appropriation, while it may have troubled (or at least interested) the Austrian neurologist and psychiatrist Sigmund Freud, appeared only to strengthen the cult of Isis and make her more all-encompassing in her attributes.

COMPARISON VIRGIN BIRTHS

Some scholars like to make comparisons between the Isis myth and the Mary of Nazareth story, for they both contain elements of parthenogenesis (the 'virgin birth', or at least having a god for a father), the nurturing bond between mother and child (recorded in iconic imagery) and the son becoming one with the father. Mary's iconic origins are often questioned: has the powerful imagery of Madonna and Child been borrowed from other cultures? The study of the Black Madonna (see pages 76–79) gained new impetus in the 20th

century, and a number of experts are building a case to say that the Madonna and Child archetype (as portrayed in hundreds of images found throughout Europe) and its Christian representations were actually predated by other cultures.

Although these various interpretations and manifestations of the Universal Woman – the Cosmic Female – may appear to be diverse and unique, perhaps we can begin to see the links, patterns and joins in the stories that enable us to piece together the many aspects of the lost Goddess. Just as Isis searched, found and brought together the dispersed parts of her murdered husband Osiris, so we have the chance to do the same for her.

Above *This Roman wall painting shows a ceremony of the Isis cult. The concept of virgin birth is just one of many similarities between the Isis myth and the Mary of Nazareth story.*

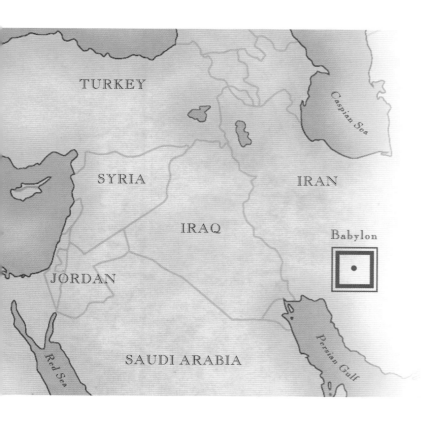

Ishtar, goddess of war, fertility and sexual love

Ishtar is the Babylonian and Assyrian goddess of fertility, sexual love and war. When her worshipping tribes first reached Sumeria, they were met by people who could identify Ishtar with their own goddess Inanna. As the second millennium developed, Inanna's myths became Ishtar's and she assimilated many of the functions of other 'smaller' goddesses.

Like Aphrodite in the Greek pantheon, Ishtar was the personification of the planet Venus, and her cult became strongly associated with sexuality and sexual fulfilment involving ritualized prostitution. Ishtar's sacred city – Erech – was also known as 'the town of the sacred courtesans' and she herself was 'the courtesan of the gods'.

ISHTAR THE ALL-POWERFUL

Babylonian scriptural texts have many names for this multifaceted goddess: Light of the World, Leader of Hosts, Opener of the Womb, Righteous Judge, Lawgiver, Goddess of Goddesses, Bestower of Strength, Framer of All Decrees, Lady of Victory, Forgiver of Sins, Torch of Heaven and Earth. She was also worshipped under a number of other

Left *The Ishtar Gate was the eighth gate to the city of Babylon. One of the original Seven Wonders of the World, it was built to celebrate the goddess Ishtar in about 575 BCE.*

sacred titles, such as Exalted Light of Heaven, She Who Begets All, Guardian of the Law and Shepherdess of the Lands. Her status as an all-powerful goddess is expressed in one early Babylonian text:

Bigger than the mountains am I,
The Empress of the gods am I,
The Queen of heaven am I
The earth's mistress am I.

As well as her powers of creation, rulership, prophecy and sexual power, Ishtar was also seen as a healing goddess. An effigy of her was once transported to Egypt in order to heal the Pharaoh Amenhotep III (ruled 1391–1353 BCE).

CULT CENTRES

Symbolically Ishtar is often seen as a lion, or seen standing on a lion – a symbol indicative of her status as a goddess of war. At her cult centres, images of the lion were common. The Ishtar Gate was the eighth gate to the inner city of Babylon and was built by order of King Nebuchadnezzar II in around 575 BCE. Originally one of the Seven Wonders of the World (until it was replaced by the lighthouse of Alexandria), the Ishtar Gate was constructed from blue glazed tiles with bas-relief figures of dragons and aurochs (cattle). The gate, 14 m (46 ft) high and 30 m (98 ft) wide, with doors of cedar, opened onto the Processional Way, which was also decorated with rows of lion images, around 120 of them in all. Each year, during the New Year's celebration, statues of the gods were brought through the gate and along the Processional Way. A reconstruction of the gate is now in the Pergamon Museum in Berlin. Ishtar also had major cult centres in Nineveh and Aleppo and was worshipped in Uruk, Akkad and Kich.

CONFLICTING ROLES

As in many early myths of ancient cultures, gods and goddesses seemed to have contradictory roles at different times. And so it was with Ishtar. She was often described as the daughter of the moon goddess Ningal and her consort Nanna (also known as Sin),

Left *This Neo-Assyrian tablet shows a typical representation of Ishtar standing on a lion. The lion was a central image in her cult and was associated with her status as a goddess of war.*

both of whom were the chief Gods of the City of Uruk. In another tradition, however, she was the daughter of the sky god Anu, and later even became his wife. She was also sister to the sun god Utu (also known as Marduk) and Ereshkigal, goddess of the Underworld. Ishtar was the highest god in the Babylonian pantheon, the *Sharrat Shame* or Queen of Heaven, who had given birth to the world and yet still remained a virgin. For the rulers of Sumeria, it was Ishtar who bestowed their right to have power over their people.

In another confusion of roles, her consort/husband was Tammuz (Dumuzi in Sumerian), the river god of the Tigris-Euphrates, who was also responsible for growth and fertility. In some versions of his myth, when Tammuz died in the summer and crops started to wither, Ishtar went looking for him, searching throughout the world. Eventually, she discovered him in the depths of the Underworld and was able to bring him back to life. With Tammuz reborn at the time of the autumnal equinox and the ritual of holy marriage with Ishtar, the rains could fall again and the crops start to grow once more.

Ishtar appears in the Old Testament, where her worship was regarded as an abomination – as was the presence of her *ishtarishtu* or sacred prostitutes. Their appearance at the doors of the Hebrew great temple brought consternation to the priests.

Above *The Epic of Gilgamesh tells the story of how King Gilgamesh refused Ishtar's advances and unleashed her wrath. This relief shows the King flanked by two bull-men.*

ISHTAR IN MYTH

Like many goddesses, one of Ishtar's most important myths revolves around a journey to the Underworld. At first it was believed that the events of the (incomplete) mythic text followed the death of Ishtar's lover Tammuz, and saw her going to confront the Queen of the Underworld and bring back Tammuz. However, the recent discovery of a comparable myth involving Inanna (Ishtar's Sumerian counterpart) has shed some doubt on the story.

What is known from Ishtar's story is that she approaches the gates in a raging mood: she demands of the gatekeeper that he open them, saying: 'If thou openest not the gate to let me enter, I will break the door, I will wrench the lock, I will smash the door-posts, I will force the doors. I will bring up the dead to eat the living. And the dead will outnumber the living.'

The terrified gatekeeper scurries away to Ereshkigal, Queen of the Underworld, who tells him to let Ishtar in, but only under the conditions of an ancient decree, which demands that Ishtar shed one piece of clothing with each gate she passes through. After the seventh gate Ishtar, both furious and naked, attacks Ereshkigal, but is captured, imprisoned and overwhelmed by a curse of 60 diseases. And while she languishes near to death, all sexual activity on Earth stops. But Ea, King of the Gods, sends a eunuch called Asu-shu-namir to revive her with the water of life – an action that Ereshkigal is forced to accept. In the ancient text, Ishtar then leaves the Underworld, restored to health, regaining a piece of clothing as she passes each gate.

In Inanna's myth, the goddess is told she can only return from the Underworld if she finds someone to take her place. When she reaches home, accompanied by Underworld demons, she discovers her husband Dumuzi unaffected by her apparent death. She furiously lets the demons take Dumuzi to the Underworld. But his sister Geshtinanna is devastated at the loss of Dumuzi and offers to take his place for half the year. It is now believed that the Ishtar myth more closely followed this model. It is also thought by some people

that Ishtar's journey to the Underworld was an attempt to discover more about death and the rites performed by Ereshkigal.

THE EPIC OF GILGAMESH

Ishtar also plays an important part in *The Epic of Gilgamesh*, one of the earliest and most important literary works in world history, originating from early Babylonia and believed to date back to at least 2000 BCE. It concerns Gilgamesh, the hero-king of Uruk, his relationship with his adventurous friend Enkidu, and his grief following Enkidu's death. Ishtar's role in the story relates to the events that unfold when she makes sexual advances towards Gilgamesh. The King, who knows the fate of her previous lovers, such as Tammuz, rejects Ishtar and unleashes a terrible revenge from the scorned goddess. She asks her father Anu to send the 'Bull of Heaven' (the constellation of Taurus) to avenge her, but when Anu refuses her, she threatens to open the gates of hell:

> *If you refuse to give me the Bull of Heaven, then I will break in the doors of hell and smash the bolts; there will be confusion of people, those above with those from the lower depths. I shall bring up the dead to eat food like the living; and the hosts of the dead will outnumber the living.*

The frightened Anu gives in to his spoilt daughter, and the Bull of Heaven wreaks havoc in Uruk, bringing drought to Gilgamesh's lands and opening up pits into which three hundred men fall. But together Gilgamesh and Enkidu use their skills to kill the Bull, remove its heart and offer it to the sun god Shamash, arbiter of justice. When Ishtar realizes what has happened, she wails in woe: 'Alas! Gilgamesh, who mocked me, has killed the Bull of Heaven.' Enkidu, now aware of Ishtar's presence, tears a bloody leg from the Bull and throws it at Ishtar, shouting provocatively: 'Had I caught you too, I'd have treated you likewise, I'd have draped your arms in its guts.' Ishtar calls her people – the dancing and singing girls, the prostitutes of the temple, the courtesans – and, over the Bull of Heaven's haunch, they mourn the animal's death.

Ishtar, though, is eventually triumphant, for Enkidu dreams that as a result of the Bull's death, either Gilgamesh or Enkidu should die. Indeed, within a short time it is Enkidu who succumbs to illness. This is, by implication, a warning to anyone who might scorn Ishtar or try to defend themselves from her wayward powers. Much of the Epic that follows Enkidu's tragic death is concerned with Gilgamesh's grief and his subsequent search for the keys to immortality.

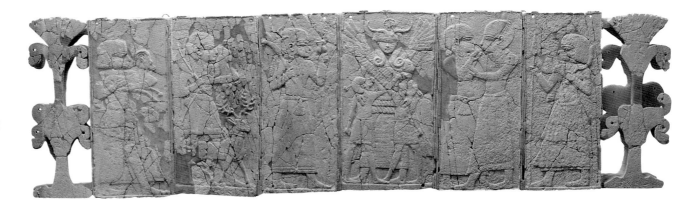

Right *A Phoenician sculpted panel from Syria depicting the goddess Ishtar accompanied by a couple embracing. The cult of Ishtar was strongly associated with sexuality and sexual fulfilment.*

The King, who knows the fate of her previous lovers, rejects Ishtar and unleashes a terrible revenge from the scorned goddess.

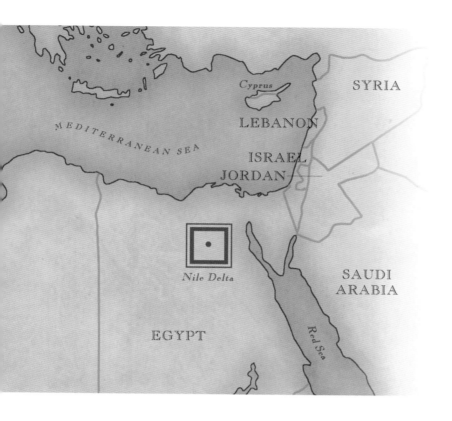

Isis, archetypal wife and mother

Isis is the most important female goddess in Egyptian mythology and was worshipped throughout much of the Egyptian era as the archetypal wife and mother. Her influence, though, is much broader and echoes of her influence appear in many other cultures. The earliest written sources that mention Isis as an object of reverence date from the Fifth Dynasty, some time between 2500 and 2350 BCE.

From this time on, her cult grew and was most prominent in late Egyptian history when the worship of other goddesses (including Astarte) was integrated into reverence for Isis. Her cult spread throughout the Middle East and Europe, with temples in Mediterranean and northern European countries. Temples to Isis have been found in Iraq, Italy, Greece, Germany and the British Isles. Perhaps the greatest centre to her was at Philae on the Nile, where she was revered well into the Christian era. Indeed, the closing of this last Egyptian temple marked the end of ancient Egypt's cultural rule.

THE ISIS–OSIRIS MYTH

It is impossible to talk about Isis without referring to the central myth or myths that surround her. The main myth of Isis–Osiris, which was so central to Egyptian belief, involves Isis, her brother and husband Osiris, their brother Set and their son Horus. It is the story of how Set, jealous of the power of the god-king Osiris, murdered his brother and cut his body into 14 pieces, leaving them by the Nile for the crocodiles to devour. But the distraught Isis managed to find all 14 parts of Osiris' body and put them together, wrapping them in bandages for the first of Egypt's ritual mummifications. The act was sufficient to bring life back to Osiris' body – or at least enough life to make one final act of love with Isis possible. This consummation,

Right *The myth of Isis-Osiris is depicted in this painted papyrus. Osiris is wrapped up in bandages and this is believed to represent the first ritual mummification in Egypt.*

prior to Osiris' journey to the Afterworld, left Isis pregnant with Horus. Following the boy's birth, Isis took care of him with great devotion and, despite Set's continued jealousies and attempts to kill the child, managed to protect him from all the monsters that his uncle could send to destroy him.

As with most Egyptian mythology, this is not the only version of the story, but its focus on the loyalty of Isis to her murdered husband, and her triumph in resurrecting him to fulfil their childbearing potential and her shepherding of the dead king to the Afterworld, are essential elements. So too is Isis' role as an idealized mother – a single mother in this case – able to protect the King-in-waiting from all the evil in the world. A number of commentators have seen parallels between the Isis–Osiris–Horus myth and the Christian story of Jesus and Mary; some have gone as far as suggesting that the early Christians were influenced in their portrayals of Mary and Jesus by statues showing Isis breastfeeding or simply holding Horus on her lap. With the transformation of Horus into his own father-god in some developments, this parallel becomes even keener.

SYMBOLS AND PORTRAYALS OF ISIS

Little is known of the early priesthood that oversaw and conducted Isis' worship, except that both men and women officiated. In the later Graeco-Roman period, many of her priests and priestesses were healers. They would conduct dream interpretation and

were credited with the ability to manipulate the weather using particular braiding of their hair. One of Isis' key symbols was the *tyet*, which resembles the *ankh* (a T-shaped cross), but is in fact the Knot or Buckle of Isis.

The depictions of Isis herself developed over time. Initially she was portrayed in art as a beautiful woman in a long dress, crowned with the hieroglyph for the royal throne. Later, when the goddess Hathor was absorbed into her identity, she was shown with a cow's horns on her head and a solar disc between them. She is usually portrayed with Horus, her son. Sometimes she holds a staff, although she is also seen with the sacred *sistrum*, or musical rattle, in her hand – another symbol of Hathor.

Right *This iconic sculpture shows Isis with her young son Horus. She is the archetypal mother-goddess figure and strong parallels have been drawn with the story of Mary and Jesus.*

A MULTIFACETED GODDESS

Isis' roles in the pantheon of gods are manifold. The Roman author Apuleius, writing in the 2nd century CE, portrayed her thus: 'I am nature, the universal Mother, mistress of all the elements, primordial child of time, sovereign of all things spiritual, queen of the dead,

queen also of the immortals.'

In the Egyptian Book of the Dead, Isis is referred to by many other names: 'She who knows the orphan', 'She who knows the widow spider', 'She who seeks justice for the poor people', 'She who seeks shelter for the weak people'. Also

referred to as the Queen of Heaven, Mother of All Gods, Great Lady of Magic, Protector of the Dead, Light-Giver of Heaven, The Brilliant One in the Sky and by many other titles, Isis represents the beneficent powers of the all-powerful feminine aspect.

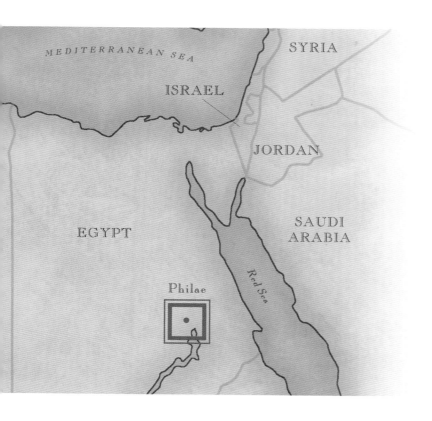

The Temple of Isis

The sacred island temple of Philae was the central focus of worship for the goddess Isis and is sometimes referred to as the 'Jewel of the Nile'. When the river levels changed during the damming of the Nile in the early 20th century, and with the increasing danger of flooding and damage to the buildings, it was necessary to move the temple complex in the 1970s from its original location at Philae to the nearby island of Agilka. There it is still possible to see many of the original buildings that formed the sacred temple.

The original island was just 400 m (1,312 ft) long and about 120 m (395 ft) wide and was made of Syenite stone, with steep sides surrounding the coastal edges. Also known as P'aaleq – the 'Remote Place' in ancient Egyptian – Philae was the last place where the Egyptian worship of Isis was practised. When religious practice ended here in around 600 CE, it was the final act of a sacred play that had lasted nearly four thousand years and had managed to survive – and even flourish during – the rise of Christianity.

As well as having a temple to Isis, Philae was regarded as one of the burying places of Osiris and the temple was thus held in high esteem by both the Egyptians to the north and the Ethiopians to the south. Such was the sanctity of the island that it was regarded as blasphemous for anyone but a priest to live there, and hence ordinary people deemed it the 'Unapproachable'. It was reported by the Roman historian Seneca that no birds flew over the island and no fish swam near its shores.

BUILDING WORK

The island temple at Philae was built over a long period and was initiated during Egyptian Pharaonic times. Amasis Khunimbre was probably the earliest builder of a temple to Isis on the small island during his reign (570–526 BCE). This was subsequently incorporated into the foundations of later parts of structures that can still be seen today, including the 'second pylons' and the Hypostyle Hall. King Nectanebo I (ruled c.379–360 BCE) also constructed significant buildings on the island, including the walls for the main enclosure and a monumental gate. He is credited with building a temple to Athor (later known as Aphrodite), who was identified with Isis, and the *Mammissi* or Birth House, whereby each ruler's descent from the gods was confirmed and celebrated.

Further ruins date from the Ptolemaic dynasty: particularly Ptolemy II or Philadelphius (ruled 284–246 BCE), who continued work on the temple and the Birth House; Ptolemy V or Epiphanes (ruled 205–180 BCE), who added the first 'pylons'; Ptolemy VI Philopator (ruled 180–145 BCE), who added the second set of pylons and the Temple of Hathor on the eastern side of the Great Temple; and Ptolemy VIII (ruled 164–163 and 145–116 BCE), who extended the Birth House.

ARRIVAL OF THE ROMANS AND CHRISTIANITY

There followed the arrival of the Romans, who, perhaps surprisingly, allowed the Isis–Osiris cult to retain its status. For them, Isis was an expression of Venus (the Greeks' Aphrodite), the goddess of love. In its prime, the island temple would have been both magnificent and awe-inspiring for those arriving across the waters of the Nile. Visitors and pilgrims would land on the island and walk through a double colonnade.

As Christianity grew in influence, so the Roman and Egyptian religious cultures came under increasing pressure, because they were viewed as pagan and, therefore, blasphemous. The island temple at Philae represented the last outpost of the Egyptian Isis cult. With increasing destruction from Christians, who defaced the sculptures and representations of any non-Christian figure, the end of the Isis culture was inevitable. In the 6th century CE the temple was finally abandoned and left to the ravages of time.

① FIRST PYLONS

Giant pyramidal *propyla* (pylons) separated the outer from the inner court. In front of the twin first pylons and its central doorway stood two enormous granite lions, and behind these were a pair of obelisks, each 13 m (43 ft) high. Consisting of two tapering towers, the pylons represented hills between which the sun set.

② SECOND PYLONS

Beyond the first pylons was the inner court containing, on the west side, the *Mammissi* or Birth House. To the north, between a further pair of smaller granite *propyla* – the second pylons, which were covered in reliefs – lay access to the Temple of Isis itself.

③ THE MAMMISSI

Between the first and second pylons lies the Mammissi, or Birth House, dedicated to the birth of the god Horus, son of Isis. In order to demonstrate his decendency from Horus the king would partake in birthday rituals here. The rooms in the buildings contained images of Isis suckling Horus as a child.

④ ISLAND LOCATION

Located 100 km (62 miles) above the cataract in the River Nile at Syene, Philae is actually the name for two small islands in the river; however, the term is more usually applied to the smaller of the islands, the original home of the Temple of Isis.

⑤ WEST AND EAST COLONNADES

The outer court was flanked by two colonnades: the longer western one contained windows that originally overlooked the island of Bigeh, before the temple was moved; the eastern colonnade (which was never actually finished) included temples to Nubian deities and a chapel to Imhotep.

Artemis, goddess of hunting

In Greek mythology Artemis was the twin sister of Apollo, both being the children of Zeus and Leto. Artemis was the maidenly goddess of hunting, wildness and wilderness, and is often seen carrying a bow and arrows. She was also regarded as a protector of girls and women. She was widely worshipped throughout ancient Greece, with many temples, sanctuaries and shrines dedicated to her in both town and countryside.

There are many stories that make up her myth and demonstrate both the positive and negative aspects of her influence. As a child, one mythic poem records, Artemis asked her father Zeus to grant her several wishes. Her first wish was that she remain chaste and unmarried all her life. Her second was for hunting hounds to attend her, for stags to pull her chariot and for virgin nymphs to be her companions. She may have remained chaste (although hunted), but she was not afraid to carry out deeds of cunning, justice and violence when required.

ARTEMIS' MANY PERSONAS
Once, when bathing on a part of Mount Cithaeron, she was discovered and spied upon by the Theban prince and hunter Actaeon. Angry at being looked at in this way, she immediately transformed him into a stag, which was then hunted and killed by his own hounds. And in some versions of the story of the Greek god Adonis, Artemis sent a wild boar to kill the beautiful young god for boasting of having the greatest hunting skills. Another example of her swift

Left *The island of Delos is one of the most important mythological sites in the Greek world. It was the birthplace of Artemis and Apollo and, as a result, became a major centre for cult worship.*

vengeance appears in the story of Queen Niobe, who foolishly boasted to Artemis' mother Leto that she was superior, as a result of having 12 children compared to Leto's twins. Artemis and Apollo, appalled by this disrespect, killed them all with poisoned arrows and oversaw the death of Queen Niobe and her husband Amphion.

Like many goddesses, Artemis had a number of other adopted identities beyond her main role as goddess of hunting. In Athens she was linked with the local goddess Aphaea. And the Greek epic poet Homer referred to her as Potnia Theron, the patron of wild animals. As Locheia, she oversaw the work of midwives; and as Kourotrophus, she was a nurse to younger people. She was also known as Phoebe, the female version of Phoebus, her brother Apollo's epithet; and as Cynthia, because she was born on Mount Cynthus. Artemis was synonymous with the goddess Diana of later Roman mythology and with Artume of the Etruscan world.

Worship of Artemis was widespread throughout the Greek world. As well as her key role as goddess of the hunt, she also became goddess of the moon, displacing Selene, the Titaness. Her most important cult-worship location was initially at the island of Delos, where she was born; other cult centres existed at Brauron, at Mounikhia near the port of Piraeus and at Sparta. At Brauron young Athenian girls were sent to Artemis' sanctuary to serve the goddess for a year. Known as *arktoi* (little she-bears), these five- to ten-year-olds were paying a debt for the death of a bear that had once visited the town of Brauron, but had been killed by a group of young men. The *arktoi* were required to act the part of the bear for this period to atone for the town's sins. In some locations Artemis was also worshipped as a fertility and childbirth goddess.

CULT IMAGES

Artistic representations of Artemis vary widely: perhaps the oldest is that of the Potnia Theron, the Queen of Beasts, which appears to originate from early Minoan culture; as a winged goddess with a stag and a leopard (or a lion and leopard) in her hands. More

Left *This marble statue survived the destruction of the Temple of Artemis in Ephesus and offers the modern world a remarkable image of the goddess as she was worshipped. The statue is adorned with multiple breasts that are said to symbolize fertility.*

regularly she is the tomboyish maiden in short skirt and hunting boots, equipped with her silver bow and quiver of arrows and accompanied by a hound or stag.

Perhaps the most extraordinary and striking and image of Artemis is as the Lady of Ephesus, which played an important role in cult worship. The most significant marble statue, which survived the destruction of the Temple of Artemis at Ephesus (see pages 54–55), now in the Archeological Museum in

Ephesus, although other versions exist. It is remarkable in many features, particularly for the gourd or egg-shaped multiple breasts. The mummy-like statue is also covered with mythical animals. This clear expression of fertility, and of the ability to feed and nurture her worshippers, is an extension of her original role as virgin hunter, but illustrates the common process of syncretism, whereby the qualities of one set of beliefs are absorbed under another religious code.

The Temple of Artemis

The Temple of Artemis at Ephesus was one of the Seven Ancient Wonders of the World; indeed, there were commentators who claimed it to be the greatest of all human creations. Philo of Byzantium wrote, 'I have seen the walls and Hanging Gardens of ancient Babylon, the statue of Olympian Zeus, the Colossus of Rhodes, the mighty work of the high Pyramids and the tomb of Mausolus. But when I saw the temple at Ephesus rising to the clouds, all these other wonders were put in the shade.'

Construction of the first major temple complex to Artemis was initiated by King Croesus of Lydia in about 550 BCE, when its fame began to spread throughout the western and central Asian worlds. Although almost nothing now survives of the original temple, save for one solitary column, archeological research and historical descriptions have enabled us to build a picture of the different versions of the great temple that have stood on this site, which was once under Persian rule.

COLONNADED TEMPLE
From pottery relics, it is now believed that the site was occupied during the Bronze Age and the later Middle Geometric times, when the original colonnaded temple was built in the second half of the 8th century BCE. This was the first example of what became known as a 'peripteral' temple – a rectangular floor plan surrounded by a covered colonnade and often by steps leading away from the structure.

In the 7th century BCE a flood engulfed and demolished the temple. Excavation has revealed amber tear-shaped drops with elliptical cross-sections, which once adorned

a carved wooden figure of the 'Lady of Ephesus' – an example of a *xoanon*, an object of cult reverence in early Greek culture, which had been destroyed in the flood.

In 550 BCE King Croesus (ruled 560–546 BCE) commissioned the Cretan architect Cherisphron and his son Metagenes to start building a new marble temple on raised ground, to avoid the same fate that had befallen the first temple. This ornate structure would have a double row of peripteral columns surrounding the main *cella* or temple structure. A new *xoanon*, carved from ebony or grapewood, was created by the craftsman Endoios and was housed in a niche known as a *naiskos*, to the east of the temple's altar.

A PLACE OF PILGRIMAGE
The Temple of Artemis soon became a major attraction for religious and more secular reasons. In its day it was a tourist attraction just as any modern-day cathedral is. Merchants and rulers, pilgrims and worshippers would come to marvel at the spectacle of such a creation. And while some would buy souvenirs and jewellery to mark their visit, more serious adherents

to Artemis' cult would worship at her image and invoke her blessings on their lives. The now-famous image of Artemis (see page 53) is likely to have graced the main frieze of the temple.

DEMOLITION
On 21 July 356 BCE the Temple of Artemis was destroyed by a fire that was started deliberately. The Roman historian Valerius Maximus wrote, 'A man was found to plan the burning of the temple of the Ephesian Diana so that through the destruction of this most beautiful building his name might be spread through the world.' Following the destruction of the temple, the Ephesians demanded that the name of the man should never be made public, so that his wish for fame should not succeed. But the Greek historian Strabo later revealed that the man's name was Herostratus.

Further destructions and rebuildings continued until 401 CE when the christian St John Chrysotom led a mob against this symbol of paganism and idolatry. The temple's final humiliation was to have its stones used in other major buildings (such as the Hagia Sophia in Constantinople).

① *CELLA*

The *cella* was the interior of the temple where the statue of Artemis was placed. The temple also housed paintings and many fine sculptures that frequently depicted the all-female warriors known as Amazons.

② PEDIMENT

The temple pediment featured a sculpture of Artemis wearing an elaborate headdress and decorated with multiple breasts or eggs.

③ IONIC COLUMNS

There were 127 columns in the temple, each 18.3 m (60 ft) high. The top section of each column, which was Ionic in style, was shaped like curving rams' horns.

④ RELIEFS

The bases of 36 of the marble columns were carved with figures in relief sculpture, an unusual feature for the period of their creation. A fragment of one of the columns is now housed in London's British Museum.

⑤ *AKROTERIA*

These were decorative features mounted at the gable ends of the roof. In keeping with the Ionic style of the building, the Temple of Artemis' *akroteria* comprised a stylized fan shape, rather than the statues used during the Doric period.

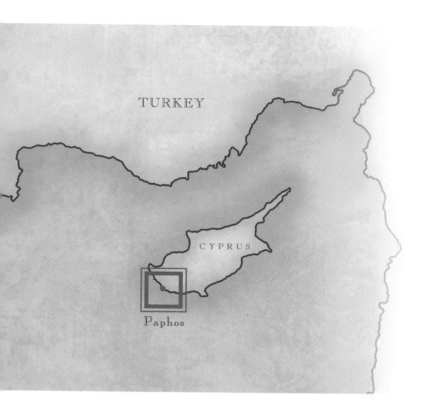

TURKEY

CYPRUS

Paphos

Aphrodite, goddess of love and beauty

Aphrodite is the Greek goddess of love, beauty and sex. She is one of the 12 great gods and goddesses of Mount Olympus. Her name in Greek literally means 'risen from the foam'. According to myth, Aphrodite was born on either Cyprus or the Greek island of Cythera and was also known by the Greek versions of her birthplace – Kypros and Cytherea.

As well as being known to the Romans as Venus, Aphrodite is associated with goddesses from other cultures: the Syro-Palestinian Astarte, Inanna from Sumeria, Ishtar of Babylon (see pages 44–47), Nepthys from Egypt and Turan from the Etruscan culture.

IMAGES OF THE GODDESS BORN FROM THE SEA

In 1485 the Italian painter Sandro Botticelli created his famous image of Venus being born from the foaming waves, carried on a scallop shell, and provided humankind with an enduring picture of her captivating and iconic beauty. The painting was actually based on an older, typical representation of Aphrodite known in ancient times as *Venus Anadyomene* or *Venus Rising from the Sea*. Perhaps the most admired of these was a painting by Apelles of Kos, which was described by Pliny in his *Natural History*. The model for Aphrodite was a woman named Campaspe, a mistress of Alexander the Great (ruled 336–323 BCE), with whom Apelles fell in love while he was drawing her. In thanks for his great artwork, Alexander is said to

have 'presented' Campaspe to Apelles. Unfortunately we have no evidence for her Aphrodisiac beauty, for the painting has been lost to time, although a Pompeiian mural of *Venus Anadyomene*, with the goddess reclining on a scallop shell, is believed to be a copy of Apelles' original.

Aphrodite's birth, fully grown from the foaming waves, is the subject of a brutal but beautiful myth. Cronos was the youngest son of Uranus (the ruler of the Universe) and Gaia (goddess of the Earth). Cronos was jealous of his father Uranus, who had fallen out with Gaia over the hiding of their two youngest and most gigantic children, the hundred-armed Hecatonchires and the one-eyed Cyclops, so that they would never see the light of day. The enraged Gaia gathered her other children to persuade them to kill Uranus with a great sickle that she had made. Only Cronos volunteered and cut off his father's genitals with the sickle. From the blood and semen that spilled onto the earth were born the Gigantes, the Erinyes and the Meliae, but from Uranus' member, which was thrown into the sea, Aphrodite later appeared, fully formed. The early Greek poet

Below *This beautiful, painting shows Venus (Aphrodite) healing her son Aeneas. Their fabled journey from Troy resulted in the founding of Rome.*

Hesiod tells the story of how 'white foam arose from the immortal flesh; with it a girl grew'. One of her two legendary birthplaces is Paphos, on Cyprus.

WAYWARD LOVER, VAIN AND POWERFUL BEAUTY

Since Aphrodite was born a fully grown, beautiful and desirable adult, she lacked the experience of childhood. In many myths that grew up around the goddess, she is often seen as headstrong, lustful and vain. Zeus – concerned that Aphrodite's beauty would cause jealousy among the other gods on Mount Olympus – decided to marry her off to Hephaestus, the rather dull god of blacksmithing and craftsmanship. Hephaestus was delighted at having captured such a beauty and created for Aphrodite some beautiful jewellery and the famous *cestus*, a stunning girdle that made her even more attractive to men. Aphrodite's temperament led her to seek other lovers: she spent much time with Ares, the god of war, but also had relationships with Adonis (her equal in beauty) and Prince Anchises.

Anchises was the cousin of King Priam of Troy, and together they produced Aeneas. The Roman poet Virgil recorded in his *Aeneid* Aphrodite and Aeneas' journey from Troy, which led to the eventual founding of Rome.

Aphrodite is often thought of as the goddess of love, but while that may be the feeling she inspired in her suitors, it was often lust rather than romantic love that appears to have driven the goddess herself. In one story Hephaestus managed to catch Aphrodite in bed with her lover Ares, and trapped them with chains he had fashioned himself. He even foolishly invited the other gods and goddesses of Olympus to come and mock the lovers. Ares, shamed, promised to pay reparation to Hephaestus, but as soon as the chains were released he and Aphrodite fled.

Numerous Greek myths and stories concern Aphrodite in her myriad roles: whether as a wayward lover, loyal mother, or vain and powerful beauty. Fascination with her complex archetype continues in modern psychological approaches to the understanding of the goddess and sacred feminine energy.

Above *Botticelli used this Roman wall painting from Pompeii as his inspiration for* The Birth of Venus. *Her mythical birth from the sea, borne on a scallop shell, naked, fully grown and beautiful, ensured an eventful life.*

SACRED SEX

The cult of Aphrodite had its initial centre at Paphos in south-western Cyprus, where she was believed to have been born and where some experts say there had already been goddess worship of Ishtar and Astarte. As befitting a goddess whose life was more about lust than love, her cult was strongly associated with sexual pleasure.

An almost universal aspect of the cult was the presence of *hierodules* or 'sacred servants' in her temples and shrines – a euphemism for prostitutes. Indeed, the practice of ritual prostitution had already been extremely familiar in the temples of Aphrodite's Near Eastern neighbours, such as those of Inanna in Sumeria and Ishtar in Babylon (see pages 44–47).

Ritual prostitution can be defined as sexual intercourse with someone who is not one's partner, for religious or sacred purposes. The women of the temple were also more usually called *hetaerae* in ancient Greece, and were often ex-slaves or women from other countries who, as well as being valued for their Aphrodisiac beauty, were talented musicians and dancers. Remarkably, the *hetaerae* were also better educated than the general female populace and were permitted to take an active part in the *symposia* – the academic (or merely entertaining) conferences at which debating, speech-making, games and consumption took place. Some *hetaerae* rose to become long-term companions of the great and good of ancient Greece, including Aspasia (lover of Pericles), Archeanassa (*hetaera* to Plato) and Thais (who accompanied Ptolemy on his expedition with Alexander the Great). *Hetaerae* were held in greater esteem than *porne*, who were 'ordinary' prostitutes in brothels. The Greek statesman and orator Demosthenes wrote: 'We have *hetaerae* for pleasure, *pallakae* to care for our daily body's needs and *gynaekes* to bear us legitimate children and to be faithful guardians of our households.'

It is clear from the way Greek men spoke about the cult of Aphrodite that there was no shame in the pursuit of sexual pleasure, whether with women or men. The cult of

Left *A Greek statue depicts the sanctioned practice of* symposium *members fraternising with* hetaerae, *or high-class prostitutes, who were the servants of Aphrodite. These women were given special privileges and were often better educated than the general female population.*

Aphrodite effectively sanctioned this process, which they saw as a celebration of a pleasure endorsed by the gods themselves. As with the Dionysian rites (see pages 18–21), by joining in the sexual pleasure they were directly worshipping and giving thanks for the gift of the gods.

THE ROMAN CULT OF VENUS

As the Roman goddess Venus, the cult is believed to have begun in Ardea and Lavinium in the ancient Italian region of Latium. The oldest temple to Venus appears to have been dedicated to the goddess on 15 August 293 BCE. Like many other Roman gods and goddesses, Venus was worshipped for a number of her roles: as *Venus Cloacina* (Venus the Purifier), *Venus Felix* (Lucky Venus), *Venus Genetrix* (Venus the Mother), *Venus Victrix* (Venus the Victorious), *Venus Obsequens* (Indulgent Venus) and even *Venus Kallipygos* (Venus of the Beautiful Buttocks). In the case of *Venus Kallipygos* (also known as *Venus Kalligloutos*), she was worshipped at Syracuse and other sites in the form of a statue depicting the goddess raising her dress above her hips and buttocks, while simultaneously looking over her right shoulder to view her naked or partially draped form.

Venus Victrix, the Victorious, was worshipped for her ability to bring increased power and winning savagery to armies. In a throwback to Ishtar, Venus could be seen armed and ready for battle. When the Roman statesman Pompey built the first stone theatre in the Campus Martius in Rome in 55 BCE, he dedicated it to Venus in her military form. Another shrine to *Venus Victrix* stood on Rome's Capitoline Hill, where festivals were held. Each year on 9 October a sacrifice was dedicated to her.

Left *Venus, the Roman Goddess, had a number of different roles. One of these was* **Venus Kallipygos** *(Venus of the Beautiful Buttocks) and in this guise she was often depicted in statue form, lifting her dress over her bottom.*

THE MODEST VENUS

Today the ideal of beauty and sensuality that Venus–Aphrodite exemplifies is still visible in some remarkable marble statues that have survived. The earliest form of the goddess was called the *Aphrodite of Cnidus*, and was fashioned by a sculptor known as Praxiteles from Attica in southern Greece. It is also known as the *Venus Pudica*, the Modest Venus, because the goddess covers her genitals with her right hand. Variants on this theme see her attempting to cover her breasts. The *Venus Pudica* is believed to have been the first life-size representation of the female naked form. It was intended to portray the moment when she prepared for the ritual bath that would restore her virginity.

Pliny tells a story that the people of Kos commissioned the artist to produce a cult statue of the goddess Aphrodite. Praxiteles decided to produce two versions: one fully clothed and the other completely naked. The citizens of Kos – perhaps prudishly – preferred the draped version. Nevertheless, some people from Cnidus in Anatolia bought the other *Aphrodite* and placed it inside a temple, where it gained a strong following for its evocation of beauty and sensual eroticism.

The Venus Pudica *is believed to have been the first life-size representation of the female naked form.*

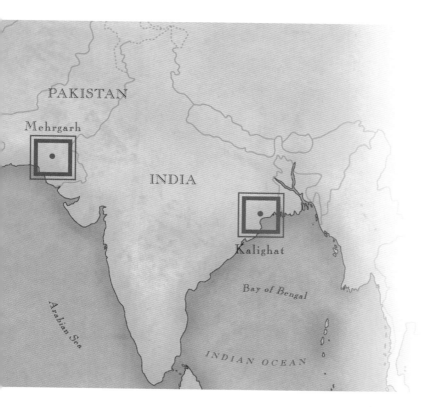

Shakti, divine mother

Shaktism is one of the four main denominations within Hinduism and is the worship of Shakti or Devi Mata, the Hindu expression of the Divine Mother. In this form of reverence, the Great Goddess, also known as Mahadevi, is considered to be nothing less than the Supreme Brahman, the infinite, immanent and transcendent reality.

Right *Devi, or the Divine Mother, has many different forms. Some are kind and beneficent while others, such as Durga, show a more ruthless, destructive side. Here, Durga is killing the buffalo Demon, Mahisha.*

Within Hindu culture, Shaktism is the ultimate form of female worship. It is, (with Saivism, Vaisnavism and Smartism) one of the four primary schools of Hinduism. As the author N.N. Bhattacharyya has written:

> *Those who worship the Supreme Deity exclusively as a Female Principle are called Shakta. The Shaktas conceive their Great Goddess as the personification of primordial energy and the source of all divine and cosmic evolution. She is identified with the Supreme Being, conceived as the Source and the Controller of all the forces and potentialities of Nature. Nowhere in the religious history of the world do we come across such a completely female-oriented system.*

Shaktism is also strongly linked with the teachings of Vedanta, Samkhya and Tantra Hindu philosophies, as well as with the devotional tradition of Bhakti yoga – a teaching that focuses on devotion to the goddesses and all the practices that lead to a heart-linked communion with the goddess in her different manifestations.

THE MOTHER GODDESS' MANY FORMS

An important feature of Shaktism is the idea that the feminine energy in the Universe represents the active principle, while masculine energy exists only in potential form and remains unfulfilled until it is activated by the dynamism of the Mother Goddess. This is demonstrated in some images, which show the god Shiva in a lesser or dependent role, as either the servant of the goddess Mahadevi or as her gatekeeper. In Shaktism all female forms, or goddesses, are merely expressions of Devi, the Divine Mother. In her beneficent aspects she is variously known as Parvati, Uma and Ambika. In her more destructive form she is the wild Kali, Durga, destroyer of demons, and Sitala, the goddess of certain illnesses. The Mother Goddess is also to be found in the forms of Lakshmi, the consort of Vishnu, who oversees wealth and material fulfilment, and Saraswati, who is invoked for her sponsorship of learning, creativity and the arts.

One link with Tantra is expressed in the practice of 'kundalini yoga'. Kundalini, a goddess in her own right, is represented in the energy that resides at the base of the spine, like a sleeping, coiled snake, awaiting activation through spiritual practice. Through meditational, breathing and sexual exercises, the energy of kundalini can be awakened and liberated to travel up through the *chakras* or energy centres of the spine, until it reaches the crown *chakra* in the top of the head. Here, the energy of the goddess is united with the energy of the god Shiva, resulting in experiences of spiritual liberation.

HISTORY OF SHAKTISM

There is archeological evidence, in the form of thousands of female statuettes discovered at Mehrgarh village in the Indus Valley, that Shaktism may date as far back as 7,500 years. The goddess does appear in the Vedas, the most sacred of all Hindu texts. Nevertheless many scholars have suggested that her worship comes from other sources, particularly the religious texts known as the Epics and the Puranas, especially the *Markandeya Purana.*

Left *Although Shaktism is thought to date back as far as 7,500 years, it has been influenced by modern approaches. The 19-century saint, Ramakrishna Paramahamsa, instigated a more universal approach to the religion.*

There are many experts who maintain that Shaktism developed within the Indian Hindu tradition between the 4th and 7th centuries CE, and that it is closely linked with the rise of Tantra (see pages 122–125). Until the 18th century, however, Shaktism was an esoteric part of Hinduism practised by Tantric ascetics and yogis, and was based on complex and subtle meditational practices. Some experts believe that the popularization of Shaktism was encouraged by the songs of poets such as Ramprasad Sen and Kamalakanta Bhattacarya. In their simpler, more devotional model of Shaktism, practitioners wished for an afterlife in the goddess' paradise, rather

than spiritual liberation in this life through kundalini practices.

In the modern age Shaktism has been influenced by a universalist approach to religion. The 19th-century saint Ramakrishna Paramahamsa of Dakshineshwar was a priest in a Kali temple who worshipped the goddess all his life. At the same time he claimed to have experienced spiritual enlightenment through the practice of other faiths, such as Islam and Christianity. This universalist spiritual theme in Shaktism can be clearly seen in the way that many modern adherents decorate their altars with symbols from many different world religions.

WORSHIP

Shakta worship is highly varied and takes many different forms. During a *puja* or ceremony, there will be offerings of flowers and sweets, the chanting of mantras, the use of *mudras* (hand gestures or postures) and some form of sacrifice.

At some sites of Shakti worship, such as Kalighat in Calcutta (West Bengal) and Kamakhya in Guwahati (Assam), goats are regularly sacrificed and, during the Durga Puja, male buffalo are sometimes killed. The brahmin, or priest, who is officiating at the sacrifice is not permitted to let the animal suffer and must cut its throat when it has submitted to the process. Blood from the animal is used in blessings and its meat is cooked for worshippers and the poor. This gift of blessed food is known as *prasad*. In some cases, where worshippers object to animal sacrifice, fruit or vegetables such as melons and pumpkins are used instead.

There are many national festivals during which Shakti worship takes place: Durga Puja in October; Divali in November; Kali Puja in October/November. Some festivals are limited to certain areas: Minakshi Kalyanam in Madurai (Tamil Nadu) in April/May; and Ambubachi Mela at the Kamakhya Temple in Guwahati (Assam) in June/July.

In many rural areas throughout India, Shaktism has blended with the more local 'grass-roots' forms of practice and may not be as recognizable as the more intellectually driven Brahmanical idea of Shakti faith.

> *In many rural areas throughout India, Shaktism has blended with the more local 'grass-roots' forms of practice.*

Local goddesses may be invoked to bring healing and cures for illnesses, to punish evil deeds and to bless the faithful.

In Bengal, popular Shaktism is mostly an oral tradition passed on by living teachers or gurus, and taking place at sacred sites known as *shakta pithas*, where the goddess dwells for ever. The two main *shakta pithas* in West Bengal – Kalighat in Calcutta and Tarapith in Birbhum district – demonstrate the different forms that Shakta worship can take. At Kalighat, the focus is on devotion to the goddess as Kali, who shows herself in a frightening form with darkened skin, sharpened teeth and a necklace made from skulls. Nevertheless she is inwardly beautiful and is a loving mother, with the power to offer her children fierce protection. Worship of Kali here is often communal and usually involves contemplation of the goddess, visualization of her form, prayer before a *yantra*, or symbol, of Kali and making offerings.

Tarapith is quite different and attracts the more yogic, Tantric practitioners. This *pitha* is actually centred on a cremation ground and is dedicated to both Tara and Ugratara, expressions of the liberating goddess. Many will come here to sit alone in the cremation area, surrounded by ashes and unconsumed bones. Practices here are closer to the shamanic tradition and are said to involve exorcism, trance transmissions and banishing dark spirits.

DEVIPURAM

As proof of the living faith of Shakti in Andhra Pradesh in India, a temple complex called Devipuram was created in the 1980s. The main temple structure is a three-dimensional expression of the Sri Chakra (or Shri Yantra), a sacred Hindu diagram or *mandala* that is central to a particular form of Tantric Shakta worship known as *Srividya upasana*. The temple itself is dedicated to the goddess Sahasrakshi (she of a thousand eyes) – a form of Parvati (Shiva's consort) and an expression of the Mother Goddess Mahadevi. The inner sanctum is reached by a set of stairways leading around the temple. On her way to the centre, the adherent will pass more than one hundred life-size *murthis*, or statues, of various *shaktis*, which express different aspects of the Mahadevi that energize this particular *mandala* form called the Sri Chakra.

Left *The* Devi Mahatmya *is an important Shakti text that follows the adventures of the goddess form of Durga. Lavish illustrations accompany the text, which promotes the benefits of praying to the goddess.*

KEY TEXTS

The *Devi Mahatmya* is a 700-verse Hindu scripture written in Sanskrit and arranged into 13 chapters. It is effectively an extract from the *Markandeya Purana*, a set of stories about the sage Markandeya and his pupils, who are all birds of different types. The verses tell of the various adventures of Durga, an aspect of the Great Goddess, and demonstrate the virtues and rewards of praying to her. The stories are both detailed and brutal, using suspense as a narrative technique to engage the reader. In all the stories, Durga faces various demonic adversaries, all with great powers, whom she eventually overcomes. The

Devi Mahatmya is thought to have been brought together during the 9th or 10th century CE and has usually been considered the work of the guru Markandeya. The original *Markandeya* is older, however, and one of the verses contained within the *Devi Mahatmya* appears as an inscription on a temple in Jodhpur dated 608 CE.

The *Upanishads*, which form part of the sacred Vedas, also contain inspiration for Shaktism. Nine out of the 108 *Upanishads* are considered to be the *Shakta Upanishads*: *Sita*, *Annapurna*, *Devi*, *Tripura*, *Bhavana*, *Tripuratapani*, *Saubhagya*, *Bahvrca* and *Sarasvatirahasya*.

Above *There are many Shakti festivals throughout the year and worship is varied. A puja, such as the Durga Puja held in Calcutta in October, involves chanting, sacrifice and making offerings to the goddess.*

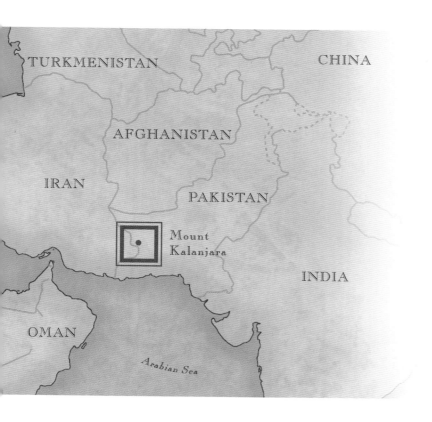

Map labels: TURKMENISTAN, CHINA, AFGHANISTAN, IRAN, PAKISTAN, Mount Kalanjara, INDIA, OMAN, Arabian Sea

Kali, Hindu Mother Goddess

Kali is one of the most popular representations of the Hindu Mother Goddess. She is depicted in two main forms: in one she is four-armed, and in the other, 'Mahakali' iconography she has ten arms (see page 67). In both she is portrayed in a disturbing way: her hair is wild, her teeth or fangs protrude from her blood-filled mouth and her tongue lolls. She is naked, save for a skirt of human arms and a necklace of severed human heads.

Kali is said to be black, although in her iconography she is also portrayed in a dark-blue colour. She is usually naked, primeval and free from any of the trappings of sophistication. She is beyond 'maya' or the world of illusion. Accompanied by serpents and a jackal, she stands on the corpse-like body of her consort Shiva, her right foot forward to indicate that she pursues the Dakshinanmarga, or right-hand path within Tantra, although she can also be found in the left-foot-forward pose, indicating a commitment to the infamous, more dangerous left-handed path. All around her are death and destruction, and it is said by some that the natural environment for her worship is the cremation ground.

Despite Kali's terrifying appearance, many Hindu worshippers view her as a kind and loving presence and, indeed as the Mother of the Universe, able to protect all beings from the dangers of mortal life. She is considered the destroyer of hypocrisy, an essential purifying force in the ongoing cycle of creation and destruction that continues throughout the Universe.

HER ORIGINS

Kali appears in a number of early Hindu scriptures. In the *Mundaka Upanishad* she is one of the seven flickering tongues of Agnr, the god of fire. The figure that we now associate with Kali first appears in the *Rig Veda*, one of the most important Hindu sacred texts from the second millennium BCE; in this work a goddess named Raartri is present, whom many scholars consider to be the prototype for both Kali and Durga, the Supreme Goddess. Kali also appears in the great Sanskrit epic known as the *Mahabharata* (6th to 5th century BCE) as a form of Durga; and in the *Harivamsha*, an early Hindu text containing material from the 1st or 2nd century CE.

In the literature of the Sangam era (c.200 BCE to 200 CE), in the area once called ancient Tamil country, a blood-soaked goddess named Kottravai first makes her appearance. She is similar to Kali in a number of key aspects: her hair is tousled, those who meet her fear her, and she consumes victims of the battleground. Some now believe that Kottravai and the Sanskrit Raartri were combined over time and were embodied in

the brutal, fearful medieval goddesses of which Kali became the most prominent. It was in the literature known as the *Puranas* that Kali was most clearly described. In the *Markandeya Purana* (written between 300 and 600 CE), Kali's origins are made clear: during a battle between the forces of divinity and those of the demonic realm, Kali appeared from the brow of Durga as a slayer of demons, symbolic of her role as the destroyer of ignorance and delusions, who enables truth to triumph. In one version she loses control and starts to destroy all manifestations of life – the trigger for Shiva to sacrifice himself beneath her feet. In the *Matsya Purana* (c.1500 CE), Kali is said to have been a mountain tribal goddess from Mount Kalanjara in northern central India.

Right *This common portrayal of the Hindu goddess Kali dancing on Shiva, shows a fearsome figure. Even though she is surrounded by death and destruction Kali is worshipped as a benevolent goddess.*

Above *In many expressions of the Hindu Tantric tradition, Kali is revered as the source of the the Hindu male trinity, making her the highest deity.*

KALI IN TANTRIC RITUAL

In the Hindu Tantric tradition (see pages 122–125), goddesses are respected just as highly as male deities. In many sources, in fact, Kali is considered the highest of the high. The *Nirvana Tantra*, one of the Hindu Tantra teachings, states that the Hindu 'male trinity' of Brahma, Vishnu and Shiva arises from the Kali 'like the bubbles in the sea', appearing and disappearing, manifesting and unmanifesting, leaving their infinite source unchanged. Many other Tantras proclaim Kali's mantras to be the most powerful, and assert that she is the essence of Mahadevi, the Supreme Divinity.

Tantric practices have always involved rituals, and one of the most important to Kali is the Panacatattva ritual, which is performed on cremation grounds, where the goddess's relationship to death is most keenly felt. In the *Karpuradi Stotra*, a Tantric text, the ritual is described thus:

He, O Mahakali, who in the cremation-ground, naked and with dishevelled hair, intently meditates upon Thee and recites Thy mantra, and with each recitation makes offering to Thee of a thousand Akanda flowers with seed, becomes without any effort a Lord of the earth. O Kali, whoever on Tuesday at midnight, having uttered Thy mantra, makes offering even but once with devotion to Thee of a hair of his Sakti [or female consort] in the cremation ground, becomes a great poet, a Lord of the Earth, and ever goes mounted upon an elephant.

Tantric practitioners, particularly those of the Bengali tradition, are encouraged to confront Kali courageously on the cremation grounds, often on the darkest of nights. While Kali may be the destroyer of all life, if the devotee can face the goddess with the humility of a child, he or she may achieve a state of acceptance with regard to death. The 18th-century writer Ramprasad Sen described Kali as being disinterested in his well-being, caring nothing for his desires or his belongings; and he found her merciless with regard to his pleas. Like a careless mother, she ignored his calling: 'It matters not how much I call you "Mother, Mother." You hear me, but will not listen.'

ICONOGRAPHY

The most common form of Kali to be seen is the four-armed version, in which she carries a sword, a *trishul* or trident, a severed human head and a skull-bowl known as a *kapala*, in which to catch the blood from the neck of the severed head. It is usually her left hands that carry the sword and the head: the sword is said to symbolize Divine Knowledge and the human head represents the human ego, which has to be killed by the sword of knowledge in order that the adherent can attain *moksha*, or liberation from the suffering of earthly life and the wheel of death and rebirth. The goddess' other two hands, which are usually those on the right, are formed into two particular *mudras* or gestures: the *abhaya* or 'no-fear' *mudra*, which bestows peace and protection; and the *varada mudra*, which signifies giving, compassion and charity – an offering or promise, to all those who would follow Kali with sincerity, that she will guide them both in this life and the next.

The necklace of severed heads around her neck usually numbers 108 (an auspicious number throughout Hinduism and Buddhism), although 51 (the number of letters in the Sanskrit alphabet) is also sometimes seen. Many Hindus who worship Kali believe that each of the 51 Sanskrit letters carries a different dynamic energy, each being an aspect of Kali. In this way she is the mother of language and represents, therefore, the power of Tantric mantras.

The ten-headed image of Kali is known, in full, as Dasa Mahavidya Mahakali. In this form she is said to represent all ten Mahavidyas or Great Wisdom Goddesses and possesses ten heads, ten arms and ten legs. Her ten hands – each of which carries a different weapon or ritual implement – represent the different powers of the ten goddesses. In this multifaceted form there is the implication that Kali is responsible for all these powers. Some *murtis* or statues are *ekamukhi*, a one-faced version with ten arms, signifying that it is through the grace of the single Kali that all the gods are able to manifest their powers.

Left *Kali is most often depicted as having four arms, as in this statue. She holds a sword, or* trishul, *and a bowl in which to catch blood from a severed human head.*

SHIVA'S ROLE

The appearance of Shiva's corpse in the iconography of Kali is at first sight mystifying, but there are a number of different explanations for his appearance in this apparently demeaning position. There is a legendary story that tells how, after Kali had overcome all the world's demons in a battle, she started a joyful victory dance. Such was the power of the goddess' dancing that the world began to shake. The gods asked Shiva, her consort, to get her to stop, but Kali was so overcome by the ecstasy of her victory that he decided to lay himself down among the corpses and attempt to absorb the power of her dancing. Kali, being at first unaware of Shiva's presence, suddenly realized that she had stepped on him and bit her tongue in shame – hence her bloodied mouth and chin.

However, not every Hindu devotee accepts this version of Shiva's presence, and the Tantric understanding of his prostration at Kali's feet is quite different. Shiva, it is said, represents Brahman or pure consciousness, sometimes described as 'the unmanifest', while Kali is his complementary opposite. She represents the creative power, or Shakti, that brings all substance into manifestation, but only through their union is this possible. For many Hindu devotees Kali is the ultimate expression of divinity.

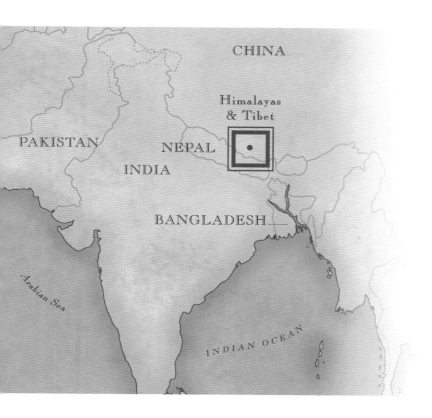

Tara, great wisdom goddess

The goddess Tara originated in Hinduism, where (as Devi) she was one of the Mother Goddesses in the company of Sarasvati, Lakshmi, Parvati and Shakti. She is the second of the ten Mahavidyas or Great Wisdom Goddesses. Her name Tara means 'star' and in this manifestation she is seen as a beautiful, self-immolating force, an unquenchable source of ineffable life and energy.

She is also an important goddess in Buddhism, and particularly Tibetan Buddhism, where she manifests in many different and powerful forms as a provider of assistance and as a multifaceted point of identification in Tantric practice (see pages 122–125).

TARA IN HINDUISM

In one version of the famous Hindu myth concerning 'The churning of the ocean of milk', Tara plays a key role. Shiva, in response to prayers, falls into a deep sickness, when he drinks poison created by the milk-churning conflict between the gods and the demons, but it is Tara who rescues him, by suckling him with her own milk and bringing him back from the brink of death. In the Hindu pantheon there are a number of similarities between Tara and Kali (see pages 64–67), and it is in this aspect that Tara shows her darker side.

Both goddesses are pictured in iconography standing on the supine or corpse-like Shiva. Both wear very little clothing, except for a necklace of human heads. Usually, though, Tara wears a skirt

made of tiger skin, while Kali's girdle is composed of severed human arms. Where Kali is always portrayed with dark or black skin, the Hindu Tara has red skin. There is a difference, too, in their weaponry. Four-armed Tara holds a sacrificial sword, a severed human head or cup made from a skull, a lotus flower and a pair of scissors, but Kali never carries the lotus or the scissors. Both goddesses are pictured with a lolling, extended tongue, and with blood oozing from their mouths.

In her 'hymn of a hundred names' from the *Mundamala Tantra*, Tara is referred to as 'she who likes blood', 'she who is smeared with blood' and 'she who enjoys blood sacrifice'. The text known as the *Tara Tantra* extols her delight in both animal and human blood, remarking that her preference is for the human type. Blood sacrifice has traditionally been made by some devotees – 'letting' some of the life-force from different places on the body, including the forehead, hands, breasts and other key points that have an energetic or spiritual significance.

Many Hindu Tantric followers of Tara use the chanting of mantras in their meditations.

They worship her in her form as Nila-sarasvati. The wording of the mantra runs:

I bow to you mother Nilasarasvati. You provide well-being and auspiciousness. You are situated on the heart of a corpse and are moving forward aggressively. You have three bright, fearful eyes. You carry a skull dish, scissors and a sword. Your form shines like a blazing fire. Give me shelter and refuge. Bless me with golden speech. May your gracious nectar fill my heart and remove all trace of pride. You wear a skirt made of tiger skin and a necklace of severed heads. You are frightening and yet you remove all fear.

In its original Sanskrit, the mantra is repeated as: *Om Tare Tuttare Ture Svaha.*

One example of the way in which Tara is physically represented is the *murti* or sacred sculpture at the Tantric sacred site of Tara Ma, at Tarapith in West Bengal. The image, generously covered with garlands of flowers, is unusual in that it is made of silver metal and shows Tara with the lower part of her face covered in blood. Also, her feet appear in a severed form, placed in front of her. Even

Tara is referred to as 'she who likes blood', 'she who is smeared with blood' and 'she who enjoys blood sacrifice'.

more unusually, it turns out that the metal *murti* portraying Tara actually contains within it a stone deity, formerly known as Chandipur, which is said to have been worshipped by the *Pujaris*, or priests of the temple, for around five thousand years. This stone was recognized as a deity for its vague likeness to a mother breastfeeding a child. The villagers of Tarapith originally likened the stone to Tara breastfeeding the child Shiva. Very few devotees get to see the *murti* in the inner temple at Tara Ma, because it is only available for viewing for a few minutes in the early hours of the morning.

Left *Tara is the feminine equivalent of the Bodhisattva, or the servant of Buddhahood and all sentient beings. This painting shows Green Tara, who protects against the dangers of the mortal world.*

TARA IN TIBETAN BUDDHISM

It was during the time of the Indian Pala empire (750–1174 CE) that the Pala rulers – strong supporters of the Mahayan and Tantric schools of Buddhism in India – oversaw the adoption of Tara into the Buddhist pantheon of gods. Their proselytizing was highly influential in the establishment of Buddhism in Tibet.

Within Buddhism, Tara is seen as the feminine equivalent of Avalokiteshvara, the Bodhisattva (or enlightened being) who embodies the compassion of all Buddhas. She has made a vow to listen to the prayers of all sentient beings and will (as will all Bodhisattvas) postpone her own Buddhahood until all on Earth have reached the state of enlightenment known as *nirvana*. Avalokiteshvara is also known as Padmapani, Holder of the Lotus, and Lokesvara, Lord of the World. In Chinese Buddhism, Tara and Avalokiteshvara are also known as Guanyin or Kuan Yin. Kuan Yin appears in both male and female forms and is typically a goddess of compassion and healing. As Chenrezig in the Tibetan tradition, Avalokiteshvara is said to be incarnated in the Dalai Lama, the Karmapa and other important lamas.

As Mother of Mercy and Compassion, Tara embodies many archetypal feminine aspects. In this role she provides compassion and gentleness to all ordinary beings suffering from the effects of karma and the wheel of birth, death and rebirth. Tara appears in a number of different colours, expressing various characteristics and qualities. As Red Tara, she is the teacher of 'Discriminating Awareness', helping her devotees to tell the difference in quality between varieties of created phenomena. She also teaches how to transform the potentially negative emotion of desire into love and compassion. As Green Tara, she provides protection from the dangers – both physical and psychological – of the mortal, illusory world. As White Tara, she extends motherly compassion and love, giving healing to the wounded in mind and body. As Blue Tara, or Ekajati in the Nyingma lineage of Tibetan Buddhism, she is a dynamic force of ferocious protection, expressing a wrathful female energy that can obliterate the barriers to spiritual transformation. Altogether Tara has 21 major forms within Tibetan Buddhism, each manifestation being linked to a particular colour and energy, which practitioners can invoke according to their spiritual and temporal needs.

One of the qualities of most Tara forms is playfulness. It is said that she often appears when practitioners are taking themselves – or their spirituality – too seriously. There are a number of Tibetan stories in which Tara appears, laughing at self-righteousness and playing light-hearted tricks on people who lack respect for the feminine aspects of life.

TARA IN TANTRA

Tara has been a focus for Tibetan Buddhist Tantric practice since the presence and teachings of the guru Padmasambhava arrived in Tibet in the 8th century CE. In Tantric 'deity yoga' the practitioner uses various meditational, mantra and visualization techniques to cultivate the qualities of the 'in-dwelling' deity within the heart. Padmasambhava gave one particular Red Tara practice to his mystic consort Yeshe Tsogyal, a semi-mythic *dakini* or female deity, believed to have lived between 757 and 817 CE. Padmasambhava asked Yeshe Tsogyal to keep the practice secret as a treasure. This same teaching was discovered in the 20th century by Apong Terton, a lama of the Nyingma lineage. A monk who had known Apong Terton later transmitted the teaching to H.H. Sakya Trizin, the current head of the Sakyapa sect and the reincarnation of Apong Terton himself. Through this arcane process this esoteric Tantric teaching, which renews Tara's presence in the world, has reached across 1,200 years.

In 1989 His Holiness the 14th Dalai Lama, whose lineage as leader of the Tibetan Buddhists can be traced back to the 14th century, spoke about Tara's role in Buddhism throughout its history:

There is a true feminist movement in Buddhism that relates to the goddess Tara. Following her cultivation of bodhicitta, the Bodhisattva's motivation towards enlightened compassion, she looked upon the situation of those striving towards full awakening and she felt there were too few people who attained Buddhahood as women. So she vowed, 'I have developed bodhicitta as a woman. For all my lifetimes along the path I vow to be born as a woman, and in my final lifetime when I attain Buddhahood, then, too, I will be a woman.'

With this important contemporary support from the Dalai Lama, Tara continues to attract the continued adherence of many Buddhist practitioners who look for a female focus.

One of the qualities of most Tara forms is playfulness. It is said that she often appears when practitioners are taking themselves too seriously.

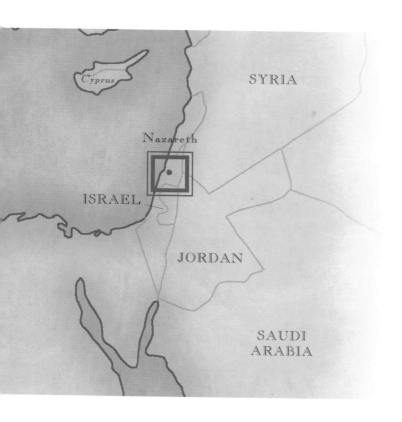

Cults of the Virgin Mary

Veneration of the Blessed Virgin Mary, mother of Jesus Christ, has a long and controversial history and encompasses many complex theological issues that continue to be the subject of debate among the different branches of Christianity. Her role as Divine Mother of Christ, her perpetual virginity, the circumstances of the Immaculate Conception and her Assumption into heaven at the end of her life have all been the subject of intellectual rifts.

Nevertheless, Mary's importance within Catholic and Orthodox Christianity is undimmed, and a series of apparitions throughout the 20th century saw a rise in the numbers of ordinary worshippers focusing on her presence and her power to bless the faithful.

The four Gospels of the New Testament tell us relatively little about the life of the historical Mary. She was a relative of Elizabeth, wife of the priest Zechariah (who was from the tribe of Levi). Nevertheless, Mary was – like Joseph – of the House of David, and so from the tribe of Judah. Her parents are believed to have been Joachim and Anne. When the angel Gabriel made the 'annunciation' to Mary that she would give birth to the Messiah, he also told her that Elizabeth – who had been barren – was going to give birth. Mary's motherhood of Jesus was seen as the fulfilment of Isaiah's prophecy that a virgin would give birth to a son who would be called Immanuel, or 'God with us'. In the Orthodox tradition, it also gave her the title of *Theotokos*, Mother of God. This is perhaps the most fundamental aspect of Mary's role: her identity with Divine

Motherhood. In Christian theology she is contrasted with Eve, the bringer of sin into the world, and – through her own sinless conception, and her role as virgin mother of Jesus – is seen as removing some of the stain left on humanity by those who dwelt in Eden.

THE IMMACULATE CONCEPTION OF MARY

All Christian groups believe that Mary conceived Jesus through a process known as Virginal Conception, or parthenogenesis. Although she was betrothed to Joseph, Mary was a virgin and the creation of the Christ Child within her womb is attributed to the action of the Holy Spirit. The Roman Catholic Church teaches that this was possible only because Mary was filled with grace from the moment of her own conception within her mother's womb. Through this Immaculate Conception – albeit through sexual intercourse – Mary was kept free from the sin that afflicts all other humans and this made her fit to carry the Christ Child. In the Catholic Church, Immaculate Conception was made a 'dogma' by Pope Pius IX on 8 December 1854,

meaning that it is mandatory for Catholics to profess this belief.

Members of the Eastern Orthodox Church and of Protestant traditions disagree with this doctrine, believing (in the case of the Orthodox Church) that Mary lived without sin all her life, but was sanctified from the moment when the Holy Spirit enabled her to conceive. Indeed, Mary is the first saint in both the Catholic and Orthodox Churches. For Protestants there are a wider variety of beliefs, depending on their specific interpretation of the Bible.

VIRGIN BIRTH

All major Christian forms of faith accept the belief that Mary conceived Jesus through the action of God working through the Holy Spirit, and that she had not had intercourse with Joseph, her betrothed, or with anyone else prior to the visitation from Gabriel telling her that she was to be the mother of the coming Messiah.

It is not known by all Christians that the Qur'an also gives a detailed account, in Suras 3 and 19, of the annunciation and birth of Jesus of Nazareth.

Right *Christians believe Jesus was conceived through the power of the Holy Spirit. This painting by Gaddi celebrates the Annunciation, when the angel Gabriel tells Mary she will give birth to the Son of God. This theme of virgin birth is shared by many goddess worship cults.*

PERPETUAL VIRGINITY

It is also believed by many Christians in the Catholic and Orthodox Churches that Mary remained a virgin all her life, although this is widely disputed by those who believe that the Bible indicates she had further children. The New Testament certainly makes references to the brothers and sisters of Jesus, although these are not referred to as being Mary's children. This may not, however, be as significant as it might seem, since the Aramaic, Hebrew and Greek languages are imprecise in this respect. The Greek term *adelphoi* – which can mean cousins as well as siblings – is used to refer to close relatives of Jesus Christ. Another piece of biblical evidence is that Jesus himself, as he is dying on the Cross, entrusts his mother Mary to the care of his 'beloved disciple' – something he is not likely to have done if she had other children. However, Protestants have disagreed (sometimes vehemently) since the Reformation as to whether Mary had further children with Joseph. In some cases this was because of the final phase of Mary's life: her Assumption into heaven.

All major Christian forms of faith accept the belief that Mary conceived Jesus through the action of God working through the Holy Spirit.

Left The Coronation of Mary *portrays the Catholic view that Mary, body and soul conjoined, was assumed into heavenly glory.*

THE CULT OF THE BLESSED VIRGIN MARY

This cult, which has continued in many forms since her death and sanctification, has been the subject of much theological debate among the different branches of the Christian Church. This debate has centred on the question of whether (and to what degree) it is acceptable to venerate Mary. It is also about what she represents within the Christian canon, her relationship with Jesus, with God and with the rest of humanity. Her cult also concerns her continuing role in the life of humanity, and whether she can intervene or provide much-needed wisdom for her Christian disciples.

At the Council of Ephesus in 431 CE the early Church Fathers sanctioned the veneration of Mary and the creation of icons bearing images of Virgin and Child. This was formal approval for a type of worship that was already popular. Many people believed that St Mary was a worthy intercessor between the prayers of humans and the help of the risen Christ. For women, she was an important figure, particularly in the Middle Ages, when devotion to Mary as the New Eve gained support. Some scholars believe that veneration of Mary as both woman and Mother of God did much to support the code of chivalry and the rise of courtly love. There is also evidence that Mary, as the human vessel for the Christ, was the human model for the Holy Grail.

In opposition to the rise of Mary was the post-Reformation Protestant opposition to what was called 'Mariolatry' or worship of Mary as a 'false idol', something banned by the Ten Commandments. This tension remains between Catholics and Orthodox Christians (who venerate the Blessed Virgin) and Protestants (who are wary of overvaluing her in relation to the Holy Trinity of Father, Son and Holy Spirit).

THE ASSUMPTION

The Feast of the Assumption of Mary, which takes place on 15 August each year, celebrates the final event in the story of Mary's earthly sojourn. Her Assumption into heaven – with body and soul still conjoined – is considered by the Eastern Orthodox and Roman Catholic religions an example of resurrection similar in character to that of Jesus.

Although there have been believers who said that Mary did not die a physical death and was simply carried into heavenly glory, the Catholic dogma does not claim this. Pope Pius XII stated in 1950 in his *Munificentissimus Deus*:

We pronounce, declare, and define it to be a divinely revealed dogma: that the Immaculate Mother of God, the ever Virgin Mary, having completed the course of her earthly life, was assumed body and soul into heavenly glory. Hence if anyone, which God forbid, should dare wilfully to deny or to call into doubt that which we have defined, let him know that he has fallen away completely from the divine and Catholic Faith.

Orthodox Christian traditions believe that the Virgin Mary, the *Theotokos*, died having lived a holy life free of sin, as an example to humanity. They believe that only 11 of the Apostles conducted her funeral, because Thomas had been delayed and arrived a few days later. When the others opened Mary's tomb to allow Thomas to offer his final venerations, they found her final resting place – as in the case of Jesus – to be empty.

APPARITIONS

Apparitions of the Virgin Mary have been a common feature of Christian history, with some 22 having been officially confirmed by the Holy See of the Catholic Church. Many more have been claimed and may be popularly accepted, but without the official stamp of approval, a Marian apparition may simply be viewed as a private or non-genuine experience that adds nothing to the faith. Many of the most famous apparitions – such as those at Guadalupe in Mexico in 1531, Fatima in Portugal in 1917 and Lourdes in France in 1858 – have been the cause of great surges of interest in Mary and her role in world history. Sometimes these events have threatened to become more important than the Church itself, based on the reality of her appearance and the wisdom of the information shared between Our Lady and those she has singled out for special attention.

At sites such as Fatima and Lourdes, the apparitions were multiple and occurred over a considerable period of time. Often Mary seems to have chosen to appear to individuals or groups of children. There have also been examples of mass experiences, such as that at Zeitoun in Egypt, where thousands of people claimed to have seen her simultaneously. These events have inspired great devotion for Mary, and subsequent pilgrimages have generated claims of other miracles. Mary's significance in the spiritual lives of believers continues, and for many her presence in the world and her intervention in human life are guaranteed.

Left *This underground shrine at Lourdes has major significance as a religious site due to apparitions of the Virgin Mary. In 2004, Pope John Paul II made a pilgrimage to the site to celebrate Our Lady.*

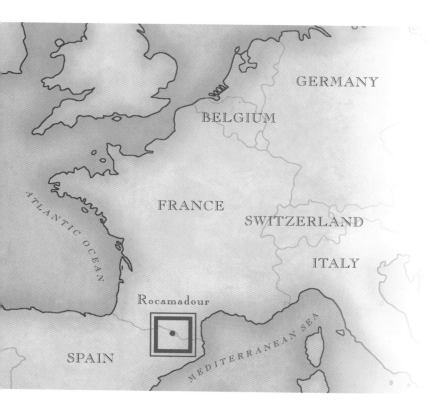

The Black Madonna

The phenomenon of the Black Madonna is one of the strangest and most unique aspects of Christian worship, and contains enigmas that have mystified religious scholars for many hundreds of years. There are estimated to be around 450–500 Black Madonna images throughout Europe, with around 180 in France alone.

Left *This statue of Isis breastfeeding Horus is one of a number of black Madonna images from around the world. Parallels have been drawn between this image and that of Mary and Jesus.*

Black Madonnas are either paintings (often in the Byzantine-icon style) or statues, predominantly carved from wood, but also found in stone. The images always feature the archetypal Mary figure and usually contain an image of the Christ Child. Some scholars contend, however, that the mother archetype found in Black Madonnas predates the Christian era and is an expression of a female spirituality that had its roots in pagan or Gnostic traditions. Many Black Madonnas have become objects of huge religious significance and are believed to be a source of important miracles. A number of them have also become a focus of intense pilgrimage.

APPEARANCE

The Black Madonnas get their name from the dark-coloured skin of the Mary and Christ figures. They are sometimes confused with Christian images of Mary and the Christ Child that originate from Africa or areas of the United States with large black populations, and which are given ethnically appropriate facial features. Black Madonnas are quite distinct: they may have dark or black-coloured faces and hands, but they have European, 'light-skinned' features. Some of the statues get their colour from the material used in their making: often ebony or another dark wood. Some commentators have suggested that the statues and icons may once have had light-skinned figures, but were darkened by years of candle soot. This theory has been questioned over the last 50 or so years – a time when a whole new theory of the Black Madonnas' meaning has taken hold in the popular psyche. At the same time there is some evidence that Black Madonnas are being rewhitened or removed from museums and churches, as religious orthodoxies start to question their real significance.

HISTORY

The history of the Black Madonna is a long one, appearing throughout texts of the medieval period and later. In a French chronicle of 1255, St Louis of France is described returning from a Crusade: '[he] left in the country of Forez several images of Our Lady made and carved in wood of black colour which he had brought from the Levant'. In a document dated 1619, the

Virgin of Myans is referred to as *La Noire* (the Black) and is also referred to in an incident in 1248. The Virgin of Pézenas is known to have been black in 1340. Reports of *Notre-Dame de Bon Espoir* (Our Lady of Good Hope) in Dijon, France, in 1591 say that she was black. Our Lady of Modene was, likewise, black in 1623. A painting from Bruges of 1676 portrays the already-famous Spanish Black Virgin of Regula. The Black Virgin of Puy is described in detail by in 1778 as black by intentional design, since its origins date from no later than the 12th century. The famous Black Virgin of Montserrat, also known as *La Moreneta*, is known to have been worshipped since the 9th century.

THE BLACK MADONNA OF CZESTOCHOWA

The icon known as Our Lady of Czestochowa, or the Queen of Poland, now resides at the Jasna Góra Monastery in southern Poland. It is believed by some to have been painted by St Luke on wood from a tabletop belonging to the holy family when they were in Nazareth It is recorded as arriving in Czestochowa in August 1382 after journeying to Constantinople in the 4th century CE, where it was credited with bringing healing from epidemic diseases to the Orthodox Christian faithful. The icon is still highly influential within the Catholic Church, and during recent public displays many thousands of Poles travelled to be in its presence. People have commented that the style of the painting is more in keeping with icons of the Eastern Orthodox tradition than with other approaches to the depiction of Mary and the Christ Child.

The icon shows Mary dressed in a robe with a distinctive fleur-de-lis pattern. She is portrayed as the *Hodegetria*, or the 'One Who Shows the Way', gesturing with her right hand towards the Christ Child, who holds a book (presumably the Gospels), indicating his role in the transmission of God's word. There are scholars who link this portrayal with older, pre-Christian figures, such as Isis and Horus of the ancient Egyptian world. There is also a legend that the Jasna Góra Monastery

was miraculously saved from destruction by fire, owing to the presence of the icon – but not until Mary and Jesus' skin tones had been darkened by the smoke. However, while the faces and hands of Mary and Jesus are dark, the rest of their clothing and adornment is still brightly painted.

Above *Some people believe that the iconic painting known as Our Lady of Czestochowa was painted on wood from a tabletop owned by Mary and Joseph. It attracts thousands of visitors every year.*

Above *The Black Virgin of Montserrat, or* La Moreneta, *is an intricate wooden statue of the Virgin Mary with the child Jesus that has been worshipped since the 9th century* CE. *The carving resides in the Santa Maria de Montserrat monastery.*

OTHER KEY SITES

Another important Black Madonna that has become a special pilgrimage site is the delicate French example at Rocamadour in the Lot. Made of walnut, together with some strips of silver, and standing 66 cm (26 in) high, this Madonna and Child – she wears a necklace and both are crowned – is attributed to St Luke, the author of the New Testament Gospel.

Enshrined in the Chapel of Our Lady in the town that clings to a cliff, high above the Alzou canyon, the Black Virgin is believed to have drawn pilgrims to make the steep ascent since the 12th century. Over the years since then, her blessings are believed to have resuscitated unbaptized babies, to have protected sailors, promoted fertility and

freed captives. Numerous monarchs and saints have visited the shrine and worshipped before the figures, including St Bernard of Clairvaux, St Louis, St Dominic, Louis XI, Henry II and, in 1172, Eleanor of Aquitaine.

WHY IS SHE BLACK?

For the Christian Church, controversy swirls around the Black Madonna. While a number of 'reasonable' proposals have been put forward to explain her blackness, many alternative theories have flourished which suggest that the inspiration for these important Christian images comes from entirely non-Christian sources. Conventional explanations are generally fourfold: Mary lived in a hot climate and, as the images attributed to St Luke show, would have been sunburned; Black Virgins were created by dark-skinned people of the Middle East, who were creating in their own image; the European creators of Black Virgins naively thought people from Palestine were dark-skinned; and prototypes of Black Virgins, made in dark wood such as ebony, set a precedent. For critics, none of these explanations is particularly convincing.

The alternatives to the conventional explanations are intriguing. They point to a longer, deeper tradition that has valued the female as mother for much longer than the last two thousand years. Examples of the arguments run as follows: Black Madonnas have emerged from the pre-Christian earth-goddess tradition, and the dark skin is either associated with these older images or with the colour of the fertile soil itself. Many of the shrines where Black Madonnas reside are the sites of temples to earlier goddesses and goddess cults, such as those of Cybele and Artemis of Ephesus (see pages 52–55).

Another important strand of thinking regards Black Madonnas as the continuation of the Isis cult (see pages 48–51), where Isis was much darker-skinned than figures of the Middle East or Europe. She is often seen breastfeeding her son Horus in poses that uncannily mirror – and possibly precede – the iconic image of Mary and Jesus. A further line of discussion gives the dark Madonna a different power that is not conveyed by the pale, virginal quality of Mary. Indeed, there are some traditions that believe some Marian statues are, in fact, of Mary Magdalene, a woman more fully acquainted with sexual power and, thus, more threatening to the medieval Church establishment. These ideas are sometimes invoked by those who wish to see female and feminist spirituality more strongly represented within Christian thinking and theology.

Black Madonnas have also been associated with the Knights Templar and with the Cathars (see pages 100–103) of medieval France. These groups followed the Gnostic traditions and saw themselves as protectors of secret, often 'encoded' information – knowledge that was sufficient to earn them the badge of heresy from the Catholic Church.

SYMBOLIC MEANING

An even more radical idea about the Black Madonnas' significance was put forward in the 20th century by Robert Graves, the famous expert on myth. He saw the Black Madonnas in quite a new light: 'Provençal and Sicilian "Black Virgins" are so named because they derive from an ancient tradition of Wisdom as Blackness.' In his book praising the enduring quality of the Black Virgins, Graves looked to a new symbolic role for both men and women:

The Black Goddess is so far hardly more than a word of hope whispered among the few who have served their apprenticeship to the White Goddess. She promises a new pacific bond between men and women … in which the patriarchal marriage bond will fade away … the Black Goddess has experienced good and evil, love and hate, truth and falsehood in the person of her sisters … she will lead man back to that sure instinct of love he long ago forfeited by intellectual pride.

With psychologists and students of spirituality taking a new interest in the Black Madonnas, it seems that these ancient, apparently fixed figures still have the power to inspire and illuminate the modern mind and the modern heart.

Right *Many worshippers who have asked for the blessing of the Black Madonna of Rocamadour, have reported miracles. This walnut statue of Madonna and child has drawn comparisons with similar images of Isis and the infant Horus.*

PART 3

MYSTERY RELIGIONS AND MYSTICAL TRADITIONS

For among the many excellent and indeed divine institutions which your Athens has brought forth and contributed to human life, none, in my opinion, is better than those mysteries. For by their means we have been brought out of our barbarous and savage mode of life and educated and refined to a state of civilization; and as the rites are called 'initiations', so in very truth we have learned from them the beginnings of life and have gained the power not only to live happily, but also to die with a better hope.

CICERO, ROMAN STATESMAN AND PHILOSOPHER, DESCRIBING THE ELEUSINIAN MYSTERIES

Unveiling the mysteries

Mystery religions are characterized by the gifts they can bestow on those who undergo their training and initiation. One of the poems of Orpheus begins with the words 'Close the doors, you uninitiated' – an acknowledgement that secrecy is a key to deep spiritual knowledge and that the leaky vessel will always end up dry. The Orphic cult of ancient Greece was typical of many mystery religions and offered a model that numerous others followed.

The Orphic cult was based on a creation myth, an archetypal story that wrapped up sacred meaning in unforgettable and resonant form: as a result of the gods' conflicts, humankind is both divine and held within the bondage of a physical body, subject to the wheel of rebirth. Thus the cult gave the devout a sense of its members' place in the Universe – a knowledge of their relationship to the gods.

EXOTERIC VERSUS ESOTERIC

Although many mainstream traditions do not accept the distinction, many mystery religions divide religious or spiritual practice into the 'exoteric' and 'esoteric'. Exoteric means 'outer' and is concerned with the formal aspect of religion: the 'going to church on Sunday' aspect, as it might be known in Christian terminology. It is also bound up with the idea that spirituality is about the performance of good acts and the exercise of morality, as a way to please God – perhaps in the hope of a better afterlife, or simply as a means of reducing stress within the conscience. The term 'esoteric', which has incorrectly taken on the meaning of obscure, is about the inner aspects of faith and spirituality. It concerns the development, by whatever means, of a connection with the Divine, the Source, pure consciousness, God. All esoteric traditions, whether they are within the Buddhist, Hindu, Muslim or Christian movements, focus on this link: the way it is formed, what is possible when it is in place, and how to maximize the internal benefit of the link for the growth of the individual's soul. It inevitably addresses many psychological aspects of the human being in a way that exoteric practice does not.

Even before the work of the great modern psychologists like Sigmund Freud, Alfred Adler and Carl Jung, many esoteric traditions possessed enormous amounts of wisdom about the human psyche, its strengths and failings. Much of this information had been codified in mythology and teaching stories, which told of people's capacity for great acts of courage and humiliating acts of folly. The Eleusinian Mysteries (see pages 88–91) were based on the telling and retelling of the same story, year after year, of Demeter's search for her daughter Persephone, and of how her search brought the knowledge of agriculture to the Earth. The mysteries also initiated its

Right *The myth of Persephone and her reappearance from the world of the dead was central to The Eleusinian Mysteries and was celebrated on artefacts like this vase.*

members into the promise of immortality as, in symbolic form, they witnessed Persephone reappearing from the death and degradation of the Underworld. In our image-soaked world, it is hard to appreciate how these staged initiations provided the conditions for contact with the Divine, but many of the greatest philosophers of their time attested to their esoteric power – their ability to connect people with their deepest soul.

The many strands of Gnosticism (see pages 96–99) have been seen as the heart of the Western mystery tradition. Although Gnosticism is usually identified with early Christianity, some scholars are willing to broaden the interpretation to include a longer tradition of gnosis, or inner knowing. Hermeticism (see pages 104–107) is considered by some to be an expression of the Gnostic search. So is Catharism (see pages 100–103), the now-famous heretical movement that was sufficiently threatening to the Roman Catholic Church that it embarked on a Crusade within Europe to wipe out its followers. The Church, so frightened of a faith that did not need a church, even created the Holy Inquisition to ensure that the truth was extracted from those who dared to threaten its rule in the name of Christ.

SEEKING THE DIVINE

Some mystical traditions may contain mystery religions of their own, while others may not involve explicit initiations into the secrets of the faith, the holy of holies. Pythagoreanism (see pages 92–95), for example, had its inner core of disciples, of whom more was demanded and to whom more was given, as well as its wider audience. Mysticism, though, is the search for connection to the Divine. In this sense, all mystical traditions have attempted to answer deep questions about whether its members were simply insignificant mortals left to fend for themselves in a world that cared not whether they lived or died, or whether – through their faithful practice – they could feel the presence of divinity in this earthly life and help, in some way, to guarantee the immortality of their souls.

Above *The Catholic Church launched a crusade against Catharism to eliminate all its followers. Troubadours, often linked to the culture of Catharism, became victims of the Crusade.*

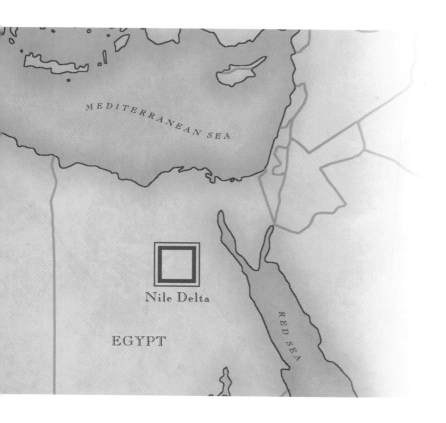

MEDITERRANEAN SEA

Nile Delta

EGYPT

RED SEA

The cult of Horus

The cult of Horus was remarkably long-lasting, continuing from Predynastic Egypt through Greek influence to the Christian era. The powerful myth of Horus, Osiris, Isis and Set, together with further stories of the gods' roles through Egyptian Pharaonic history, promised rebirth and resurrection, both in this earthly life and in the celestial worlds beyond the veil of Death.

During the Hellenic period, under the influence of Platonic ideas, the cult of Horus became a mystery religion in its own right, which is now generally known by the name 'Osiris–Dionysus'.

THE EYE OF HORUS

This is one of the most potent and evocative ancient Egyptian symbols. Before it was identified with Horus, it was known as the Eye of the Moon and the Eye of Ra, and is an image associated with protection and royal power. In Egyptian, the symbol was known as *wadjet* and was a form of deity in its own right. In its 'right-eye' form, it represents Horus' peregrine-falcon eye, the eye of the sun and the more powerful of the god's two eyes. The left-eye form was associated with the moon and the god Thoth. A clear demonstration of the ancient Egyptians' belief in the power of the symbol, and of its ability to bestow immortality, was the discovery of an Eye of Horus hidden beneath the 12th layer of Tutankhamun's mummificatory bandages, following the opening of the Great Pyramid, which took place in 1923.

HORUS' PLACE IN THE EGYPTIAN PANTHEON

Throughout his long cult worship, Horus took many different forms. It is believed that his original form was as a sky god. He was seen as the falcon, with his wings spread out across the sky; his right eye represented the sun and his left eye the moon. He became known as 'Harmerty', meaning Horus of two eyes. He

Right *This Eye of Horus was discovered in the tomb of Tutankhamun. The symbol had particular relevance in Ancient Egypt where it was known as* wadjet *and was worshipped as a distinct deity.*

is commonly portrayed in papyri, but as a human figure with the head of a falcon.

Horus' place in Egyptian myth needs to be understood in the light of the story of Osiris (the god of life, death and fertility) and Isis (his sister and wife, see pages 48–51), who was worshipped as the archetypal mother and wife. Osiris, who had his own cult, is one of the oldest gods for whom records have been

found: the first references appear in the Pyramid texts of around 2400 BCE, when his cult was already well established, and he continued to be worshipped until paganism was suppressed in the Christian era. In the most common version of the myth, Osiris and Isis had a brother named Set, who was the god of the Underworld. Set was jealous of his brother Osiris and decided to kill him, cutting his body into 14 pieces and leaving them along the banks of the Nile for the crocodiles to devour. But Isis searched throughout the land and finally found all 14 pieces. She gathered them together and, with the help of Thoth (or Anubis in some tellings), wrapped his body in linen to bring him back to life. This first act of mummification would set a precedent that lasted for thousands of years. In some versions of the story, Osiris was sufficiently resurrected for Isis to impregnate herself with his seed before he made his journey to the Afterworld. Isis' pregnancy led to the birth of Horus, who grew up to discover the painful knowledge that his own uncle Set had killed his father.

THE CONTENTIONS OF HORUS AND SET

This powerful myth, which exists in a number of versions, explains Osiris' promise of eternal life to his people, with Horus acting as the continuation and promise of new life. The myth continued with the story of Horus' revenge on Set. In some of the myths Horus was portrayed as Set's brother (rather than his nephew). During 80 years of conflict, known as the 'contentions of Horus and Set', there were many fights between the two aggressors. During one of them, Horus managed to remove one of Set's testicles – reducing his fertility and explaining (in mythological terms) the desert's barrenness. But Set also managed to gouge out Horus' left eye. As Horus was the sky god, this helps to explain the lesser light of the moon in relation to the sun. In some versions of the story he lost both eyes, but had his sight restored through the healing magic of Hathor, his mother in this tale and an equivalent of Isis.

Below *This statue of Horus shows him in his original form, as a sky god. The right eye of this imposing figure represented the sun and the left eye, the moon.*

Some scholars have seen links between the story of Horus-Osiris and that of Jesus.

HISTORY

It is possible that the story of Horus and Set had a correlation with historical and political events. According to the Shabaka stone, one of the Egyptian mythic sources from the reign of the Pharaoh Shabaka in the 8th century BCE, Geb – the god of the Earth – wishing to settle the ongoing conflict between Set and Horus, divided Egypt into two halves. Upper Egypt (the desert region to the south) was given to Set, while Lower Egypt (around the Nile delta) was given to Horus. Later, however, Geb revised his decision and gave all of Egypt to Horus. In around 3000 BCE Lower Egypt fought with Upper Egypt for supremacy, but Upper Egypt was victorious, apparently contradicting the myth. Nevertheless, with the eventual union of the two Egypts, Seth and Horus were portrayed together during the enthronements of new pharaohs. Queens of the first dynasty were given the title 'She who sees both Horus and Set' to demonstrate their ability to synthesize the powers of the competing gods. This resolution of the conflict between Horus and Set became an important symbol for peace and harmony within greater Egypt: if the gods, who had so many reasons to fight to the death, could give up their conflict, there was a chance for pharaohs and other humans.

FORMS OF THE GOD HORUS

Through the different periods of Egyptian history, Horus was worshipped in many different forms, according to his function. Generally these forms divide Horus into his two roles as the son of Isis and Osiris and as a solar god.

As the innocent child of Osiris and Isis, he was worshipped in a number of forms. As Harpokrates, he represents the newborn sun and can be seen being suckled by Isis or seated with his thumb in his mouth and wearing the royal crown and *uraeus* (serpent emblem). As Harsiesis (Horus, son of Isis), he is defended from his wicked uncle Seth by his mother Isis. Living on the floating island of Chemmis in the marshes of Buto, the frail child Horus was under constant attack from serpents and other beasts sent to kill him. Isis' magic was strong enough to defend him, and he grew up to be powerful in his own right and to become Harendotes (Horus, the avenger of his father).

Many of Horus' forms are related to his role as a sun or sky god. As Ra-Harakhte, he is identified with Ra, the original sun god, as he makes the journey across the skies from east to west. In this form he is portrayed as the falcon or falcon-headed man wearing the solar disc and double crown on his head. He is also seen as Harmakhis (Horus of the Horizon) and represents the rising sun and the keeper of wisdom. In this guise he was sometimes seen as a falcon-headed sphinx. At Edfu in Upper Egypt, Horus was worshipped as the representation of the midday sun and was portrayed as a winged sun disc or falcon-headed lion.

As Haroeris (Horus the Elder), he is seen as the patron of Upper Egypt. In this incarnation he is said to be the son – or sometimes the husband – of Hathor, who is identified with Isis. This makes him the brother of Osiris and Seth. It is in this form, in around 3000 BCE, that he is seen conquering Seth, uniting the two parts of Egypt and wearing the double crown of both. In this guise Horus has numerous wives and four sons, generally said to be mothered by Isis and known as Duamutef, Imsety, Hapi and Qebehsenuef. They took on the funerary duties of mummification, the ritual known as the 'Opening of the Mouth' – the burial of all men according to the way of Osiris. Horus the Elder was also worshipped as Horus Behdety, at Behdet in the Western Delta. He was usually seen as a sun disc or falcon accompanying pharaohs during battles.

Right *Horus was worshipped in different forms throughout Egyptian history. This papyrus drawing shows him as Ra-Harakhte, the falcon. Ra was the original sun god and Horus wears a solar disc and double crown on his head.*

The Eleusinian Mysteries

GREECE

Aegean Sea

Eleusis

AEGEAN
ISLANDS

MEDITERRANEAN SEA

Sea of Crete

CRETE

The Eleusinian Mysteries were initiation ceremonies held each year as part of the rituals for the cult of Demeter and Persephone. They took place at Eleusis in ancient Greece, west of Athens, where they began in around 1500 BCE. They became the most important of all cult mysteries of the Hellenistic era and even spread eventually to Rome.

The great Roman statesman, lawyer and philosopher Cicero had nothing but good to say about the civilizing influence of these spiritual mysteries:

For among the many excellent and indeed divine institutions which your Athens has brought forth and contributed to human life, none, in my opinion, is better than those mysteries. For by their means we have been brought out of our barbarous and savage mode of life and educated and refined to a state of civilization; and as the rites are called 'initiations', so in very truth we have learned from them the beginnings of life and have gained the power not only to live happily, but also to die with a better hope.

THE STORY OF DEMETER AND PERSEPHONE

The Eleusinian Mysteries that provoked such admiration and loyalty were based on the story of Demeter and her daughter Persephone, a rich feminine myth that explained much about the natural cycles of life. The legend is recorded in the *Hymn to Demeter*, a poem of 495 verses originally attributed to the Greek poet Homer, but now of disputed origin. Demeter was the Greek goddess of life, fertility and agriculture, and her daughter Persephone was a beautiful, innocent image of her mother. One day when she was picking flowers with her friends, Persephone was seen by Hades, god of the Underworld, who instantly fell in love with her. To impose his love he kidnapped Persephone and took her to his Underworld realm. Demeter, sick with grief, embarked on a journey to find her lost daughter. Having taken the form of an old woman named Doso, she travelled for miles and had many encounters, but her neglect of her duties as a fructifying goddess caused the land to suffer grave drought. At one point in her wanderings she met Triptolemus, the son of King Celeus of Eleusis, and, because of his kindness, taught him the secrets of agriculture – a gift that he later passed on to the whole Greek nation.

In despair at the loss of Persephone, Demeter finally consulted Zeus. As the highest-ranking Greek god, Zeus could not allow the Earth to perish, so he ordered Hades to return Persephone to her mother. But Hades cunningly fed Persephone

Above *The Eleusinian Mysteries, which centred around the myth of Demeter and Persephone, were based around initiation ceremonies, as depicted in this terracotta tablet.*

pomegranate seeds, knowing the Fates had already decreed that anyone who consumed food in the Underworld would be condemned to spend eternity there. Zeus' power was great, and a compromise was agreed: Persephone would spend four months as goddess of the Underworld with Hades; during this time Demeter was filled with sadness and neglected the Earth until her daughter finally returned to her again.

This powerful story provided the Greeks with an explanatory myth for the seasonal variations in crop growth. Some experts refer to Persephone's time in the Underworld as winter, when the seed is in the dark ground, although most associate Persephone's absence with drought during high summer, and her return with the time when seeds are planted and the first rains begin to fall. The timings of the Eleusinian Mysteries reflect these key seasonal events.

THE GREATER AND LESSER MYSTERIES

There were two versions of the mysteries – the Greater and Lesser – which each had a distinct character. The Lesser Mysteries were performed each year in the month of Anthesterion (March), although the exact date was not fixed. They expressed some of the miseries of life while the soul is imprisoned in the body. The Greater Mysteries, whose regularity is disputed, were of a more uplifting nature and offered participants an intellectual and spiritual vision of the soul's potential joys, both on Earth and in the world to come. These Greater Mysteries took place in Boedromion (the first month of the calendar), which equates with late summer and the return of the rains.

Four categories of people were permitted to take part in the mysteries: priests and priestesses; those who had already learned the greatest mysteries of Demeter and were said to have attained *epopteia*; those who had already participated once (*mystes*) and were eligible to reach *epopteia*; and initiates, for whom these were their first experience of the mysteries.

From its inception during the Mycenaean age, it is believed that the cycle of Lesser and Greater Mysteries continued with little change for almost two thousand years. Under Pisistratus, the ruler of Athens at various times between 561 and 528 BCE, the mysteries were opened up to people across and beyond Greece and, with Greek state control starting in around 300 BCE, they became even more popular. Nervertheless, the entry requirements for initiates were a lack of 'blood guilt' (never having murdered anyone) and not being a 'barbarian' (not able to speak Greek).

The Eleusis sanctuary

Because much about the Eleusinian Mysteries was never written down, there has been a great deal of speculation about some of their more esoteric ritual content. Even so, much more is known about the spiritually more important Greater Mysteries – which took place at Eleusis over nine days in late summer – than about the more frequent Lesser Mysteries.

Events began the day before the official first day, when the *Hiera* – a set of mysterious holy objects – was brought from Eleusis to the Eleusinion, a temple at the base of the Acropolis in Athens.

THE NINE-DAY RITES

On the first official day, the Archon Basileus (an Athenian magistrate) summoned the people to the main marketplace in Athens, known as the Agora. In the presence of the Hierophant (the high priest from Eleusis) and the Dadouchos (the torchbearer), he called forth the initiates to join the mysteries. People forbidden to participate included anyone who had committed murder and those who could not understand Greek. Initiates entered the Eleusinion after washing their hands in purificatory water.

On the second day the participants processed to the sea close to Athens and cleansed themselves in the water. A small pig that accompanied them was similarly washed, and on their return to the city the pig was ritually killed. The third day was known as the Day of Sacrifices, when it is probable that the Archon Basileus made sacrifices on behalf of Athens. The fourth day was named *Asklepia* after the Greek god Asclepius; legend stated that he arrived a day late for his purification ritual, but was allowed his own rites so that he could be initiated into the mysteries. So, in an age when travel was uncertain, *Asklepia* was a day for those who had arrived late to go through their own purification.

The fifth day, called the *Pompe* or procession, was when the sponsors and initiates made their way on foot from the Athenian cemetery to Eleusis along the Sacred Way. The priests, priestesses and the Hierophant would mostly travel by horse-drawn carriage. At the head of the procession a statue of the boy-god Iacchos, who embodied the noise and excitement of the event, was carried. Once they crossed the bridge over the River Rheitoi, the initiates would each be decorated with two saffron-coloured ribbons – one on the right hand, one on the left leg. This event was known as the *Krokosis*, after a legendary man named Krokos, the first inhabitant of the area. At the River Kephisos a less friendly reception awaited the procession. A group of men known as the *gephyrismoi*, their heads covered, would appear and start hurling insults and abuse at some of the most important citizens of Athens. On arrival at Eleusis, dancing and festivities took place for the excited initiates.

On the sixth day, called the *Telete* or 'rites', there was fasting to commemorate Demeter's fast during her search for Persephone. The initiates' fast was broken only by the drinking of *kykeon*, a potion made from barley and the herb pennyroyal, known for its psychotropic qualities. The seventh and eighth days of the mysteries represented the climax of the initiatory process, during which thousands of initiates experienced the mysteries inside the sacred building known as the Telesterion.

'THINGS ENACTED, THINGS SAID AND THINGS SHOWN'

In the middle of the Telesterion stood the Anaktoron or palace, which was only accessible to holy officials and was where sacred relics were stored. In the vague descriptions given by ancient sources, we are told that in the Anaktoron were 'things enacted, things said and things shown'. Various interpretations of this phrase have been given, but a consensus suggests that the 'things enacted' would have included a

sacred drama telling the story of Demeter and Persephone and requiring the initiates to participate in a search for Persephone, which might have climaxed in her reappearance in a blaze of torchlight.

The 'things said' are likely to have been a series of prayers and invocations. The 'things shown' were a revelation of the sacred objects, the *Hiera*, believed to have been passed down directly by Demeter and Persephone: scholars say they may have included stalks of cut wheat, serpents, special bread, sculptures of a male phallus or a female pudendum. Whatever was revealed to the initiates, the sanctity of the moment would have been life-changing.

The evening of the eighth day saw a feast with dancing and music, which took place in the Rharian Field where Demeter's first grain grew. A bull sacrifice also occurred that night or the following morning, on the ninth day.

The support that many great intellects and philosophers gave to the Eleusinian Mysteries over two millennia is a testament to their enduring psychological power.

① KALLICHORON WELL

Demeter is believed to have grieved for Persephone at Eleusis, at the spot marked by the holy well of Kallichoron, situated outside the precinct wall.

② TELESTERION

The Telesterion was rebuilt during the 5th century BCE. Following this time it went through a number of changes to increase its capacity, so that it could accommodate several thousand people at once.

③ ANAKTORON

In the centre of the Telesterion stood the oldest and most sacred part of the site, the Anaktoron or palace. Only holy officials could enter this small stone building, inside which the sacred relics were stored.

④ PLUOTONION

This cave within the sanctuary was dedicated to the god of the Underworld, Hades, and was believed to be the site of Persephone's return to Earth from the Underworld.

⑤ SITE OF ELEUSIS

Situated about 22 km (13 miles) west of Athens on a ridge above the bay of Eleusis, ancient Eleusis flourished in Roman times. During that period shops, a council chamber, houses, temples and triumphal arches surrounded the central Anaktoron and Telesterion.

Pythagoreanism and the *mathematikoi*

The work of the Greek philosopher and mathematician Pythagoras of Samos in the areas of natural philosophy, mathematics, ethics and cosmology influenced many of his own times, as well as many who adopted his ideas and passed them on to subsequent generations. Both Plato and Aristotle, perhaps the greatest Greek philosophers, appear to have been deeply affected by Pythagoras' thinking.

Pythagoras of Samos, who lived from around 575 BCE to around 496 BCE, is probably best known for a theorem learned by most schoolchildren; given the lengths of two sides of a right-angled triangle, Pythagoras' theorem predicts the length of the third side. But his influence ranges considerably wider and deeper.

THE CULT OF THE *MATHEMATIKOI*

The movement that Pythagoras started – Pythagoreanism – may have been regarded as a controversial cult, but its ideas can now be seen as ahead of their time, and many other metaphysical and spiritual orders have drawn on the philosopher's revolutionary thinking. The Pythagoreans were often called *mathematikoi*, Greek for 'those that study all'. In this sense, mathematics was the all-embracing search for knowledge and was seen as a spiritual activity, rather than merely a scientific one. Pythagoras and his followers believed that numbers represented the ultimate reality and that, through the study of numbers, all manifestations of the Universe could be predicted through patterns and cycles. The Greek philosopher and historian

Iamblichus quotes Pythagoras as saying 'Number is the ruler of forms and ideas and the cause of gods and demons.'

Born on the Greek island of Samos in the eastern Aegean Sea, Pythagoras was the son of Mnesarchus (a Phoenician merchant father) and Pythais (a native woman of Samos). While he was still a young man he fled to Calabria, in present-day southern Italy, to evade the oppressive regime of the tyrant Polycrates (ruled c.538–522 BCE). At Croton in Calabria, Pythagoras started a secret religious society based on the Orphic cult. He aimed to transform the lives of Croton's inhabitants and established strict rules of behaviour and conduct. Both men and women initiates lived at the school and were treated equally. Those who were part of the inner teaching – the *mathematikoi* – were forbidden personal possessions and had to follow a strict vegetarian diet. Pythagoreans were required to follow a structured, monastic form of life, which included communal mealtimes, study and reading times as well as group exercise. Many of the activities also included music, with the *mathematikoi* regularly singing hymns to

Apollo. The music of the lyre was used in the treatment of physical and mental conditions – an early form of music therapy.

Quite early on in the development of the Pythagorean cult, Thales – one of the seven sages of Greece, and perhaps the first scientific philosopher – advised the young Pythagoras to go to Memphis in Egypt. There he studied with the priests and it is believed that he learned much about geometric principles. He is also thought to have studied at the temples of Tyre and Byblos in Phoenicia, his father's home.

CODES OF CONDUCT

In the wider society of Pythagoreans there were also *akousmatikoi* (listeners), who were not required to give up possessions or to be strictly vegetarian. They were only permitted summary versions of the esoteric knowledge available to the *mathematikoi* and could only listen to Pythagoras' lectures from behind a fabric veil.

The inner circle of Pythagoreans followed a rule of absolute silence – *ethemythia* – and it is believed that they could be punished by death if they spoke out loud. Pythagoras

Right *Born on the
Greek island of Samos,
Pythagoras was much
more than solely a
mathematician.
He began the
Pythagoreanism
movement, which also
embraced cosmology,
ethics and natural
philosophy, and was
viewed as controversial
at the time.*

thought that a man's words rarely expressed his truth: if someone was in doubt, silence was always preferable. Other rules meant that they should help a person pick something up, but not help him put it down, for this might encourage laziness. They also said (in an echo of Orpheus) that, on leaving your house, you should never look back, 'for the Furies will be your attendants'. It is possible that some of the 'superstitious' ideas were more metaphorical in nature, and were only intended for the exoteric *akousmatikoi*, rather than the *mathematikoi* whose knowledge was more esoteric.

One of the most important tenets of Pythagoreanism is that of 'metempsychosis', or the transmigration of souls. This idea seems to have been adopted throughout the Orphic cult and the teachings of Pherecydes of Syros, one of Pythagoras' most important teachers. In the Pythagorean understanding, a man or woman's soul could, following death, find a new home within a new person, animal, plant or other form, depending on the moral quality of the person's life.

It is believed by some scholars that Pythagoras himself never wrote anything down, and certainly none of his work survives in written form. The study of Pythagoreanism is the study of those who came after him – in particular Parmenides, Empedocles, Philolaus and Plato. Philolaus recorded Pythagoras' ideas in the most detail, and it is his works that are often believed to be most representative. Even though he was born in the year following Pythagoras' death, he was initiated into the Pythagorean school and was only 16 when he escaped the burning of the Pythagorean meeting place and fled, eventually living in Thebes, where he would teach many important writers and philosophers the ideas that stemmed from Pythagoras (in an echo of Orpheus' trip to the underworld). These included the idea that the earth was not the centre of the universe and that there was another counter-earth to balance our own.

Left *Pythagoreans were responsible for many groundbreaking theories of the time. This Copernican model of a heliocentric universe resulted from Philolaus' idea that the earth was not the centre of the universe.*

THE SACRED NUMBER TEN

Cosmology was a great concern of the ancient Greeks, and their attempts to find our correct place in the Universe absorbed much study. It is extraordinary that Philolaus was apparently the first person in Western culture to posit a model of the Universe that did not have the Earth at its centre. These cosmological ideas foreshadowed the work of Nicolaus Copernicus at the turn of the 16th century, proposing a heliocentric or sun-centred Universe. In his model based on the ideas of Pythagoras, Philolaus proposed that the Earth, the moon, the sun, the known five planets and the fixed stars of heaven all revolved around a 'Central Fire'. Since these only came to a sum of nine, Philolaus added what he called a 'counter-Earth' to bring the total number of objects in the Cosmos to ten.

The sacred significance of the number ten is embodied in the symbol known as the Tetractys, which is a triangle made up of the first four numbers: 1, 2, 3, 4. Together the four numbers total ten, which represents another level of order in the decimal system. The first four numbers are also related to another Pythagorean idea: the music of the spheres. And they symbolize the four elements of earth, air, fire and water. In another way, the four levels of the triangle represent the very organization of space: the first level is simply a point, with no dimensions; the second level creates a line, which has one dimension; the third level defines a triangle, a plane that has two dimensions; and the fourth level represents three dimensions and the figure of the tetrahedron, created from four equilateral triangles of the same size.

OATHS TO THE TETRACTYS

To demonstrate the spiritual importance of the number ten and the Tetractys to the Pythagorean school, it is known that they prayed regularly to the Tetractys and even took their sacred oaths on it when they were initiated into the cult:

> *By that pure, holy, four-lettered name on high,*
> *Nature's eternal fountain and supply,*
> *The parent of all souls that living be,*
> *By him, with faith find oath, I swear to thee.*

Right *The Pythagorean music system was based on intervals between individual notes. He experimented with new forms of music, as seen in this woodcut, and endeavoured to alter the structure to create a more spiritual sound.*

This would signal the start of a three-year period of silence while they fulfilled the duties of novices. One of their prayers also conveys their devotion to the Tetractys:

Bless us, divine number, thou who generated gods and men! O holy, holy Tetractys, thou that containest the root and source of the eternally flowing creation! For the divine number begins with the profound, pure unity until it comes to the holy four; then it begets the mother of all, the all-comprising, all-bounding, the first-born, the never-swerving holy ten, the keyholder of all.

THE PYTHAGOREAN MUSIC SYSTEM

The Tetractys is also the foundation of the Pythagorean music system, in that it defines the 'intervals' between notes and the ratios of their musical frequencies. Pythagoras had maintained that the existing music of his time was not sufficiently harmonious, and that it should be possible to create new forms of music with more spiritual, or mathematically pleasing, structure. In answer to his own question he attempted to develop a system of tuning based on a ratio of 3:2, or the 'fifth' interval as we know it. His system is not perfect and has since been adapted to avoid some of its inherent problems. Nevertheless his intuitive leap led to progress within Greek music.

Pythagoras claimed that it was possible to hear the 'Music of the spheres' – the actual sounds of the planets as they moved through space. Whether this was meant to be a mystical or metaphorical experience is not wholly clear, but it points to the idea that Pythagoras made 'planetary sojourns', or astral journeys, in order to perceive what he described. It is interesting that recent advances in astronomy have indicated that different celestial objects do indeed produce harmonic sounds that can be described as a form of music.

On initial study it may appear that Pythagoras' philosophy was almost too wide-ranging to be coherent. Nevertheless, there are certain themes that bind Pythagorean thinking together, and it is often mathematics and the esoteric meaning of numbers that bring harmony to the whole of his extraordinary acheivement.

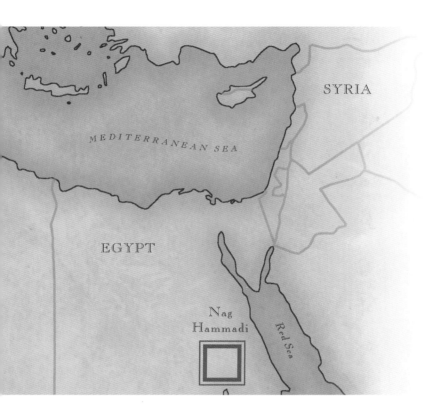

Gnosticism and the Gnostic gospels

The word Gnosticism comes from the Greek word gnosis, *meaning knowledge. Gnosis, though, when referred to in the context of Gnosticism as a religious tradition, means a very particular kind of knowledge: a direct experiencing of the Divine. Gnosticism can be understood as the search for states of mystical experience in which true 'gnosis' occurs.*

Gnosticism has perhaps two aspects: it is a description of the tools and conditions required by seekers, if they are to reach their goal of *gnosis*; it is also represented by the texts that are the result of mystical experiences – descriptions by mystics of what they have discovered through their searches.

DIFFERENT SCHOOLS OF THOUGHT

Gnosticism is also used as a term to describe a number of sects and religious groups, both pre- and post-Christian, in which seekers practised particular forms of mysticism and approaches to the Divine. In the Syrian-Egyptian school, these different groups were all influenced by Platonist ideas, which saw the Universe as the result of a series of emanations from the 'Monad', the primal Source. At the same time they included Christian texts and source material in their studies and often viewed themselves as Christians outside the mainstream of Roman Catholicism or Orthodoxy. These groups included the Sethians, who promulgated the idea that Seth (the third son of Adam and Eve) was a mystic and a teacher of *gnosis*. The

School of St Thomas the Apostle had as its main text the Gospel of Thomas, which has gained modern popular interest since its rediscovery at Nag Hammadi in Upper Egypt. The followers of Valentinius were active in the 2nd to 4th centuries CE, after their teacher developed a new cosmology outside the Sethian tradition. And adherents of the teacher Basilides were present at around the same time; his works are best known to us through the criticism of one of his theological opponents named Irenaeus, in his work *Adversus Haereses* (*Against Heresies*).

Of the schools that continued the Gnostic line, the early Christian teacher Cerinthus depicted Christ as a Divine Spirit separate from the human personage of Jesus. He also credited the 'Demiurge' with the creation of the material world, although – unlike most Gnostics – his version of the Demiurge was a holy one. He also taught Christians to observe the Jewish Law and believed in the Second Coming of Christ. At around the same time, or soon afterwards, there were the Ophites, who worshipped the serpent in Genesis as the bringer of knowledge; and the Cainites, who worshipped Cain, son of Adam,

Above *The prophet Mani was the founder of Manicheism, a branch of Gnosticism, denounced as being heretical by more mainstream religions.*

Esau, Korah and the Sodomites – their apparent heresy was to view the mortal flesh as evil, and therefore indulgent sin became, ironically, the key to their salvation.

In Persia there developed Manicheism, which had an influence on the Paulicians, the Bogomils and, later in the Middle Ages, the Cathars (see pages 100–103). Its distinct heritage was initiated by the prophet Mani in the 3rd century CE, and although there are connections with Jesus Christ, Manicheism is a quite different set of beliefs. Indeed, Manicheism was not simply an heretical sect; in Persia in the 8th century CE it became the state religion of the Uyghur empire. In general, though, Gnosticism in all its forms has attracted the negative attention of mainstream religions (particularly Christianity), which have been keen to brand its ideas heretical and to attempt to suppress its influence.

GNOSTIC PRINCIPLES

What are the common features of religious groups that have called themselves, or been called, Gnostic? Gnostic belief is usually founded on 'dualism' – the idea that the world, the Universe, is explicable as an interplay between two fundamental entities. There are various versions of dualism in which the two forces – of light and dark – are seen in different relationships. Some see the two as balanced, while others view the material world as created by an 'evil' Demiurge into which the Divine is trapped. Through Gnostic, mystical contact with the Divine, it is possible for the spirit to seek salvation from matter.

The *gnosis* is the wisdom and knowledge that makes this process possible. In each school this *gnosis* is a little different, but prayers of invocation are sent to the mediating force, such as the Christ figure or Seth or Sophia, the representative of the wished-for wisdom.

There is often a distinction between the Abrahamic God of the Old Testament, Yahweh, and the God of the New Testament or Christ figure. Some Gnostics pointed to the works of God in the books of the Old Testament: to the killing and warring that led

Right *This tiny piece of manuscript depicting Manichean priests was discovered in Idikut Shahri. Manicheism had major influences on other branches of Gnosticism.*

to conflict and death. This could hardly be the work of a benevolent Divine Creator, they maintained, and came to the conclusion that Yahweh must indeed be the Demiurge who has tricked the Spirit of Man into the confusion of the material world it inhabits.

GNOSTIC GOSPELS

The Gnostic Gospels is the name for a group of texts about the life and teachings of Jesus Christ, which are believed to have been written around the 2nd and 3rd centuries CE. They do not form part of the Bible, but are often referred to as part of the New Testament 'apocrypha'. They are not the results of a single 'find', but a series of discoveries that were made mostly in the last hundred years or so.

The most well-known and important of the Gnostic gospels are: the Gospel of Mary, recovered as part of the Akhmim Codex in 1896; the Gospel of Thomas, first discovered in Oxyrhynchus, Egypt, in 1898 and in a further version at Nag Hammadi in 1945, also

Egypt; the Gospel of Truth and the Gospel of Philip, both found in the Nag Hammadi Library; and the Gospel of Judas, originally discovered in Egypt in the 1970s and recovered from the black market in 1983, before being at least partially reconstructed and published in 2006.

THE GOSPEL OF JUDAS

This Gospel has gained much recent interest for its portrayal not just of the role of Judas in the life and death of Jesus, but about the Gnostic perspective on Jesus' teachings and beliefs. Carbon-dated to around 280 CE, the Gospel completely revises our understanding of Judas as simply the evil betrayer of Jesus for 30 pieces of silver. Rather, it shows how Jesus

required and directed Judas to turn him in to the authorities as part of a pre-planned and spiritually necessary set of events. In this way Jesus lived out the Gnostic understanding that death is a desirable release from the imprisonment of the material body. The Gospel implies that Judas was the only one of the disciples who had been fully initiated into Gnostic ideas by Jesus. Mysteriously the Gospel quotes Jesus as saying to Judas: 'You shall be cursed for generations ... You will come to rule over them ... You will exceed all of them, for you will sacrifice the man that clothes me.'. Perhaps the most important, and heretical, feature of the Gospel of Judas' story is that it undermines the conventional Christian idea that Jesus died to wipe away

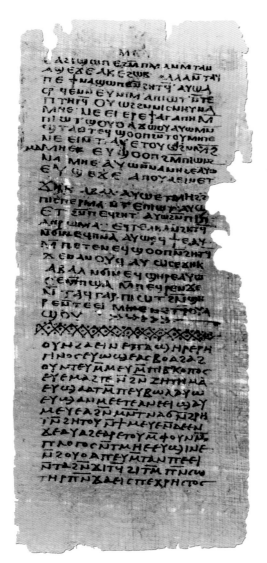

Above *These fragments of manuscripts were discovered in Nag Hammadi. They are Gnostic gospels that speak of the life of Jesus Christ and are referred to as part of the New Testament 'apocrypha'.*

the sins of humankind. An early Gnostic sect known as the Cainites took the view that Judas, in handing Jesus over to the authorities, was an instrument of the 'Sophia' or Divine Wisdom and in this way earned the hatred of the Demiurge for Jesus' triumph over death and the carnal world.

THE GOSPEL OF THOMAS

The discovery of the Nag Hammadi Library in 1945 was an important step forward in the understanding of Gnosticism. Since 1975, when it was first made publicly available, the Gospel of Thomas has been one of the most influential of these texts. (Fragments of the Gospel had been found in 1898, but it was not until the Nag Hammadi discovery that the identity of the material was uncovered.) Unlike the biblical gospels, the Gospel of Thomas is not a narrative story: it is, rather, a collection of 114 sayings attributed to Jesus, written down by Didymus Judas Thomas.

It starts with the words: 'These are the secret sayings which the living Jesus spoke and which Didymus Judas Thomas wrote down. And he said, "Whoever finds the interpretation of these sayings will not experience death".' The sayings stress the mystical route to salvation through direct, unmediated experience of God. In Thomas verse 3, Jesus says, 'the Kingdom of God is within you ...'. This is the essence of Gnosticism. In verse 70, Jesus goes on to say, 'If you bring forth what is within you, what you have will save you. If you do not bring it forth, what you do not have within you will kill you.'. In the Gospel of Thomas, Jesus offers everyone the opportunity to become an anointed Christ, as he is. This picture of the role of Christ is in stark contrast to the conventional Christian view.

Right *This section of papyrus concludes a Gnostic dialogue between Jesus and his disciples. It is a Coptic translation of a lost Greek original and such dialogues have sparked much discussion about early Christian thought.*

THE DA VINCI CONNECTION

Since the arrival of Dan Brown's bestselling novel *The Da Vinci Code* and its use of the Gnostic Gospels in the story, there has been an increased knowledge of their existence and importance in religious history. Further books and television documentaries have focused increased attention on the Gnostic Gospels and on Gnosticism as an independent strain of religious and spiritual thought, which has continued to challenge the mainstream religions and offer seekers an alternative means of growth and salvation throughout history.

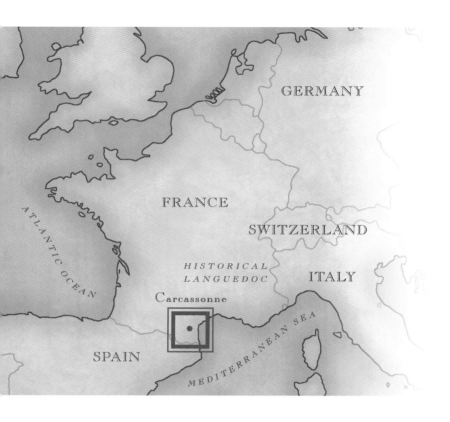

Catharism and the Catholic inquisition

Catharism is generally thought to be a strand of Christian Gnosticism (see pages 96–99) that emerged during the 11th and 12th centuries in south-west France. The sad truth about this influential religious movement is that it became more famous for its brutal extinguishing in the 13th century by the Albigensian Crusade of the Catholic Church than for its flowering as a peaceful expression of unconventional Christian ideas.

Some say that the roots of Catharism lay in the Paulician movement in Armenia. There is also believed to have been influence from the Bogomils of Bulgaria.

GUIDING PRINCIPLES

One of the central themes in Cathar ideology seems to have been an adherence to 'dualism', which draws on Manichean concepts of good and evil in the world. Dualism, as expressed in Cathar thought, is the idea that the manifest world we live in was created by a satanic, demonic or 'Demiurge' force, and that humans had to endure the lessons from a series of reincarnations on Earth before they were liberated and able to dwell permanently in the presence of a Loving God. Although they worshipped Jesus as a teacher and guide to a successful spiritual life, the Cathars differentiated between the Demiurge God of the Old Testament – as personified by Jehovah – and the Loving God, the Father of Jesus, who appears in the New Testament. Some modern scholars have said that their belief in reincarnation put the Cathars closer to Pythagorean ideas (see pages 92–95), and even to Buddhism, than to Christianity.

Other key tenets of the Cathar way of life were vegetarianism and an avoidance of Christian marriage, which has been taken by some to be not only heretical, but also 'anti-life' – in the sense that it expressed a rejection of child-bearing into a fallen world. In practice, however, Cathars were perfectly clear about the necessity to procreate in order that future souls might eventually find liberation.

Left *Some schools of thought place the evolvement of the Troubadour movement in Languedoc in France. However, related movements soon spread throughout Europe, until they were sent underground by the Albigensian Crusade.*

Although there was a priesthood in Catharism of *Parfaits* and *Parfaites* – the Perfected Ones – who were celibate, their role was not to mediate between God and the ordinary man or woman, as a Catholic priest might. As a Gnostic tradition, Catharism taught that direct contact with God was available to everyone and the priests' role was to facilitate this experience, rather than act as the bridge between one world and the next. *Parfaits* and *Parfaites* earned their title by undergoing a ceremony known as the *Consolamentum*, the central and only ritual that Cathars acknowledged as part of their faith.

To receive the *Consolamentum* in the prime of life would mean that the participant was committing to a life of abstinence from eating meat, complete chastity in sexual relations and regular fasting. Although this may sound like a depressingly ascetic recipe, there are those who see this commitment as being similar to the life of the Indian yogi. Indeed, when *Parfaits* came to face the wrath of the Catholic Inquisition and execution by burning, it is said that many went into the flames willingly and appeared to suffer no pain. It is also true that there were many 'ordinary' Cathars who would make a pact, or *Convenanza*, which meant that they would receive the blessings of the *Consolamentum* on their deathbeds – a privilege that many might see as a spiritual convenience.

THE ROLE OF THE INQUISITION

It is partly through the accuracy of the Holy Inquisition's scrupulous record-keeping that we know so much about Cathar life. When Pope Innocent III launched the Albigensian Crusade against the growing Cathar heresy, he could have had no idea that more than seven hundred years later another Pope would have to ask forgiveness for his actions. The Inquisition recorded both the relationships and involvements of those who lived out this important faith, as well as the treatment meted out against them. That the Catholic Church felt the need to stamp out Catharism with such force is an indication of the movement's influence at the time. Not only had its liberal brand of dualism created a challenge to the Roman spiritual leadership, but there was also a cultural movement emerging from the Languedoc (literally the 'language of the Occitane region') in the form of the

Above This 14th-century painting shows the excommunication of the Albigense by Pope Innocent III. This resulted in the Crusade, endorsed by the Roman Catholic Church, which eradicated the Cathar movement.

troubadour. Embracing poetry, art and music, troubadours were part of a chivalric code that brought together ideas about spiritual and human forms of love. When the Crusade came to wipe out Catharism, it also drove the troubadours underground. Some scholars believe that the troubadour movement was an early renaissance, and that the actions of the Catholic Church effectively delayed the new flowering that would later appear in Italy.

Whatever the truth, it seems that this strand of Gnosticism has never been fully extinguished; that it continues to reincarnate itself in different ages and different times, and that its dualistic ideas will, in some form, always be a part of the European spiritual tradition.

Carcassonne

The walled city of Carcassonne is one of the most spectacular sights in the region of south-western France known as Languedoc-Roussillon. The fortified town, which stands on the top of a hill some 90 km (56 miles) south-east of Toulouse, was significantly restored from 1853 onwards by the architect Eugène Viollet-le-Duc, but can still claim to have been an important Cathar site.

It is believed that there was human settlement on the site as early as 3500 BCE, but Carsac – as it was known by its Celtic name – developed as a trading place in the 6th century BCE. The Romans held the fortified site from 100 BCE until 462 CE, when they ceded it to the Visigoths, although it was later held by Saracens in the 8th century CE.

CATHAR HISTORY

It was 1067 when Carcassonne came under the control of Raymond Bernard Trencavel, Viscount of Albi and Nîmes, after he married Ermengard, the sister of the last Count of Carcassonne. The Trencavels were an important family in Cathar history, and it was to be Raymond-Roger Trencavel who confronted the might of the Roman Catholic Church in the Crusade.

In 1208 the Catholic Church under Pope Innocent III sent a legate named Pierre de Castelnau to meet the ruler of the area, Count Raymond VI of Toulouse, a known protector of the Cathars. Castelnau delivered the news to Raymond VI that he was to be excommunicated for his Cathar sympathies. But, on his way back to Rome, the legate was murdered by a knight in Raymond's service. The blue touchpaper had been lit: Pope Innocent announced that there would be a Crusade against the Cathars, and named a number of leaders to carry it out.

The first Albigensian Crusade was led by the Pope's legate, the Abbot of Cîteaux, Arnauld Amaury, and was empowered to root out and destroy the Cathar heresy wherever – and however – it found it. It was Raymond-Roger Trencavel, the 24-year-old Viscount of Béziers and Carcassonne, who was to face the full force of Amaury's attack. Raymond-Roger lived in the Château Comtal within the walls of the fortified city of Carcassonne. Even though it was difficult for anyone to ascertain that he was a Cathar, it was known that he took a relaxed approach to the practice of Catharism in his midst. He was also a patron of troubadours and poets, who were often Cathar, and his wife Agnes of Montpelier is believed to have been a Cathar.

THE DESTRUCTION OF BÉZIERS

By June 1209 the Crusaders had gathered at Lyons, north of the Languedoc: they included many French noblemen from the north, hopeful of gaining new lands. Realizing the gravity of the threat, Raymond-Roger was eager to protect his people. He sought a settlement with Amaury, but was rejected. As he returned to Carcassonne, the Crusaders advanced on the nearby town of Béziers. On 22 July the Crusaders initiated an attack on the Cathars who had sought refuge in the town and its church. Amaury was reputedly asked by one of his co-Crusaders

how they could tell Cathars from Catholics. The Cistercian abbot famously replied, *'Caedite eos. Novit enim Dominus qui sunt eius'* – 'Kill them all, the Lord will recognize His own.' After savagely slaughtering the 20,000 people they found, the crusading army razed Béziers to the ground. Writing to Pope Innocent III after the event, Amaury boasted of his success: 'Today, your Holiness, twenty thousand heretics were put to the sword, regardless of rank, age or sex.'

THE FALL OF CARCASSONNE

Carcassonne knew it could expect the same treatment, although its fortifications gave it greater protection. On 1 August 1209 the advancing army – now led by Simon de

Montfort – laid siege to the city and its inhabitants. By cutting off the water supply, they quickly made conditions within the *cité* intolerable, as water ran out and illness spread. There are many stories that during the siege a number of Cathar *Parfaits* and *Parfaites* managed to escape, carrying with them their valuable treasures, although similar stories are also related concerning the later siege of Montségur castle. After two weeks Raymond-Roger was offered the opportunity to speak with de Montfort, but the talks were a trap – Trencavel was taken prisoner. Perhaps surprisingly, the inhabitants of the city were allowed to make their escape. *Parfaits* and other inhabitants of Carcassonne sought refuge in towns and castles throughout the region, where they were relentlessly pursued by de Montfort and his crusading troops.

In the meantime, de Montfort was declared Viscount of Carcassonne by the Army Council, thereby taking ownership not just of the city, but also of the surrounding lands. Raymond-Roger was imprisoned in his own jail and died some three months later.

① BASILICA OF SAINT-NAZAIRE

Simon de Montfort was briefly buried in the cathedral, before his remains were exhumed three years later and reburied in a monastery close to Montfort-Amaury. The Siege Stone in the basilica purportedly depicts the siege of Carcassonne in 1209.

② CHÂTEAU COMTAL

A fortress within the fortress of Carcassonne, the moated Château Comtal was where Raymond-Roger lived. It included five towers and ramparts with wooden galleries to assist in its defence.

③ *LICES*

This space between the inner and outer walls of the town could be used for tournaments and jousting events. Re-enactments of such jousting events still take place in the *lices* today.

④ BISHOP'S TOWER

The Bishop's tower was built between 1270 and 1285 during the reign of King Philippe III. Its presence, linking the two walls, helped to strengthen Carcassonne's extensive fortifications.

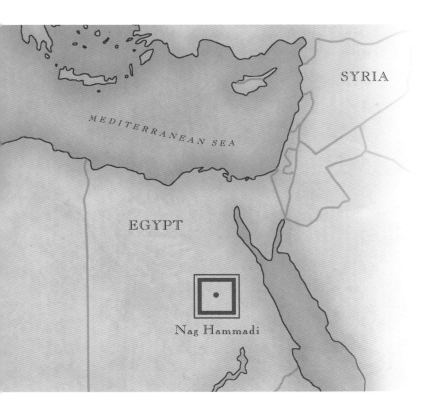

Hermeticism and alchemy

Hermes, or Hermes Trismegistus ('Thrice Greatest'), was a legendary wise man and priest from Egypt who fathered Hermeticism and was responsible for writings that have influenced the Western mystery tradition for many hundreds of years. He is often seen as an embodiment of the Greek god Hermes, who is synonymous with the Egyptian god of writing and magic, Thoth.

Above *Hermes Trismegistus was regarded by many as an embodiment of the Greek god Hermes and is the patriarch of alchemy and natural mysticism.*

Hermes Trismegistus is the patriarch of natural mysticism and alchemy, and was known in the early centuries of the Christian era through a series of Hermetic texts. This Hermetic movement was part of a rebirth of syncretistic and polytheistic thought that included the works of Neoplatonism, late Orphic and Pythagorean thought (see pages 92–95) and the writings and teachings of Gnosticism (see pages 96–99).

THE *CORPUS HERMETICUM*

In Renaissance times renewed interest in Hermetic works led to the bringing together of a *Corpus Hermeticum* – a surviving group of texts from the 2nd and 3rd centuries CE in the Greek language, part of a large group of works in other languages such as Arabic, Armenian, Syriac and Coptic. An agent of Cosimo de Medici named Leonardo reputedly recovered the texts from a monastery, where it may have been translated from its original Arabic. Analysis in the 17th century by Isaac Casaubon, a Swiss philologist, placed the work within the Christian Era, although there are still scholars who believe that the texts record a much older oral tradition. Indeed,

knowledge of Hermes Trismegistus' works exists within the writings of the Greek historian Plutarch during the 1st century CE, and the philosophers Tertullian, Iamblichus and Porphyry in the 2nd and 3rd centuries CE were all conversant with Hermetic texts.

The *Corpus* is generally considered to include 18 texts, mostly in the form of dialogues between Hermes and a disciple, and concerning subjects such as alchemy and magic. They are characterized partly by an absence of reference to existing religions such as the Jewish and Christian faiths, which generally viewed Hermeticism as heresy. Different translators have given the texts a variety of names. G.R.S. Mead gave 13 texts the following names: *Poemandres, the Shepherd of Men*; *To Asclepius*; *The Sacred Sermon*; *The Cup or Monad*; *Though Unmanifest God is Most Manifest*; *In God Alone is Good and Elsewhere Nowhere*; *The Greatest Ill Among Men is Ignorance of God*; *That No One of Existing Things doth Perish, But Men in Error Speak of Their Changes as Destructions and as Deaths*; *On Thought and Sense*; *The Key*; *Mind Unto Hermes*; *About the Common Mind*; and *The Secret Sermon on the Mountain*.

THE EMERALD TABLET

One particular Hermetic text, known as the *Emerald Tablet* or *Tabula Smaragdina*, justifies Hermes Trismegistus' Moses-like role for alchemists and esotericists by revealing the divine commandments of the alchemical arts. Also referred to as *The Secret of Hermes*, the Emerald Tablet is a short cryptic text made up of 14 or 15 theses, which became a vital document for all those involved in alchemy. Sir Isaac Newton, the discoverer of the laws of motion and an enthusiastic and committed alchemist, was one of many translators of the text. His version begins:

> *Tis true without lying, certain and most*
> *true. That which is below is like that*
> *which is above and that which is above is*
> *like that which is below to do the miracles*
> *of only one thing.*
> *And as all things have been and arose from*
> *one by the meditation of one: so all things*
> *have their birth from this one thing by*
> *adaptation. The Sun is its father, the*
> *moon its mother, The wind has carried it*
> *in its belly, the earth its nurse.*
> *The father of all perfection in the whole world*
> *is here.*

The Emerald Tablet surfaced in around 800 CE as part of an Arabic compendium of advice for rulers, and was subsequently translated into Latin in the 12th century as *The Secret of Secrets*. It became a key alchemical text for many important figures, including the English philosopher Roger Bacon, the occultist Aleister Crowley, the German theologian Albertus Magnus and even the psychologist Carl Jung, who wrote that he had first encountered it in a dream in 1912.

OTHER DOCUMENTS

In 1945, with the discovery of 13 leather-bound papyrus codices from the 2nd century CE at Nag Hammadi in Egypt, more information from the Hermetic corpus appeared, along with Gnostic texts. One of these was already known from the *Corpus Hermeticum* and is composed of a conversation between Hermes and Asclepius (the Greek god of healing); it concerns the art of imprisoning demons and angels in statues – using gems and herbs – in order that the statue can speak and make prophecies. Another text, known as *On the Ogdoad and the Ennead* and written in late-Egyptian Coptic, describes the Hermetic mystery schools.

Above The Emerald Tablet *is a particularly significant Hermetic text as it purports to reveal the divine commandments of alchemy.*

Inside the oval border: **MAGNVS · ALBERTVS BOLSTADIVS COGNOMENTO**

Mitra pedumq oneri tibi quondam, Alberte, fuerunt.
Dulcius est Sophiæ delituisse sinu.

Left *An engraving of Albertus Magnus, the most important German theologian, alchemist and philosopher of the Middle Ages.*

The practical development of the art from medieval times followed an often-hidden and obscure evolution. It was always a lonely road, and one that suited the outsider. One of the most well-known alchemists, Albertus Magnus, set down his guidelines for the aspiring alchemist:

First: He should be discreet and silent, revealing to no one the result of his operations.
Second: He should reside in a private house in an isolated position.
Third: He should choose his days and hours for labour with discretion.
Fourth: He should have patience, diligence and perseverance.
Fifth: He should perform according to fixed rules.
Sixth: He should use only vessels of glass or glazed earthenware.
Seventh: He should be sufficiently rich to bear the expenses of his art.
Eighth: He should avoid having anything to do with princes and noblemen.

THE SEARCH FOR THE PHILOSOPHER'S STONE

Writing in the late 13th century, the Majorcan philosopher Ramón Lull introduced the idea of *prima materia* or first matter, which was identified with *Argent Vive*, 'Quicksilver' or mercury, which was always associated with the god Hermes. This substance, said Lull, was the source of other matter, including human life; but his own life was cut short when he was stoned to death by a group of Muslims in 1316 on arrival in Africa.

Late in the 14th century Nicholas Flamel, a French scrivener, came across a large gilded book by an author called Abraham Eleazar, which contained many obscure symbolic

ALCHEMY

In popular thought, alchemy is understood to be the study of transformational techniques: the ability to turn base metals such as lead into precious metals, particularly gold. Alchemy has also been seen as the epitome of folly, the pursuit of the impossible, greed wrapped up as mystery. In 1317, Pope John XII issued an edict warning against its dangers: 'Poor themselves, the alchemists promise riches which are not forthcoming; wise also in their conceit, they fall into the ditch which they themselves have digged.'. But this is to misunderstand the true nature of the search that alchemy entailed for those who made it their lives and who referred to it as 'The Great Work' or 'The Sacred Art'.

The writings attributed to Hermes Trismegistus became extremely important to alchemists for their magical, healing and astrological content. It is possible, though, to divide the Hermetic writings into those that are philosophical (ones concerned with personal transformation and the human place in the Universe) and those that are practical (ones dealing with the many uses of magic). There are also texts that synthesize these two aspects of the art – as above, so below – where, seemingly, Mammon and God are brought into dialogue. Through the chemical process in which they are involved, the alchemists are seeking to be transformed inwardly, to be brought closer to God, who is the One, and the divine essence of all for which they seek.

illustrations and a mystifying text. On a pilgrimage to Spain, Flamel finally found a man named Master Canches who interpreted the pictures for him. Back in Paris, Flamel embarked upon his own 'great work' and finally succeeded in making the 'first agent' on 17 January 1392, recognizing it by its strong smell. The 'first agent' is another name for the 'Philosopher's Stone', the catalyst that makes the transmutation of matter possible. Next Flamel transmuted mercury into pure silver; then he made a 'projection' of 'the red stone' (the Philosopher's Stone) onto mercury and transmuted it into gold. Wealth led to the founding of hospitals, building of churches and restoration of cemeteries. When his life-story was encapsulated in a book of 1612, Flamel's fame was ensured.

NEW DIRECTIONS

In the 16th century the German physician Paracelsus took alchemy in a new direction by maintaining that its real function was the creation of medicines to heal body and soul. He argued that – as a part of the Universe – we have an inner being or *astra* that governs our health. If we are sick in body, we need another substance from the Universe's rich abundance of material to bring it back into balance. Paracelsus was the first 'holistic' healer and the father of many forms of medicine, including homoeopathy.

With the rise of science in the early 17th century, the focus of European alchemy changed and became more interested in the inner person. Mystics such as Jakob Boehme in Germany and Robert Fludd in England led this movement, which continued through to the rise of psychology at the end of the 19th century and the arrival of Carl Jung. In the modern era, Jung above all others probably expressed most about the mysterious process of inner transformation, and how the more 'base' elements of the human psyche can be transformed into a more essential, more spiritualized and individuated Self.

Perhaps the symbolic and metaphoric works of Hermes Trismegistus have been able to speak to each generation in new ways, according to their needs.

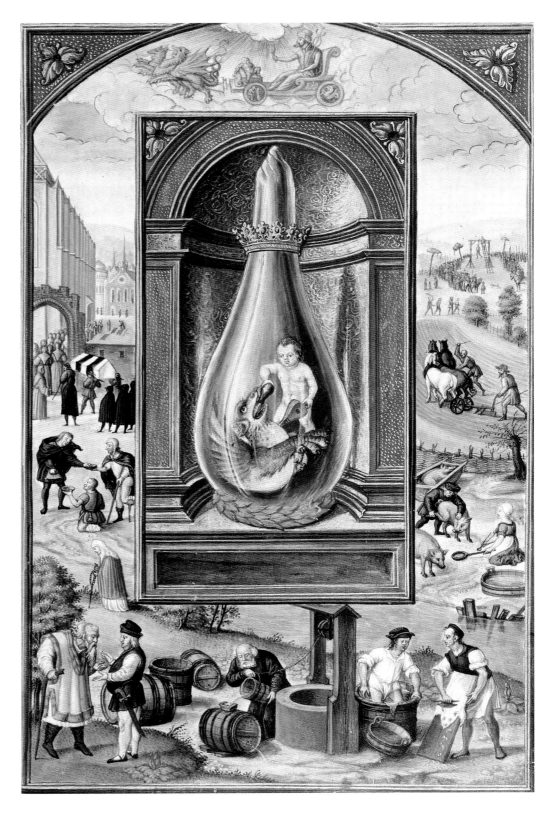

Above *This 16th-century painting depicts the Philosopher's Stone or 'first agent'.*

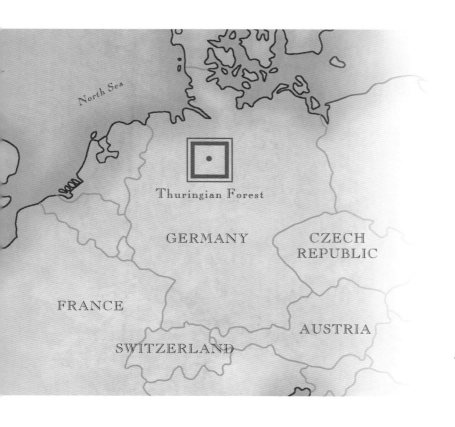

Rosicrucianism and Christian Rosenkreuz

Rosicrucianism – the doctrine of the Rosy Cross, the Cross and the Rose – is a form of esoteric Christianity that first appeared publicly in the 17th century, when a series of three Manifestos were published between 1614 and 1616 detailing a secret brotherhood headed by a mysterious figure called Christian Rosenkreuz.

Many readers at the time were confused as to whether the characters, descriptions and stories contained within the Manifestos were real or simply allegorical. Either way, Rosicrucianism as a religious or spiritual impulse took hold in the world and led to the formation of groups, teachings, sub-teachings and cults. In all its forms Rosicrucianism's resonant influence has continued until the present day. And yet many questions about Rosicrucianism remained largely unanswered. However, for those who have sought inspiration and a spiritual path through this teaching, it seems that many have been rewarded.

THE REVELATION OF CHRISTIAN ROSENKREUZ

At the heart of the questions about Rosicrucianism is the mystery of its apparent founder. His appearances in the three Manifestos are frequent and vital. In the first document, the *Fama Fraternitatis* (*Discovery of the Brotherhood*), the founder is named as 'the most godly and highly illuminated Father, our Brother, C.R. a German, the chief and original of our Fraternity'. In the second,

the *Confessio Fraternitatis* (*Confession of the Brotherhood*), he is named as 'our Christian Father'; his date of birth is given as 1378 and the reader is told that he lived for 106 years. In the third document (*The Chymical Wedding of Christian Rosenkreuz*), a long allegorical story taking place over seven days appears to be narrated by Christian Rosenkreuz himself, although authorship is widely attributed to the Lutheran theologian Johannes Valentinus Andreae, who is also thought to have been involved in the writing of the *Fama* and a member of the Brotherhood – namely Brother I.A.

As well as being written in a metaphorical and symbolic tone, there are some indications within both the *Fama* and the *Confessio* that the text is intended to be taken literally. Other brothers are identified by their initials – Brother P.A.L., Brother J.A. and Brother J.O. – and their particular skills and areas of knowledge and experience are noted. Details of Brother C.R.'s journeys to the East, to Damasco (Damascus), Jerusalem and Egypt, are given. And we are told of a search for esoteric knowledge in the East, which the character of Rosenkreuz then

applied to the establishment of a secret teaching, a form of esoteric Christianity: the Brotherhood of the Rosy Cross.

Readers were asked to believe that Rosenkreuz died in 1484 and was buried in a specially constructed vault that was not only structurally symbolic, but also contained many sacred objects. On the reopening of his tomb 120 years after his death, his body remained intact and uncorrupted – a sure sign of a saintly person. In some mystical way this recovering of Rosenkreuz marked the beginning of the more public revelation of Rosicrucianism. It was as if, by some alchemical process, the mystical value of his life was now being resurrected and made available to a wider group of seekers.

The Manifestos made clear that the aim of this organization was a reformation of religious and spiritual life in Europe. But far from being a 'top-down' attempt to topple and overthrow the old order, it would be a 'ground-upwards' movement of the pure in heart and mind. People of good intention were invited to make contact with the Brotherhood so that they might play their part in the healing of European spiritual culture.

Christiani Rosencreutz.   127

sahe ich Fraw Venerem gantz bloß (dann die
Decken hatte er auch auff gehebt) in solcher zierd
vnd schöne da ligen / das ich schier erstarret / auch
noch nicht weiß / ob es nur also geschnitten / oder
ein Mensch wer hie lig / dan sie war gantz vnbe=
weglich / noch dorffte ich sie nicht anrühren. Hie=
mit wurde sie wider bedeckt / vnd der fürhang
fürgezogen. Wir aber war sie noch als in Augen /
doch ersahe ich bald hinder dem Bett ein Taffel /
Darauff stund also geschrieben :

[symbolic cipher script, four lines of characters]

Ich fraget meinem Knaben vber die Schrifft /
Er aber lachet / mit versprechen / ich solte es noch
wol erfahren / Also leschet er die Fackel auß / vnd
stiegen wir wider herauff : Da besahe ich alle

Left *This extract forms part of the third manifesto of the Rosicrucians, entitled* The Chymical Wedding of Christian Rosenkreuz. *This secret brotherhood aimed to reform spiritual and religious life in Europe.*

Below *A pictorial plate entitled the* Monas Hieroglyphica, *for the frontispiece of* The Chymical Wedding of Christian Rosenkruez, *produced by the Queen's astrologer, Dr John Dee, demonstrates the movement's status.*

MONAS HIEROGLYPHICA
IOANNIS DEE, LONDINENSIS,
AD
MAXIMILIANVM, DEI GRATIA
ROMANORVM, BOHEMIÆ ET HVNGARIÆ
REGEM SAPIENTISSIMVM.

a movement that called for a peaceful spiritual revolution at a time of conflict refused to blow over, and frustrations at the organization's secrecy led many to conclude the entire event had been a hoax.

Among its supporters was the leading philosopher, astrologer and physicist Robert Fludd, who wrote spirited defences of the Rosicrucian project. The initials of Elizabeth I's Attorney-General Sir Francis Bacon – FB – appear as a latter-day member of the Brotherhood in the Manifestos. This led many to believe that Bacon was at least a member of the Brotherhood, if not even the founding force. And a pictorial plate – the *Monas Hieroglyphica* – by the Queen's astrologer and mentor Dr John Dee appears on the frontispiece of *The Chymical Wedding of Christian Rosenkreuz*. Clearly the movement had friends in high places – perhaps even the highest of all: the English monarch herself.

RESPONDING TO THE INVITATION

The response among the intellectual and spiritual elites of the time was highly significant. Many well-known figures attempted to RSVP to the Rosicrucian invitation, but it seems that few were able to find the Brotherhood. René Descartes, the famous philosopher and author (and source of the phrase *Cogito ergo sum* – 'I think therefore I am'), was unable to track it down. Some people declared themselves publicly as members of the Rosicrucian Brotherhood, only to be denounced or criticized as charlatans. The intellectual storms over

Above *The occultist and mystic Aleister Crowley incorporated certain Rosicrucian ideas into his own Hermetic Order of the Golden Dawn. He was a controversial figure whose exploits gained him much notoriety.*

At a certain point Johannes Valentinus Andreae stepped into the fray, saying that things had got out of hand and that 'the game' was now over. Although this confirmed many sceptics in their suspicions that the whole publication had been an elaborate scam, there were others for whom this simply confirmed the real need for further secrecy to protect the Brotherhood's identity and purpose. Pandora's box had been opened, though, and the Rosicrucian impulse to contribute to spiritual and cultural life through devotion to certain principles had been set free.

WIDER LINKS

A number of organizations started to absorb Rosicrucian ideas and ideals: one of the foremost was the Freemasons, whose rituals still bear the mark of Rosicrucian and alchemical symbology. Indeed, through the participation of the Jesuits within Freemasonry, a Rosicrucian Order was established. Even now, the Golden Rose Cross, for instance, is still an important symbol within the Brotherhood of Freemasonry. In the 19th and 20th centuries the ideas were incorporated into new esoteric movements and teachings. The Hermetic Order of the Golden Dawn, headed by the occultist Aleister Crowley, incorporated (though some say distorted) a number of important Rosicrucian ideas.

Max Heindel's Rosicrucian Fellowship and Jan van Rijkenborgh's Lectorium Rosicrucianum are both expressions of the broader idea of 'esoteric Christianity'. And in the early part of the 20th century, Rudolf Steiner, originally a Theosophist and the founder of Anthroposophy (see pages 146–151), Waldorf Education and Biodynamic Farming, lectured at some length on the importance of Christian Rosenkreuz's life and spiritual mission. In

America, AMORC (the Ancient Mystical Order of the Rosy Cross) appeared and then gained a significant following. Rosicrucianism as a strand in the Western mystery tradition seems to have a built a resonance that is likely to continue.

THE REAL CHRISTIAN ROSENKREUZ

Perhaps predictably, the response from many was to question the reality of the message, the reality of the intention and of the man Christian Rosenkreuz. A number of writers, occultists and spiritual seekers have put forward versions of the life history of Rosenkreuz, some of which claim to have access to esoteric knowledge of the man's real history and spiritual mission. The oral tradition regarding him tells an extraordinary story.

The most important version of the Rosenkreuz story starts back in the time of the Albigensians, or Cathar people, who lived in the south-west of France during the 12th and 13th centuries (see pages 100–103). When the Cathar doctrines were wiped out as a heresy by the Catholic Inquisition in the 13th century, the few Albigensian survivors went to ground and attempted to maintain their precious spiritual teachings in secret. Some of these cells took root in Germany, where Inquisitions continued with the approval of Pope Gregory IX.

One German family that held on to the Cathar beliefs of reincarnation and the possibility of direct contact with the Creator was the Germelhausens, who lived in a castle in the centre of Thuringian Forest in the Rheon district. But they came under attack from Count Conrad of Thuringia and, after many sieges, the castle was overrun and all the family killed, except for their youngest son, aged five, who was smuggled away by an Albigensian monk. He had recognized the

A number of organizations started to absorb Rosicrucian ideas and ideals: one of the foremost was the Freemasons, whose rituals still bear the mark of Rosicrucian and alchemical symbology.

child's exceptional intelligence and spiritual abilities, and brought the boy up in a hidden monastery where only the monk and three further brothers were party to the child's existence. The boy became known by his symbolic name of Christian Rosenkreuz.

ROSENKREUZ'S JOURNEY

The small group that formed around this exceptional young man determined that they would search for spiritual truth in the East, and so began the Rosicrucian Brotherhood that would later be described (if incompletely) in the Manifestos. The searches for spiritual truth started when Christian Rosenkreuz, then 15, set off with one of the brothers (Brother P.A.L.) ostensibly on a pilgrimage to the Holy Sepulchre. In fact they were looking for a centre of initiation. When Brother P.A.L. died in Cyprus, Rosenkreuz continued on to Damascus alone – now in the disguise of a Muslim pilgrim.

This was the time of the destructions of Baghdad and Nichapur, when their universities and libraries were ransacked and there were fears that civilization was on the point of ending. These feelings were not calmed by reports of earthquakes in Syria and a rain of scorpions in Mesopotamia. But Rosenkreuz's only interest was in the knowledge that could be accumulated in this place. Here he read the great texts of the time, listened to the poetic works of Omar Khayyám and consumed his extraordinary and advanced mathematical books on algebra and Euclid. He encountered the Sufi teachings contained in the sacred Masnavi text, which bears interesting comparison with the spiritual ideas of the Cathars that formed his earlier education. His broad absorption of ideas only confirmed in him the need for deep spiritual ideas to be kept alive and transmitted to people of the West in a form they could understand and appreciate.

Above *The Rosy Cross, is the symbol of the Rosicrucian movement. The rose is the female element and the cross itself is male.*

Left *Sir Francis Bacon was believed by many to be the incarnation of Rosicrucian founder, Christian Rosenkreuz. According to one school of thought, he could have been just one of many incarnations, all of whom were prominent historical figures.*

From Damascus, Rosenkreuz travelled on to spend time in a desert monastery at Damcar, where he was initiated more deeply, before his pilgrimage took him to Egypt and Fez, where he studied in a school of magic and astrology. Crossing the Mediterranean to Spain, he joined a secret school called the Alumbrados, where he learned more of the sciences, of alchemy and mystical philosophy. He was to leave shortly before the school was destroyed by the Inquisition.

Travelling back through France, he reached his homeland at a time when the persecution of mystical groups – some of them based on the Albigensian teachings – was still brutal and merciless. Finding the three remaining monks, Rosenkreuz re-established the Brotherhood and increased its number to eight. Though he wished for a total transformation of spiritual activity in the West, he realized that his approach must be slow and almost completely invisible. In some traditions it is believed that once the Brotherhood was in its full form, Rosenkreuz underwent mystical rituals that were almost as important to the spiritual growth of the planet as Christ's crucifixion and resurrection and the Buddha's enlightenment under the Bodhi Tree. These rituals were believed by some to have helped unify the various strands of spiritual influence and tradition that are expressed in different cultures, and to have made their cross-fertilization and mutual understanding more possible.

THE SHAKESPEARE CONNECTION

The question of the identity of William Shakespeare is, in certain ways, similar to that of Christian Rosenkreuz. Scholars have long debated whether William Shakespeare of Stratford was really the person who wrote the greatest, most profound and psychologically sophisticated plays ever created in the English language. Some have postulated that they could have come only from the minds of those who were educated and initiated into certain mystery schools that understood the workings of the human psyche to the degree that the plays achieve. Others have detected codified information, hidden using ciphers, in the First Folio edition of Shakespeare's plays. This codified information appears to confirm the idea that the author of the plays was Sir Francis Bacon, Attorney-General at the time of Elizabeth I (ruled 1558–1603), and, in some people's version of history, one of Elizabeth's two sons by her lover, the Earl of Leicester.

Not only is it believed among certain occult circles that Francis Bacon was a Rosicrucian, but – even more startlingly – that he was actually the reincarnation of Christian Rosenkreuz. There is a school of thought that sees both Rosenkreuz and Bacon as part of a succession of incarnations, which started well before biblical times and took in a number of significant human personalities. This series of lives, often referred to under the name of the St Germain line, also includes: Joseph, father of Jesus; Roger Bacon, the early natural philosopher; Christopher Columbus, the 'discoverer' of America; and the 18th-century Count of Saint-Germain, who unsuccessfully attempted to avert the violent excesses of the French Revolution. This 'lifestream' can be seen as an influence in the spiritual culture of Europe in a similar way to the Dalai Lama's many incarnations in Tibetan culture over the centuries. In the person of Francis Bacon – if his authorship of Shakespeare's plays is to be accepted – the ideas, understanding and mission of Christian Rosenkreuz found a continuing resonant outlet that still filters through our lives today.

Following his death, Rosenkreuz's body was interred in such a secret place (a construction of sacred geometry and meaning) that it was never found except by members of the Brotherhood – only to be rediscovered more than a century later with its occupant in an uncorrupted state.

THE REAL TEACHINGS OF ROSICRUCIANISM

To some people it seems impossible that a character of such apparently vague history can really have made such a contribution to the evolution of spiritual consciousness on Earth. There are, however, respected figures who value Christian Rosenkreuz's role in the world's spiritual history to the highest degree. One of these was Rudolf Steiner, the founder of Anthroposophy (see pages 146–151). In some of his most important lectures in 1912 and 1913, entitled 'Esoteric Christianity and the Mission of Christian Rosenkreuz', Steiner laid out his understanding of Rosenkreuz's task. At the time when Rosenkreuz was alive, there was

the potential for the world to split into two types of people: the practical types, who carried out all the functional work that was required to maintain life and were almost totally lost to a material view of life; and the spiritual, more monastic types, who simply lived for an experience of the Divine or mystical. Steiner described St Francis as being an example of the latter category. Many esotericists believe that through his spiritual practice and his large personal influence, Rosenkreuz was able to avert evolutionary disaster and keep alive the possibility of spiritual progress for all on planet Earth.

Left *Rudolf Steiner, the founder of Anthroposophy, was an advocate of the teachings of Christian Rosenkreuz. He incorporated Rosenkreuz's teachings into a number of his key lectures.*

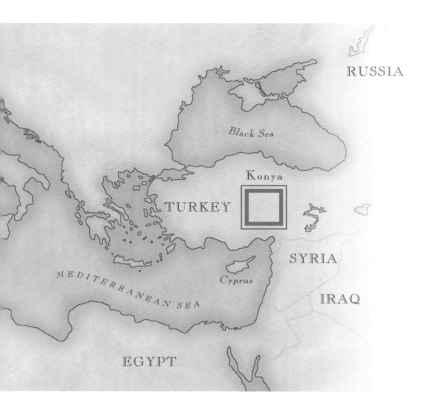

Sufism – touching the hand of God

Made famous by the ecstatic dances of the whirling dervishes, Sufism is an ascetic and mystical movement within Islam. Its followers, the Sufi, seek to find divine love and knowledge through a direct personal experience of God. While Sufism is said to have incorporated elements of Christian and Indian mysticism, its origins are traced back to the formative period of Islam.

The term *Sufi* (Arabic for 'man of wool') was coined in the early 9th century CE as a name for mystics whose ascetic practices included wearing coarse woollen garments, or *sufu*; soon the term referred to all mystics, whether or not they followed ascetic practices.

The Sufi mystic is described as a pilgrim on a journey who follows a path comprising seven stages, as follows: repentance, abstinence, renunciation, poverty, patience, trust in God and acquiescence to the will of God. Then a higher level of consciousness is attained, in which knowledge, the knower and the known become one.

Sufi orders were willing to assimilate aspects of local religious traditions, helping Sufism to play a major role in the expansion of Islam into sub-Saharan Africa and throughout Asia. The Sufi emphasis on intuitive knowledge and the love of God increased the appeal of Islam to the masses and largely made possible its extension beyond the Middle East. Sufi brotherhoods multiplied rapidly from the Atlantic coast to Indonesia; some spanned the entire Islamic world, others were regional or local.

THE WHIRLING DERVISHES

Although Sufi practitioners have often been at odds with the Islamic mainstream, the importance of Sufism in the history of Islam is incalculable. Sufi literature – especially love poetry – represents a golden age in Arabic, Persian, Turkish and Urdu languages.

The greatest mystical poet in the Persian language, Jalal ad-Din ar-Rumi, who lived in the 13th century, was also a key figure in Sufism. Known in the West as Rumi, he instituted devotional dances, particularly those of the whirling dervishes, who sought ecstasy through an elaborate dancing ritual, accompanied by superb music.

Each order has its own form of ritual. Among the most widely known and perhaps the earliest of the dervishes are the Kadiris,

Left *Rumi was buried in the former monastery of the whirling dervishes of Konya. Today it is both a museum and shrine and each year on 17 December tens of thousands of pilgrims pay their respects at Rumi's tomb.*

whose order was founded in 1165 and who are known in Europe as the howling dervishes because of their peculiar chant. Also celebrated are the Rifais, famous for their feats of eating glass and hot coals and of swallowing swords; and the Kalenderis, who vow to travel perpetually.

MONASTIC COMMUNITIES AND SHRINES

From the 8th century onwards, Sufi monastic communities began to be founded where devotees practised mystical exercises. In the Middle Ages the great Sufi orders, which had several million adherents, were established; about one hundred orders still exist, many of them in Iran. In addition to the members of these orders, numerous wandering Sufi mendicants, or *fakirs*, have appeared over the centuries. Many have been genuinely pious, but some who were merely fraudulent beggars brought disrepute to Sufism.

Rumi's disciples, called the Malawiya (in Arabic) or Mevlevi (in Turkish), have their headquarters at Konya in Turkey. Situated high in the vast Anatolian steppe, Konya is one of the world's oldest cities, with excavations revealing settlement from as early as the 3rd millennium BCE. Konya's golden age came in the 12th and 13th centuries under Seljuk rule; the city still contains many magnificent buildings and mosques from that period. It was during this time that Rumi came from his birthplace on the Eastern shores of the Persian Empire to live in Konya.

The distinctive whirling and circling dance of the dervishes is known as *Sema*. The *Sema* ceremony represents the mystical journey of an individual on his or her ascent through mind and love to union with the Divine. Dressed in long white gowns (the ego's burial shroud) and wearing high, cone-shaped hats (the ego's tombstone), the dervish dances for hours at a time. With arms held high, the right hand lifted upward to receive blessings and energy from heaven, the left hand turned downward to bestow these blessing on the Earth, and the body spinning from right to left, the dervish revolves around the heart and embraces all of creation with love.

In the centuries following Rumi's death, many hundreds of dervish lodges were established throughout the Ottoman domains in Turkey, Syria and Egypt. With the secularization of Turkey following the First World War, the Mevlevi Brotherhood was seen as reactionary and dangerous to the new republic and it was banned in 1925. Members of the Brotherhood continued their religious practices in secret until their ecstatic dances were allowed again in 1953.

Above *This manuscript illustration of the 16th century shows whirling dervishes in the midst of their ecstatic dance accompanied by musicians.*

Shah Rukn-i-Alam Tomb

The mausoleum of Shah Rukn-i-Alam is widely considered to be one of the most beautiful architectural creations of Sufism, and to signify the glory of Multan. The city of Multan, in Pakistan's Punjab, has become famous for its ornate and beautiful mausoleums, but these are dominated by the dome of the shrine dedicated to Sheikh Rukn-ud-Din Abul Fath, who is more commonly known by the name Shah Rukn-i-Alam, meaning 'the pillar of the world'.

The mausoleum was built from red brick, supported internally by timber beams of shisham wood, which have now turned black with age. The exterior has ornate and colourful decoration, and includes panels of raised, glazed tiles among the polished brickwork. Some of the decoration is geometric, but the building also carries floral and calligraphic patterning. The actual tomb within the building is made of plain brickwork covered with plaster. During the 1970s the whole mausoleum was significantly restored, and the glittering, glazed interior is as much a testament to the skills of modern Kashigar craftsmen as it is to the building's original architects.

ORIGINS OF THE MAUSOLEUM

It is believed that the mausoleum was originally constructed between 1320 and 1324 by Ghias-ud-Din Tughlak, who was once the Governor of Depalpur, for himself. Following his death in 1330, however, it is understood that his son Muhammad Tughlak surrendered the structure to the descendants of Shah Rukn-i-Alam. When

Rukn-i-Alam died in 1335, he was buried (according to his own will) in the mausoleum of his grandfather Shaikh Baha-Al-Din Zakariya, but after some time his coffin was transferred to its present position in the Rukn-i-Alam shrine.

A MASTER OF METAPHYSICS

Throughout his life Shah Rukn-i-Alam, who was born in 1251, gained a reputation as a master of metaphysical subjects. He taught a form of 'metempsychosis' – the doctrine that souls migrate, taking different forms in different lifetimes on a path to perfection and reunion with God.

He is also known to have been friends with the saint known as Nizam-ud-Din of Delhi, and this link led to a number of visits by the emperors of Delhi, who were seeking enlightenment. Part of Rukn-i-Alam's legacy is the continued existence of 'Mukhdums of Multan', a group of hereditary guardians who oversee both his shrine and that of his grandfather Shaikh Baha-Al-Din Zakariya. The Mukhdums are spiritual teachers with many thousands of adherents throughout the Punjab and Sindh.

Multan's reputation as the 'city of saints' is well earned, and the many examples of Muslim- and Sufi-inspired architectural achievement that can be seen here are possibly as great as those to be found anywhere in the world.

① OCTAGONAL PLAN

The structure of the mausoleum is based on an octagonal floor plan, with a diameter of more than 27 m (90 ft). Its walls are 12.5 m (41 ft) high and more than 4 m (13 ft) thick. On top of this base, a smaller octagonal structure with walls 8 m (26 ft) high supports a hemispherical dome with a diameter of 17.5 m (58 ft).

② LEANING TOWERS

Eight inward-leaning round towers topped with domed pinnacles support the main structure – much as flying buttresses serve the same purpose on a cathedral.

③ DOME

The dome glistens with a light-blueish verdigris surface, a feature that is repeated in miniature on the 16 smaller domes that sit atop the apexes of the octagons. It is purportedly one of the biggest domes in the world, after St Peter's in Rome and Gol Gumbad in the Bijapur district of India.

④ WALKWAY

Between the larger, lower octagon and the smaller upper octagon supporting the dome is a narrow walkway on which the *Moazzan*, the person who calls the Muslim faithful to their regular prayers, stands and performs his sacred duties.

⑤ FORT

The shrine to Rukn-i-Alam, which is located in the south-west part of the Multan fort complex, is visible from 45 km (28 miles) away, because it is built on the fort's artificial mound and is therefore a prominent feature on the horizon.

⑥ WHITE MOSQUE

Next to the mausoleum of Shah Rukn-i-Alam stands a small white mosque, which is raised slightly above the ground on a shallow platform. Though it is overshadowed by the larger Tomb building, the mosque nevertheless attracts many adherents.

Zoroastrianism and Zarathustra

Zoroastrianism is a unique philosophy within the history of world religions because it appears to function as the spiritual link between the major strands of Eastern and Western traditions. As the theologian Mary Boyce wrote in 1979, '[As] the oldest of the revealed credal religions, Zoroastrianism probably had more influence on mankind directly or indirectly than any other faith.'

The religion was based on the life, beliefs and written works of the Iranian prophet and poet Avestan Zoroaster. There are widely differing ideas about when he lived, ranging from as far back as the 17th century BCE to the 1st century BCE. Many scholars place his birth around the 6th to 9th centuries BCE.

Relatively little is known of the man Zoroaster (or Zarathustra), and many mythologies have grown up around the events of his life. In the *Avesta*, the most important collection of Zoroastrian texts, we are told that he was married to a woman named Hvovi and had three sons and three daughters. He received illumination from the Creator God when he was 30. When he first attempted to promulgate his teachings, he encountered fierce opposition from the priests of existing traditions, as well as from local princes and aristocrats. Zoroaster and his early converts – including his wife, children and cousin – fled their homeland, but still faced resistance. Eventually Zoroaster received an audience with King Vishtaspa and convinced him of the importance of his new philosophy. As a result, the King decided to adopt the Zoroastrian faith and urged his people to join him. Zoroaster then spread his teachings throughout the country, before they began to spread to nearby countries through his disciples. There are a number of different stories about his mysterious death, including an account by the Persian poet Firdousi that he died a martyr's death at the hands of the Turanians during the storming of the city known as Balkh.

BELIEFS

Zoroastrians believe there is one universal Creator God, whose name is Ahura Mazda and who is the focus of all worship. Ahura Mazda created the Universe as an expression of order or *asha*, but this is opposed by *druj* or chaos. The conflict between them requires that humanity play an active part through the expression of good thoughts, words and deeds, so that happiness can be maintained and chaos stopped from overwhelming the Universe. This active principle and its demand on human behaviour means that Zoroastrianism does not condone or permit monasticism. It also reinforces the notion of

Right *This carving shows Ahura Mazda, the Creator God of the Zoroastrian religion. It was believed that the universe was created to represent order and this was opposed by chaos. It was up to the human race to strike an equilibrium between the two.*

Left *Zoroastrianism was based around the beliefs of Avestan Zoroaster. Little is known about the Iranian poet and prophet, including exactly when he lived.*

'Free Will' – a concept that Zoroastrianism developed more strongly than any preceding tradition. While the conflict between *asha* and *druj* has perpetuated itself for aeons, Ahura Mazda will eventually be victorious and at the end of time, in the final 'renovation', all souls – both alive and dead – will be reunited with the Creator.

One of Zoroaster's developments was to bring the many aspects of divinity into a cohesive whole under the Supreme Creator. In his system, Zoroaster says that the first of Ahura Mazda's creative actions was the emanation of six divine sparks, jointly referred to as the *Amesha Spenta*. As Zoroastrian thought developed, this came to be personified as archangels with responsibility for a specific domain of life: Vohu Manu was responsible for Animal Life; Asha Vahishta oversaw the powers of Fire; Kshathra Vairya was in charge of Metals and Minerals; Armaiti was patron of the Earth; Haurvatat was responsible for Water; and Ameratat oversaw Plant Life.

THE AHUNA VAIRYA

In Zoroastrianism, the destructive principle in the Universe is known as *Angra Mainyu*, while the positive or 'Bountiful' principle, representing Ahura Mazda's wish for order, is called *Spenta Mainyu*. The latter can be considered a form of 'Holy Spirit' and functions in addition to the six aspects of the *Amesha Spenta*. The dialogue between *Angra Mainyu* and *Spenta Mainyu*, and the eventual triumph of the latter, is expressed in the most sacred texts of Zoroastrianism, the *Ahuna Vairya*. This is believed by Zoroastrians to have particular invocatory powers: 'This utterance is a thing of such a nature that if all the corporeal and living world should learn it, and learning hold fast by it, they would be redeemed from their mortality.' It is also believed to help people in distress, repel demons, and ensure health and safety in many of life's most difficult situations. The *Ahuna Vairya* is used at least once in every Zoroastrian ritual.

Although it is always thought to have more power in its more original Avestan-language version, many superficially quite different English translations have attempted to capture the essence of its meaning. For example:

Just as the righteous Creator of the world is powerful, in the same way
Any person will be powerful according to his/her righteousness.
The gift of the Good Mind is both the effect and the cause of serving God's Will.
One who dedicates one's life to serving the needs of the world will have the help of God's powers and glory.

OTHER KEY TEXTS

The *Avesta* is the most important collection of sacred texts for Zoroastrians. Written in the Old Iranian 'Avestan' language during the first millennium BCE, it includes the 'Gathas', a group of 17 hymns attributed to Zoroaster himself. They consist of just 238 verses, spoken in the voice of Zoroaster. Some of these address the audience that has come to hear him speak, encouraging them to live according to the direction of Ahura Mazda. Zoroaster prays to his god to help his people live this life according to the principles of *asha*. Some of the hymns in the 'Gathas' are devotional and are addressed directly to the Creator, Ahura Mazda. The Prophet asks for guidance and blessings and for answers to his most difficult questions.

In the 28th verse Zoroaster asks for blessings: 'I approach you with good thought, O Mazda Ahura, so that you may grant me the blessing of two existences (on Earth and in paradise), the material and that of thought, the blessing emanating from Truth, with which one can put your support in comfort.' In the 48th verse the Prophet pleads for good temporal leadership: 'Let good rulers assume rule (over us), with actions of good insight, O right-mindedness. Let not bad rulers assume rule over us. The best insight, which purifies progeny for mankind, let it also be applied to the cow. Her You breed us for food.'

The 'Gathas' cover different periods of Zoroaster's life, from initial doubts about his ability to carry the message of *asha*, through troubled times to a more peaceful and resolved state of mind as he oversees the wedding of his youngest daughter. It seems likely that what we know of Zoroastrian texts may only be the tip of a much larger iceberg of works that failed to survive the ravages of history.

ESCHATOLOGY

Zoroastrian eschatology (the theological study of the 'last things') is the oldest recorded 'end-time' tradition, dating from before 500 BCE. According to Zoroastrian philosophy:

at the end of thy tenth hundredth winter ... the sun is more unseen and more spotted, the year, month and day are shorter; and the earth is more barren; and the crop will not yield the seed; and men ... become more deceitful and more given to vile practices. They have no gratitude ... a dark cloud makes the whole sky night ... and it will rain more noxious creatures than winter.

Below *Zoroastrians worshipped outdoors until the introduction of fire temples, such as this example in Iran.*

FIRE TEMPLES

Fire temples were a distinctive development of Zoroastrian worship, although they did not first appear until the 4th century BCE. Prior to this, the Greek historian Herodotus recorded in the mid-5th century BCE, Zoroastrians worshipped in the open air, climbing to the tops of mounds and hills to light their fires. Fire temples acted as a ritualized container for the hearth fire, and some fires were kept burning continuously. Eventually fire temples spread throughout the Persian Sassanid empire. Typically they were built on a square ground plan, with four pillars supporting a domed sanctuary above the fire-altar. Following the arrival of Islam in the 7th century CE, all fire temples were either destroyed or converted into mosques.

At the end of these Earth changes and the battle between the supporters of *asha* and the supporters of *druj*, a Final Judgement will start. Those who have sinned will be punished for three days, but will then be forgiven. The world will then reach perfection, when all its ills are wiped away: poverty, disease, hunger, thirst, old age and death are all ended.

ZOROASTRIANISM TODAY

Today the tradition of Zoroastrianism is maintained by the Parsee community based mainly in India. Parsees are the descendants of Persian Zoroastrians who travelled to India initially in the 7th century CE, following the Arab conquest of Persia and the fall of the Sassanid empire, which had practised Zoroastrianism. In order to protect their religion and culture, the founding fathers of the current Parsee community travelled to the port of Hormuzd on the Persian Gulf, from where they journeyed to the island of Div near the coast of Kathiawar, part of Gujarat state; there they stayed for 19 years, before making their home on mainland Gujarat. They were given permission to stay by the local ruler on condition that they spoke Gujarati and started the formation of the first of many major Parsee communities that still survive today. They continue to practise their faith and worship according to Zoroastrian tenets and the teachings of the sacred texts.

Above *A section of the Avesta, a collection of sacred texts that held immense significance for followers of the Zoroastrianism religion. The texts were written in Avestan, which was the Old Iranian language.*

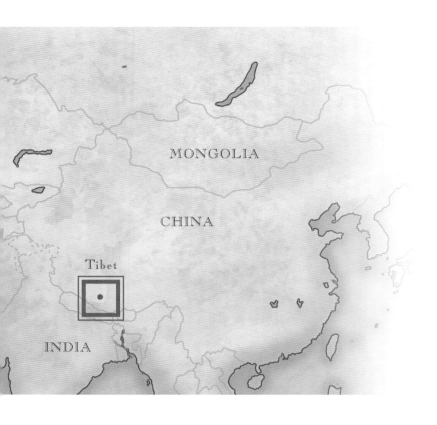

Tantric traditions and practices

Tantric practitioners seek to work with the energies that are available – either inside or outside their body – to transform their experience of the present moment and potentially have a positive effect on the greater whole. Normally this process is not embarked on alone: a guru is required to help students avoid the traps and dangers that await those on the transformational path.

Tantra is a slippery concept: it is not one spiritual practice or organized religion; it belongs to no particular organization or group; many religions and countries claim a Tantric thread within their spirituality. Since *Tantra* means continuity, it also means change and flow as well as all the other aspects of spirituality that make it hard to pin down. Recently it has become associated in the modern mind with various sensual and sexual rites, which may have distorted people's understanding of the elusive roots of the Tantric tradition. Amidst this complexity and confusion, the Tantric scholar David Gordon White has attempted a definition:

Tantra is that Asian body of beliefs and practices which, working from the principle that the universe we experience is nothing other than the concrete manifestation of the divine energy of the Godhead that creates and maintains that universe, seeks to ritually appropriate and channel that energy, within the human microcosm, in creative and emancipatory ways.

SACRED TEXTS

Tantra is often thought to have come from the Hindu Vedic tradition. The *Vedas* are a large group of Hindu sacred texts that form the oldest recognized Sanskrit literature. According to Hindu tradition, they are *apauruseya* or not of human origin: they are regarded as 'revealed' works. There are four main *Vedas*: the *Rig-Veda*, the *Yajur-Veda*, the *Sama-Veda* and the *Atharva-Veda*, each of which is a collection of mantras or chants, although the term *Veda* can also refer to knowledge of many other kinds. The *Vedas* appear to date from about the 2nd century BCE. Some orthodox followers of the *Vedas*, however, reject the veracity of Tantra and maintain that it is anti-Vedic in character. At the same time

Left *Mantras, or mystical poems, are recited by many spiritual groups. They are chanted and act as a means of evoking internal spiritual energies, which enables the devotee to identify with the divine.*

Above *This painting shows Brahma holding a page of the* Vedas. *This group of sacred Hindu texts represents the oldest known Sanskrit literature.*

there are supporters of Tantra who maintain that the *Vedas* are not appropriate for our current age, and that modern Tantric texts are easier for the general populace to follow in their spiritual practice.

The *Tantras* (literally 'weavings') is also the name for a group of 92 scriptures: 64 of these – the *Bhairava* or *Kashmir Saivite Tantras* – are *Abheda* ('without differentiation' or monistic); a further 18 – known as the *Rudra Tantras* – are *Bhedabheda* ('both with and without differentiation' or monistic and dualistic); a final ten are *Bheda* (completely dualistic) and are known as the *Siva Tantras*. Hindus, particularly those of the Kashmir Shaivism tradition, consider that all 92 *Tantras* were revealed by the Lord Siva in the form of Svacchandanath at the beginning of the period known as Sat Yuga, the first of the four great eras, the age of Truth. Svacchandanath was distinctive for having five heads with five mouths, each representing one of the five universal energies: the *cit shakti* (energy of all-consciousness), *ananda shakti* (energy

of all-bliss), *iccha shakta* (energy of all-will), *jnana shakti* (energy of all-knowledge) and *kriya shakti* (energy of all-action). It is said that the revelation of the *Tantras* at the start of the Sag Yuga illuminated the whole universe. As humans descended into increasing darkness through each subsequent era, the masters of Tantra hid themselves, and the Tantras were lost from view to more and more people.

Although Tantra may have developed initially in the Hindu tradition, it evolved quite discretely in Buddhism and is a constant feature of the Vajrayana school of Buddhism. Buddhist Tantra spread from northern India, particularly to Tibet, and had some influence on both Chinese and Japanese (Shingon) Buddhism. Tantric practices can also be found in Bonpo (the native religion of Tibet) and in the Jain faith.

RITUAL PRACTICES AND GURUS

There are certain defining features to Tantric practices, which in some ways represent an eastern mirror to the Gnostic tradition of the

West. In particular Tantrism involves the seeking of mystical experiences through a number of means: the different yogas of mind, body and spirit; the use of visualizations of deities; and the use of mantras to evoke the presence of spiritual energies within the devotee, to the point of complete identification with the deity.

A key feature of all these practices is that they are not to be undertaken alone: the presence, experience and teaching of the guru are considered essential for the disciple to remain spiritually and psychologically safe and protected on the 'razor's edge' of progress towards the Divine.

Below *Tantric sex sculptures are a common adornment on many Hindu temples. Sex was intrinsic to early Tantric rites and has many connotations in the modern notion of Tantra.*

The current 14th Dalai Lama has spoken about the relevance and purpose of Tantra as a spiritual practice within the Vajrayana tradition of Tibetan Buddhism: 'Tantra is limited to persons whose compassion is so great that they cannot bear to spend unnecessary time in attaining Buddhahood, as they want to be a supreme source of help and happiness for others quickly.'

INNER AND OUTER RITUALS

Some scholars distinguish between the outer, more generally practised rituals of Tantra and the secret rituals that characterize the most powerful, and perhaps psychologically dangerous, aspects of practice. Normally these would require that the disciple had already travelled some way along the path of ordinary Tantra before being permitted to take part. They would include aspects of the ordinary ritual, but would also involve other 'sensate' rites and initiations, including heightened experiences – both real and metaphoric – related to food, sex, death and bodily purification. Some Western observers of these practices have been impressed by Tantra's positive, affirming approach to all experience. The Tantric method involves sublimation and transformation of apparently negative aspects of attachment to the Earth: through purification and practice of his or her nature, the disciple can discover his or her identity with pure consciousness.

SEX

It is possible that early Tantric sexual rites were intimately involved in the process of offering sexual fluids to the Tantric deities. Just as offerings of food might be sacrificed to the gods, so might the produce of the human reproductive system. Early sects are believed to have focused on the apparent production of 'clan fluid' (*kuladravya*) and 'clan nectar' (*kulamrita*) from the female's womb. Males were transformed into clan members by being inseminated or insanguinated with the sexual fluids of a female consort. Sometimes the guru's semen was added to the woman's fluids. Later, these physical rites were replaced with sexual practices that put greater emphasis on the experience of bliss and union with the Divine.

In the modern world, Tantra has become heavily associated with sexual practice. When rock stars and other celebrities claim an intimate knowledge of Tantric sexual practices, the world stands to attention. But do these 'Neo-Tantric' practices have any connection with the original purpose of Tantra? Certainly Tantra involved an

understanding of the sexual energies within the body and their relationship to the process of spiritual growth, but Neo-Tantra can often be seen to have jettisoned both the guru–disciple relationship and many of the basic Tantric spiritual practices.

Some original Tantric texts express the idea that sex has three functions: procreation, pleasure and liberation. Liberation is experienced when the energies generated and exchanged between sexual-spiritual partners are consciously used to make the participants more receptive to higher and higher levels of spiritually transformative energy. Sexual acts between Tantric practitioners involve detailed preparatory rites of purification in mind and body before any contact can take place. Abstaining from certain foods and drinks is quite normal, as is the performance of prayers and meditation.

During the sexual act there is a stress on the balancing of energies flowing through the pranic *ida* and *pingala* channels, and this is controlled through breathing and visualization. Through this work on the subtle bodies, kundalini energy – which resides in the base *chakra* – starts to rise up through the *chakra* systems of both participants. Often 'frictional' activity is avoided and the partners remain in static positions, experiencing only the flows of energy within and between them. Properly performed, this process leads to *samadhi*, or the blissful state in which the human individuality dissolves and cosmic consciousness, free of the ego, is experienced. For many Hindu Tantric practitioners, this represents the linking not just of male and female, but of Siva and Shakti, the representations of the gender principles. For each, the blending of male and female is also an explicit aim. In Jungian terms, the man is linked with his *anima*, the female with her *animus*, where the aim is spiritual and psychological progress above all else.

The 14th Dalai Lama wrote:

In Tibetan Buddhism, especially if you look at the iconography of the deities and their consorts, you can see a lot of very explicit sexual symbolism which often gives the wrong impression. Actually, in this case the sexual organ is utilized, the energy movement which is taking place is, in the end, fully controlled.

The energy should never be let out ... What is required for a Tantric practitioner is to develop the capacity to utilize one's faculties of bliss and the blissful experiences which are specifically generated due to the flow of regenerative fluids within one's own energy channels. It is crucial to have the ability to protect oneself from the fault of emission. It is not just a purely ordinary sexual act.

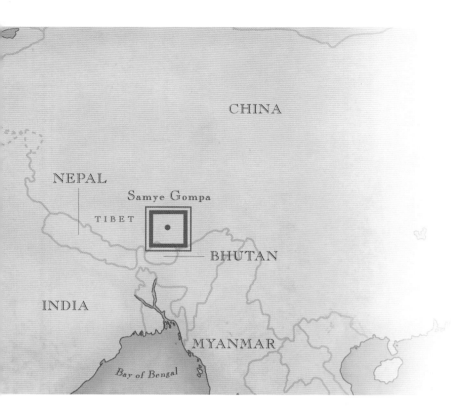

Tibetan Buddhism – a Mahayana tradition

Tibetan Buddhism has been influential throughout the Himalayan region for around a thousand years. This form of Buddhism took root in Tibet, Nepal, Bhutan, parts of north-east India, as well as areas of north-eastern China, parts of Mongolia and the Russian territories of Kalmykia, Tuva and Buryatia.

In Buddhist scholarship, Tibetan Buddhism is understood to be an example of a 'Mahayana' (or Greater) vehicle set of teachings, which also encompasses the teachings of Vajrayana, or Tantrism (see pages 122–125). It is a Mahayana tradition because it embraces the goal of individual enlightenment in order that the practitioner can assist all other sentient beings in their own journey to *nirvana*. This intention is enshrined in the 'Bodhisattva vow', a declaration to work for the complete enlightenment of all life, even if it means the Buddhist delaying his or her own liberation.

HISTORY OF THE FOUR LINEAGES

There are four main 'lineages' in Tibetan Buddhism, which – although they may differ on matters of Buddhist teaching and belief – are generally held to be of equal stature within the Tibetan Buddhist movement. They are Nyingma, Kagyupa, Sakyapa and Gelukpa. They have evolved over the last 1,300 years to become an important strand of world religious thought, and the esteem in which His Holiness the Dalai Lama is now held reflects this. The Dalai Lama is a

Below *His Holiness the Dalai Lama is a member of the Yellow Hat sect of Tibetan Buddhism. Buddhism is a key influence in world religious thought.*

member of the Gelukpa lineage, also known as the Yellow Hat sect.

In 747 CE the 38th King of Tibet, Trisong Detsen, invited the Indian Buddhist master Padmasambhava to travel from Afghanistan in order to rid the country of evil mountain deities. The King was so impressed by Padmasambhava's Tantric abilities that he asked him to teach Vajrayana Buddhism in Tibet. Padmasambhava founded the first monastery, the Samye Gompa, and initiated the first monks. This transmission of wisdom was the beginning of the Nyingma school, the first of the lineages of Tibetan Buddhism. According to legend, during his life in Tibet, Padmasambhava hid various spiritual treasures throughout the Himalayan landscape. One of these was the *Bardo Thodol* – the *Tibetan Book of the Dead* – which was later found on top of Mount Gampodar by Karma Lingpa, an important Tantric practitioner, when he was only 15.

Early Tibetan Buddhism was brutally suppressed during the 9th century CE by King Langdharma, whose reign ended amid chaos and assassinations. He was followed by Lha Lama Yeshe Yod, who was committed to the

Buddhist Dharma, or doctrine. Through his efforts new teachers came to Tibet, including Atisha, who was originally from Bengal. Atisha spent many years in Tibet and started the Kadampa school, which focused on monasticism. Under the guidance of Tsong Khapa in the 14th and 15th centuries, the philosophy of the Kadampa school was developed into the Gelukpa lineage. Tsong khapa stressed both the importance of Mahayana ideas of compassion for others and the Vajrayana techniques of 'emptiness' meditation, while also offering protection against the pitfalls of both traditions. Although successive Dalai Lamas have always originated from the Gelukpa lineage, the Dalai Lama is not technically their leader – this honour in fact belongs to the Ganden Tripa, or head of the Ganden monastery.

Later on, Marpa – who was born in southern Tibet, but travelled and studied

Buddhism throughout India – returned to his native land. There, as well as teaching and giving initiatory transmissions, he translated many of the great works of Buddhism into Tibetan. His school of teachings, which became the Kagyupa lineage, was eventually inherited by his disciple Milarepa, who was considered one of Tibet's most important poets, magicians and meditational experts.

The Sakyapa lineage of Tibetan Buddhism started in 1073 CE with the building of the original Sakya Monastery near Shigatse in southern Tibet by Khon Konchog Gyalpo. The tradition is based on the study of specific Tantric texts and practices provided by a group of four patriarch translators. Sakyapa differs from the other three lineages in that it contains two distinct forms of teaching: one for a general audience based on *Sutras* or written teachings, and a second that is private and based on Tantric practices.

Above *Samye Gompa was the first Buddhist monastery built in Tibet. It was founded by the Indian Buddhist master Padmasambhava, who travelled to the country to eliminate evil mountain deities.*

Many masters from the other three lineages have received the teachings of the Sakya in addition to their own. As with the monks of most sects, the Sakya are not allowed to marry. Their spiritual leader is, however, permitted to have a consort, since leadership of the Sakya has been passed down a male hereditary line. The current leader is the 41st Sakya Trizin, or holder of the Sakya throne.

LINEAGE OF THE DALAI LAMA

The Dalai Lama, or 'Ocean of Wisdom', is the name for the spiritual and temporal leader of Tibet. The current Dalai Lama, Tenzin Gyatso, is the 14th to hold the title in an unbroken succession dating back to Genden Drub in 1391. In fact the first person to hold the title was the 3rd Dalai Lama, Sonam Gyatso, but on accession the two predecessors in his personal lineage were posthumously conferred with the title. Within Tibetan Buddhism it is believed that each Dalai Lama is a reincarnation of the previous title-holder. On the death of a Dalai Lama, and after a suitable period of time has passed, a search is initiated for the child who is the new reincarnation of the lineage. In times past, this search would have been within the boundaries of Tibet, and monks and lamas familiar with the previous Dalai Lama would perform tests on a number of young

candidates to see whether they could recognize objects belonging to the previous lifetime. It is said that when the current Dalai Lama was first brought to the Potala Palace in Lhasa (see pages 130–131), he immediately found a significant object hidden within a cupboard. This process is not limited to the Dalai Lama, and there are similar searches for many of

the major lamas or *tulkus* after their death and rebirth. In some cases the departing lama will leave information about the details of his next incarnation and where he is likely to be found.

Since the invasion of the Chinese People's Liberation Army in 1950 and his flight from Tibet to Dharamsala in India in 1959, the current Dalai Lama has supported a policy of non-violent resistance to Chinese rule in Tibet. The Dalai Lama is both the spiritual and temporal leader of the people of Tibet, so his leadership role extends beyond the esoteric to encompass all their worldly concerns. With the increased awareness of Tibetan Buddhism that the Dalai Lama's exile has created, interest in it has spread throughout the world, and this previously hidden tradition is now considered more mainstream than at any time in its long history.

Left *Copper statue of Sonam Gyatso. Although he was the first person to hold the title, he was, in fact, the third Dalai Lama. The two predecessors in his personal lineage were awarded the title posthumously.*

Right *Each Dalai Lama is believed to be a reincarnation of the previous title-holder. The current Dalai Lama confirmed his identity by finding a significant object at the Potala Palace.*

VAJRAYANA AND TANTRA TECHNIQUES

Tibetan Buddhism is often thought of as an embodiment of Vajrayana Buddhism, the third major vehicle of Buddhism, after Mahayana and the earlier Hinayana traditions. In fact, however, Tibetan Buddhism contains elements of all three vehicles. The word *vajra* means thunderbolt, and this dynamic idea is embodied in the common translation of Vajrayana as 'The Diamond Vehicle'. For those who practise Vajrayana, it is seen as an accelerated path to enlightenment, meaning that practitioners can more quickly fulfil their vows to liberate others. Vajrayana does not invalidate Mahayana or Theravadan (Asian) Buddhism; rather, it insists that those traditions are essential to lay the foundations of the path on which the techniques of Vajrayana can be employed. As well as forming a vital part of the teachings transmitted by all four Tibetan lineages, Vajrayana Buddhism is closely identified with the Japanese Shingon tradition that was initiated by the monk Kukai – albeit via a very different geographical and intellectual development.

Using specific *vajra* techniques, and under the guidance of teachers who have trodden the path before, the student can hasten his or her progress. These techniques focus on the development and use of certain mind-body states to transform the consciousness of the practitioner. These states include those experienced during meditation, dreams and death. The application of the techniques is often described by a set of yogas. Guru yoga involves the disciple focusing on the guru or spiritual teacher during meditation, as an example of one who has 'gone before' and already overcome some of the obstacles to Buddhahood. Deity yoga is a set of techniques in which practitioners identify themselves with images, *mandalas*, statues or other visualizations in order to experience what the Dalai Lama describes as 'the celestial mansion, the pure residence of the deity'. Death yoga is a complex set of teachings that use the death process – including the experience of the after-death *bardo* realm and rebirth – to assist the process of enlightenment. This is not to be confused with common Buddhist meditations on death and 'mortality' as a way of releasing mental attachment.

Tantra techniques are taught within Tibetan Buddhist schools according to strict and careful rules. They are transmitted directly from teacher to pupil within the wisdom of the relationship. In this way it has been possible to maintain the numerous lineages that result in progress towards enlightenment over a number of lifetimes.

Potala Palace

The Potala Palace is widely considered to be the most important building in all Tibet. The home of the last eight Dalai Lamas and the seat of government in Tibet, the Potala's importance for Tibetan Buddhists remains very great, despite the Chinese invasion of Tibet in 1950 and the flight of the 14th Dalai Lama to northern India in 1959.

In the 7th century CE the Emperor Songtsen Gampo used a cave within Marpo Ri Hill, on which the Potala Palace is built, as a meditation retreat before deciding, in 637, to build a palace on the hill. He named the palace 'Potala' after the sacred mountain Potalaka in southern India, which is often regarded as the spiritual abode of the Bodhisattva Chenrezig.

THE WHITE AND RED PALACES

The construction of the palace that visitors and pilgrims see today was begun in 1645 during the reign of the 5th Dalai Lama, Lozang Gyatso. Within three years the *Potrang Karpo*, or White Palace, was complete; the *Potrang Marpo*, or Red Palace, was added to the structure between 1690 and 1694. The construction of the great palace involved the work of thousands of builders, artists and craftspeople. In 1922 the 13th Dalai Lama carried out renovations on many of the chapels and halls in the White Palace and built a further two storeys onto the Red Palace. The whole remarkable edifice now contains more than one thousand rooms and covers an area in excess of 130,000 sq m (1,400,000 sq ft).

The Red Palace is the most spiritually important structure in the complex. Its West Hall leads to the four great chapels – North, South, East and West – as well as the Saint's Chapel.

THE CHAPELS

The Saint's Chapel dates from the 7th century CE and is the most sacred shrine in the whole of the Potala Palace. It contains an entranceway to the 'Dharma Cave', where the Emperor Songtsen Gampo is believed to have spent time in contemplation and Buddhist study. Libraries within the Red Palace contain the main Tibetan scriptures: the *Kangyur* in 108 volumes and the *Tengyur* in 225 volumes.

The North Chapel contains figures of the Shakyamuni Buddha, the 'sponsor' and inspirer of Tibetan Buddhism, and of the 5th Dalai Lama. Also here is the tomb of the 11th Dalai Lama, who died in childhood and whose remains are contained within a gold *stupa*, or funeral mound. In addition there are representations of Avalokiteshvara and his earthly incarnations: the Emperor Songtsen Gampo and the first four personages of the Dalai Lama lineage.

The South Chapel is dedicated to Padmasambhava, the 8th-century Indian Tantric Buddhist mystic who came to Tibet at the request of the King and subsumed the Bon faith into his Buddhist teachings. Padmasambhava is regarded as the true founder of Tibetan Buddhism and was responsible for establishing the Nyingma tradition, the first of the four great lineages of the faith (see pages 126–127). In the chapel his figure sits between eight holy manifestations of

meditating power and another eight 'wrathful' manifestations of magic power subduing the demons of the Bon faith.

The East Chapel is devoted to Tsong Khapa, the founder of the Gelukpa tradition, to which the Dalai Lama belongs. His representation is surrounded by lamas from the Sakya Monastery, who ruled Tibet for a short time until Tsong Khapa established the new ruling tradition.

The West Chapel contains five great golden *stupas*, including the dominant central one, which contains the mummified body of the 5th Dalai Lama, Lozang Gyatso. Two of the other *stupas* contain the funerary remains of the 10th and 12th Dalai Lamas.

SURVIVAL OF THE PALACE

In the years since the Chinese arrival and the Tibetan uprising of 1959, the Potala Palace has remained a symbol of Tibetan Buddhism, despite the many changes and threats that the Tibetan people have had to suffer. Remarkably, it was not destroyed by the Chinese Red Guard, after personal interventions during the 1960s and 1970s by the Chinese Premier, Chou En-lai (Zhou Enlai). Today it is a state museum.

① MARPO RI HILL

The Potala Palace is perched on Marpo Ri Hill, some 130 m (425 ft) above the Lhasa Valley at an altitude of 3,700 m (12,135 ft). The hill, a solitary mound, was originally believed in Tibetan legend to be the home of a sacred cave belonging to the Bodhisattva Chenrezig (also known as Avalokiteshavara), one of the most important personages in the Tibetan Buddhist canon.

② THE WHITE PALACE

The function of the White Palace is mainly secular: the building makes up the living quarters of the Dalai Lama, as well as a seminary, offices and a printing area. A central courtyard, painted yellow and known as a *Deyangshar*, separates the White Palace from the Red Palace.

③ THE RED PALACE

Although the Red Palace was built after the White Palace, it is the more spiritually important structure within the overall Potala complex, because it contains the most holy and revered sanctuaries of Tibetan Buddhism. It is completely dedicated to prayer and study.

④ THE WEST CHAPEL

Within the red palace is the West Chapel, which contains the five golden *stupas*. The central *stupa* in this chapel contains the mummified body of the 5th Dalai Lama. It rises more than three storeys high, and is believed to be covered with as much as 3,000 kg (6,600 lb) of gold.

⑤ CHAPEL OF THE 5TH DALAI LAMA

Also known as The Saint's Chapel this building contains the holiest shrine in the palace. A passage leads from the shrine to the Dharma cave where Songsten Gampo is believed to have studied Buddhism in the 7th century.

PART 4

CULTS OF THE NEW AGE

Keep your highest ideal, strive ever towards it; let naught stop you or turn you aside, for mine is the secret door which opens upon the door of youth.

DOREEN VALIENTE, *CHARGE OF THE GODDESS*

Live through deeds of love, and let others live as they will, with understanding for their own individual intentions.

RUDOLF STEINER, *PHILOSOPHY OF FREEDOM*

Exploring the Age of Aquarius

The idea of the New Age emerged in the later part of the 20th century and has its roots in astronomy and astrology. It is based on the idea that the Earth is involved in a 25,800-year-long cycle known as the Great Siderial Year and that, astrologically at least, this cycle can be divided into the 12 signs of the zodiac. Currently it can be said that the Earth is moving out of the Age of Pisces, the fish, into the Age of Aquarius, the water bearer.

Opinions differ as to the exact moment, or range of time, when this transition takes place, but it is believed to signal a change in the influence that guides humanity from the emotionality and divisiveness of Pisces to the imaginative thinking of Aquarius.

OUR PLACE IN THE WORLD

The New Age of Aquarius is expected by some to bring great transformations in human consciousness, as well as changes in the Earth's living conditions. These ideas were already known within esoteric circles during the late 19th and early 20th centuries, long before public concern about climate change was even a subject of discussion or research. The religious movements described in this section have all aimed to bring about changes in spiritual consciousness for practitioners at a time when the world requires great shifts in the way we think and feel about its stewardship. They focus on our place in the world, the Universe, and demand an individual response to what many people now agree is a planet (and a human race) in crisis.

Most of the organizations under discussion have been led by at least one charismatic leader, and while this may not be an identifying feature of a religion, it is often the case that the presence of a particular individual is capable of inspiring great loyalty and devotion. In the case of the Theosophical Society (see pages 142–145), it is also possible to see what happens when divisions occur within an organization and one person – their new Christ figure, Krishnamurti – decides to go his own way. From its peak in the 1920s, when the young Krishnamurti was due to make his appearance as the coming avatar, the Theosophical Society fell spectacularly from

Right *The Maya document known as the* Codex Troano *is reputed by some researchers to document the destruction of the fabled lost civilization of Mu or Atlantis. Some new-age movements have picked up on this idea as a confirmation of alternative world histories.*

Left *Mistletoe has special significance in druidry and here, members of the Mistletoe Foundation gather at the largest mistletoe auction in the UK. Many new age movements focus on our treatment of the planet.*

public favour, in a way from which it never fully recovered.

Rudolf Steiner, the founder of the Anthroposophical movement (see pages 146–151), had his own background in Theosophy, but always maintained an individual path and teaching, which, once launched, became an important new strand in world teaching. He also wrote about the lost civilization of Atlantis (see pages 152–155), as did many other prominent figures. Sir Arthur Conan Doyle was a key figure in Spiritualism (see pages 136–141) in the early 20th century and spent much of the second half of his life promoting its cause – often to the detriment of his public reputation. George Ivanovich Gurdjieff (see pages 156–161) was both charismatic and enigmatic, and attracted interest from the intellectual elite throughout Europe. In the end, though, many were called, but few were chosen. His harsh brand of conscious-awareness development was too much for

some, and they never discovered where the path might have led. In the area of nature religions, Gerald Gardner's reinvention of Wicca (see pages 162–165) in the 1950s and the rise of Neo-Paganism (see pages 166–169) have been remarkably influential and, in terms of the world's concerns, prescient.

One of the key things that mark out these movements is that they all developed in a time when our sense of the world was shrinking rapidly. Owing to technological and scientific developments, it was possible for people to look well beyond the boundaries of their own country – both in sourcing ideas and inspiration, and in thinking about the effects their influence might have. The Theosophical Society moved from London to America to India. Gurdjieff's work was present in St Petersburg, Paris, London and New York. The Anthroposophical Society, which started in Germany and moved its headquarters to Switzerland, now has a presence in many

other countries through its teachings, the businesses it spawned, the therapies it initiated and the schools it started. Spiritualism began in America, and travelled initially to Europe and then throughout the world. Now Spiritualist mediums perform regularly on global television, fulfilling the original aim of providing evidence of survival after death to those in a scientific age.

If we look closely, we can see the threads of these spiritual philosophies and ideas sewn into the fabric of modern society, just as clearly as the much older influences which were provided by the main religions and ancient myths. Renewal, it seems, is a necessary process and if the mainstream cannot provide it, then teachers and ideas from outside conventions will step forward and make their own contributions. Here are some of those movements that have made their presence firmly felt and may well continue to influence spritual thought in the years to come.

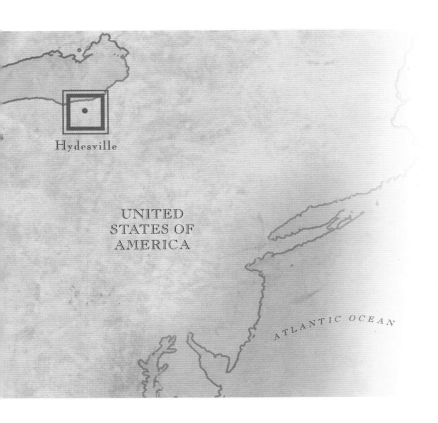

Hydesville

UNITED
STATES OF
AMERICA

ATLANTIC OCEAN

Spiritualism and spiritualist phenomena

Spiritualism emerged in 1848 when two sisters named Kate and Margaret Fox of Hydesville, New York, reported that they had made contact with the spirit of a murdered pedlar, Charles B. Rosma, who communicated with them via a series of audible 'rappings' in their home. The 'Hydesville rappings' were an example of evidential phenomena that became the touchstones of Spiritualist belief.

In the case of the Fox sisters, this 'physical' evidence appeared to prove the existence of a spirit world in which the dead continued to exist and could communicate with the living about matters temporal and spiritual.

WHAT HAPPENS WHEN YOU DIE?

The idea of life after death was not new; virtually all religions and faiths contain beliefs about the transcendent nature of the soul. With Spiritualism, however, the notion that those who had passed over wished to make contact with the living through tangible, physical and evidential means contained within it the possibility of a scientific approach to religious phenomena. It was for this reason that the growing movement attracted scientists and other apparently rational types who might otherwise eschew religion. It seemed that Spiritualism could offer an answer to the most fundamental question of existence: 'What happens when you die?'

Within ten years of the Fox sisters' first experiences, more than a million people professed support for Spiritualism in America. But the growth of this movement

was to take some very strange twists and turns. In addition to physical phenomena such as rappings, table-turnings and levitations, Spiritualism was, from its earliest inception, linked with the work of mediums and clairvoyants, who offered evidence of survival after death and

information about life in the spirit world. One of the most important figures in early Spiritualism was Andrew Jackson Davis, an American from Poughkeepsie, New York. Davis was a clairvoyant, faith healer and hypnotist who became famous for his book *The Principles of Nature, Her Divine*

Right *American Sisters Kate and Margaret Fox can be credited with the emergence of the Spiritualist movement in 1848. They claimed to have communicated with the spirit of a murdered peddler and this was taken as physical proof of the spirit world.*

Left *New Yorker Andrew Jackson Davis was one of the key figures in the early Spiritualist movement. He was a faith healer, hypnotist and clairvoyant who dictated a number of books while in a trance state.*

Revelations, and a Voice to Mankind, published the year before the Hydesville rappings. His work was spoken in a trance state and recorded by a friend – an example of the phenomenon now known as 'channelling'. Davis also drew on the inspiration of two important figures: the Swedish mystic Emanuel Swedenborg and the discoverer of hypnotism Franz Mesmer, both of whom gave specific information about contact with spirits and the afterlife.

SPIRITUALIST PHENOMENA

Spiritualism developed through mediums offering evidence of the reality of the afterlife, and the variety of phenomena providing this evidence also increased. Some clairvoyants performed seances with small groups, attempting to contact the spirit world; others offered automatic writing – letting a spirit control the writing hand of the medium to produce messages (William Stainton Moses was an Anglican priest who became well known for his 'automatic writing', producing a number of books that described conditions in the spirit world). Some mediums were fully conscious while transmitting messages from spirits, while others were in a trance state. There were also those who played host to manifestations such as apportation (the mysterious and sudden appearance of objects in the seance room), audible phenomena such as the playing of musical instruments (apparently by the more musical spirits) and the production of ectoplasm (a kind of 'spirit-matter' that issued from the nose and mouth of the medium).

As with many spiritual movements that rely on the quality of its proselytizers, there were some practioners who fell below the required level, and this new religion was soon criticized as little more than a series of magic shows.

At this point the sceptics stepped in to test and potentially discredit the work of the so-called clairvoyants: evidence that mediums were faking their messages would be enough to tar all with the same brush; it would prove that the whole thing was a piece of entertaining flim-flammery performed on a gullible public for the purposes of relieving them of their money.

SPIRITUALISM DEVELOPS

In the UK the first organization to take the study of Spiritualist phenomena seriously was the Society for Psychical Research, which was founded in 1882 by a group of eminent thinkers of the time – both Spiritualists and non-Spiritualists. While taking a serious approach to Spiritualism, it was also responsible for exposing a number of frauds and charlatans. Its work has continued to the present day and, although its research has implicitly endorsed the work of some mediums and clairvoyants, the organization as a whole has never explicitly given its backing to Spiritualism.

In the 1920s the magician and escapologist Harry Houdini embarked on a crusade to uncover fraudulent mediums, and although he made it clear that he did not oppose Spiritualism *per se*, he was widely believed to have set out to destroy the movement. The timing of his effort was historically relevant: during the First World War and the flu pandemic that followed, many had lost their loved ones and the desire for an answer to questions of life after death had, perhaps, never been so widespread.

While some sceptics set out to expose charlatanism and trickery within Spiritualism, many people of a scientific and rational mind were converted to the ideas of the philosophy. Robert Owen, a prominent atheist and socialist, became an avowed believer in Spiritualism following experiences in the seance room. The well-known chemist William Crookes became an avid supporter, as did the famous physicist Sir Oliver Lodge and the evolutionary biologist Alfred Russel Wallace. But perhaps the most famous champion of Spiritualism was the author Sir Arthur Conan Doyle.

CONAN DOYLE AND SPIRITUALISM

As the creator of Sherlock Holmes, Conan Doyle was probably the most successful writer of his generation. A number of profound personal losses had led him to formulate important questions about 'survival' beyond death. In 1906 his first wife Louisa died, but he was (like many others) to suffer further family losses during the First World War, when his son Kingsley died after being wounded at the Battle of the Somme in 1916. Conan Doyle's brother, two brothers-in-law and two nephews were also to perish as a result of the conflicts. Much like his fictional detective, Conan Doyle – blessed with a curious and determined mind – set out on a path to discover the truth about their fate.

Among a sceptical public, however, Conan Doyle's involvement with Spiritualism was to cost him much of the goodwill he had built up through his creation of the Sherlock Holmes stories. Nevertheless, he was indefatigable. The incident of the Cottingley Fairies would again lower his esteem with fans of his books, and he would eventually regret some of his original impulsiveness in supporting the claims of two young cousins – Frances Griffiths and Elsie Wright – to have played with Nature Spirits at Cottingley Glen in Yorkshire. Whatever the truth of the

matter, his book *The Coming of the Fairies*, and the controversy that followed him until after his death when the girls revealed their childish hoax, did him little public good.

Conan Doyle's later life was almost exclusively focused on the promulgation of Spiritualism. As a convincing and inspiring speaker, he embarked on many series of public lectures – even travelling to Australia to spread the Spiritualist word. His relentless enthusiasm knew no bounds and, as he neared the end of his life, he decided on an audacious experiment. With the help of his medium colleague Grace Cooke – better known to some as Minesta – he would prove survival personally, by returning with a message after his own death. Some months following his death on 7 July 1930, a large public meeting was organized at the Albert Hall, at which Doyle is believed by some to have communicated his first message from beyond the grave to Grace Cooke.

The events and the messages received from Conan Doyle by Cooke eventually formed a book called *The Return of Arthur Conan Doyle*. They were also to start a new movement, an offshoot of Spiritualism influenced by Cooke's other spirit guides and known as 'The White Eagle Lodge'. It would incorporate the messages of Conan Doyle and his more sophisticated perspective of the earthly world from his new vantage point in the spirit world.

While his presence is still felt most keenly through the works of Sherlock Holmes and Dr Watson, there are those who claim to feel the continuing influence of Sir Arthur Conan Doyle in the Spiritualist movement and, more broadly, in the spiritual affairs of human beings.

Left *The hoax of the Cottingley Fairies cost Arthur Conan Doyle much of the credibility he had built up among fans of the Sherlock Holmes books.*

THE LAST ENGLISH WITCH TRIAL

It is a surprising fact that the last witch trial in England did not occur in the 17th or 18th century, but in 1944. The accused was a 46-year-old Scottish woman called Helen Duncan, who had worked as a 'materialization medium' and clairvoyant since her teens. One of her particular gifts was the ability to produce ectoplasm, the substance that mediums claim can be used by spirits of the departed to clothe themselves and appear more physically present to their living relatives.

Throughout her life Duncan attracted strong adherents and ardent detractors. To some she was a graceless, dour and rather shambling figure, while others saw her as the mouthpiece of the Divine and the comforter of the bereaved. As a prominent figure in the Spiritualist movement, she was also a subject of study by organizations such as the Society for Psychical Research and its chief researcher Harry Price, who took an interest in her work and came to the conclusion that there was some charlatanism involved. Nevertheless, Duncan's popularity grew,

particularly during the Second World War among relatives of those who had lost loved ones in combat. In May 1941, while she was living in Portsmouth, one of her seances was attended by Brigadier R.C. Firebrace of the British Army. While Helen Duncan was in a trance state, she gave information that a British battleship had sunk. When Firebrace later discovered that HMS *Hood* had been destroyed with the loss of 1,100 sailors' lives, he reported his experience to Military Intelligence.

Later that year the spirit of a sailor appeared in the seance room, wearing a cap bearing the name of his ship, HMS *Barham*, and reported that his ship had been sunk in action. The editor of *Psychic News*, Maurice Barbanell, contacted Military Intelligence and requested confirmation or denial of the ship's fate. The British Government denied that the ship had been destroyed, but some months later it emerged that the ship had indeed been torpedoed by a German U-boat, with the loss of 861 seamen.

Over the next few years Military Intelligence is believed to have monitored Helen Duncan's seances more closely, believing that she might be a spy. On 19 January 1944, with detailed planning for D-Day under way, one of her seances was disrupted by a naval lieutenant and a plain-clothes policeman, who made a grab for the ectoplasmic spirit figure in the room, but was disappointed when it dematerialized in his hands. Nevertheless, Duncan and three members of the audience were arrested on a charge of vagrancy, later changed to conspiracy – a hanging offence; this was changed to contravention of the 1735 Witchcraft Act when the case finally came to the Old Bailey in April 1944.

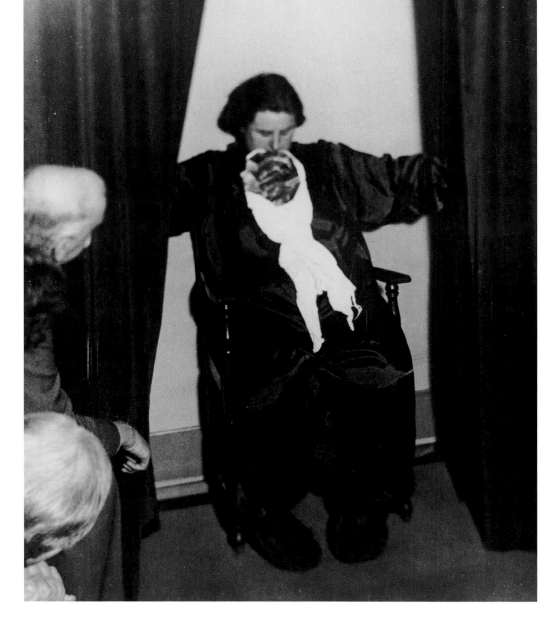

Left *This photograph shows Helen Duncan purportedly producing ectoplasm, the substance used by spirits to manifest themselves. Duncan was the last person to be tried as a witch, in 1944.*

WINSTON CHURCHILL'S INVOLVEMENT

Despite 44 witnesses testifying to Duncan's credibility and a further three hundred ready to take the stand, the seven-day trial found her guilty under the Witchcraft Act. Her right to appeal was withheld and she was sentenced to nine months in Holloway women's prison. While she was there, however, she received the most surprising of visitors: the Prime Minister, Winston Churchill. He was outraged by her trial and conviction and sent a stern note to his Home Secretary, Herbert Morrison: 'Let me have a report on why the Witchcraft Act 1735 was used in a modern Court of Justice. What was the cost of this trial to the state, observing that witnesses were brought from Portsmouth ... and the Recorder kept busy with all this obsolete tomfoolery.'.

It is known that Churchill's interest in the paranormal was more than cursory. As well as being a Mason, it has been suggested that his interest in Spiritualism and psychic phenomena led him to employ clairvoyants during the war to gain an advantage over Hitler. Today this work might be compared with the 'remote viewing' used by the US army in the last 20 years or so. It is even believed by some that Churchill attended one of Helen Duncan's seances.

Whatever the truth, when Churchill was re-elected Prime Minister in 1951, one of his first actions was to repeal the Witchcraft Act of 1735 and replace it with the Fraudulent Mediums Act (the name itself being an assertion that there must be 'non-fraudulent' or trustworthy mediums). In 1954 Spiritualism was recognized as an official religion in the UK; Helen Duncan's contribution, as well as her suffering, seemed to have paved its way.

It was not to be so simple. In November 1956 the police again raided one of her seances. This time their actions were so violent that Duncan's health was badly affected. Having been strip-searched for evidence of fraud, she was later found with second-degree burns across her stomach. Within five weeks she was dead. The victor was now the martyr.

Left *Winston Churchill was an apparently unlikely campaigner for the convicted Helen Duncan. In fact his interest in the paranormal resulted in the use of clairvoyants during the war and he repealed the Witchcraft Act soon after his re-election in 1951.*

It is known that Churchill's interest in the paranormal was more than cursory. His interest in Spiritualism and psychic phenomena led him to employ clairvoyants during the war to gain an advantage over Hitler.

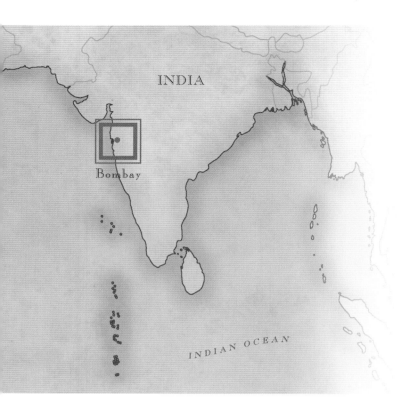

INDIA

Bombay

INDIAN OCEAN

Theosophy and rediscovering the East

Theosophy has played an influential role in bringing the ideas of Eastern religions into Western consciousness. Led by Helena Petrovna Blavatsky, one of the leading occultists and mediums of her generation, Theosophy inspired many thinkers and public figures to reject both conventional Christianity and intellectual atheism and join a search for truth and wisdom among the treasures of the East.

lthough she was, later in life, undermined by controversy and effectively stripped of her role as the figurehead of Theosophy, Blavatsky remained an important figure in the development of spiritual life in the West throughout the 20th century. Without H.P.B. (as she was known to many), Theosophy continued to gain attention and admirers through the works of Charles Leadbeater, Annie Besant, Rudolf Steiner and the young Krishnamurti, before its star began to wane.

HELENA PETROVNA BLAVATSKY

Born on 12 August 1831 in southern Russia, Helena Petrovna von Hahn grew up to be an

Left *Helena Petrovna Blavatsky spent 22 years receiving wisdom teachings all around the world. She then, along with Colonel Henry Steel Olcott (also shown here), launched the Theosophical Society and helped formulate its objectives.*

exceptionally gifted child. She also knew she was somewhat different from other children and was aware of beings that others could not perceive. From early on she had a strong feeling that her life had a specific purpose.

On her 20th birthday, while visiting the 1851 Great Exhibition in London, she met a figure she had only previously seen in childhood visions: Mahatma Morya (also known later as M.) was a spiritual initiate from Rajput and outlined to the young Blavatsky a picture of the work she would be doing on behalf of spiritual forces. Over the next 22 years she travelled the world with her spiritual master, underwent many initiations and received different wisdom teachings. In 1868 she met the Tibetan master Koot Hoomi in the Himalayas. Together with M., K.H. was to be Blavatsky's other main spiritual teacher, or Mahatma.

By 1871 the masters believed she was ready for the transmission of Eastern wisdom teachings, or *Theosophia*, to the West. This knowledge – 'The accumulated Wisdom of the ages, tested and verified by generations of Seers' – was intended to counter the dual illusions of conventional Christian theology

Science; and 3) to investigate unexplained laws of Nature, and the powers latent in man.

In 1877 Blavatsky's first major written work, *Isis Unveiled*, was published in New York; its first printing of one thousand copies sold out in ten days. It painted a picture of the perennial, yet often hidden, philosophy that runs through every religion, but which is obscured by the outer forms of that same belief system. Its impact among occult circles was great and it attracted many more adherents to the ideas of Theosophy.

The following year Blavatsky received citizenship of the United States, but left with Colonel Olcott for Bombay in India, to establish a new headquarters for Theosophy. There they met A.P. Sinnett, a journalist and writer, who was to play an important part in the promulgation of Theosophical ideas. H.P.B. put Sinnett in written contact with her two Mahatmas, M. and K.H., and there followed an exchange of correspondence that was to form the basis of a number of important Theosophical books and teachings. In 1880 both Blavatsky and Olcott took the vow of 'Pancha Sila' and became Buddhists, in an act that was seen by many as a final rejection of the Western spiritual tradition.

Following a scandal in which she was accused of falsifying psychic phenomena, which forced her to resign her leadership of the Theosophical Society, H.P.B. returned to London, where she continued to write what would be regarded as her master work. *The Secret Doctrine* – an assimilation of many aspects of occult knowledge – was finally published in two substantial volumes in 1888. She also started a new 'Blavatsky Lodge' to promulgate Theosophical ideas and formed the Esoteric School.

and the hold of scientific materialism. Through her mediumistic access to occult teachings, H.P.B. would be the channel through which this spiritual-cultural phenomenon would propagate. She would also challenge the teachings of Spiritualism, which she perceived to be offering an erroneous view of spirit lives.

THE THEOSOPHICAL SOCIETY

On 7 September 1875 the Theosophical Society was formally founded in America and was publicly launched with an inaugural address by Colonel Henry Steel Olcott, an ex-civil-war military man who had also served in the government. Together with William Quan Judge, a young Irish lawyer, Olcott and H.P.B. formed the triumvirate that took Theosophy forward in its first years, with a general objective 'to collect and diffuse a knowledge of the laws which govern the Universe'. Over time there was a refining of the Society's aims until they were enshrined as: 1) To form a nucleus of the Universal Brotherhood of Humanity, without distinction of race, creed, sex, caste or colour; 2) To encourage the study of Comparative Religion, Philosophy and

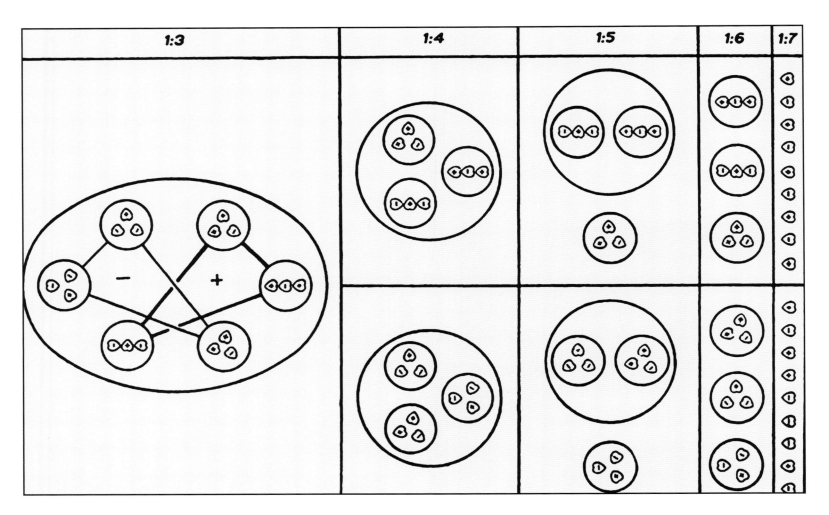

THEOSOPHY REBORN

Following Blavatsky's death in May 1891, control of the Theosophical Society was taken by a newer generation of occultists, led by Annie Besant and Charles W. Leadbeater, who shared her orientialist leanings as well as an anti-Christian tendency. Besant had been an activist working for women's suffrage as well as a well-known 'free-thinker', and her powerful personality found an outlet through Theosophy. Together with Leadbeater, she embarked on a number of occult experiments, perhaps the most successful of which was published in 1908, detailing the results of their psychic exploration into the nature of physical matter. Besant and Leadbeater embarked on a series of yogic 'micro-psi' exercises in which they clairvoyantly looked into nuclei of the chemical elements, as they were then known. What they were to perceive and record has, over the last hundred years, been gradually vindicated through the stunning discoveries of modern particle physics, while at the same time leaving a number of mysteries unsolved.

Through their clairvoyant techniques, Besant and Leadbeater initially looked into the hydrogen atom, before going on to investigate all 92 known elements. They were the first scientists to say that the nucleus of atoms contains both protons and neutrons, some three years before conventional science put forward a nuclear model that involved neutrons, and 24 years before the uncharged particle was finally discovered. They also proposed that the proton was not the smallest particle (as was believed at the time), but was in fact composed of six groups of three 'omegons' or 'ultimate physical atoms', which the two Theosophists saw as the smallest particles in the Universe, acting as a bridge between energy and matter. It as not until 1964 that physicist Murray Gell-Mann put forward his controversial theory that protons

Above *Leaders of the Theosophical Society embarked on a series of experiments to examine the composition and structure of chemical elements.*

were in fact made up of three sub-particles called 'quarks' – important confirmation of the Theosophists' psychic findings.

By 1907 around 60 elements had been psychically analyzed by Leadbeater and Besant. The larger elements were classified into seven basic types according to their shapes: Spike, Tetrahedron, Cube, Bars, Dumbbell, Octahedron and Star. All of the five platonic solids are contained within these forms, as well as the Fibonacci series and the Golden Section. Surprisingly a number of the elements showed variations of atomic weight. These results were published, initially in *The Theosophist* magazine, some six years before Frederick Soddy, later winner of the Nobel Prize for Chemistry, introduced the idea of 'isotopes' to conventional science.

In retrospect, many observers consider the occult scientific work of Besant and Leadbeater between 1895 and 1932 – the results of which are still being vindicated today – to be the crowning achievement of Theosophy.

STEINER AND KRISHNAMURTI

When Blavatsky was being laid to rest in 1891, a young Austrian named Rudolf Steiner was receiving his doctoral degree for refuting the philosophy of Immanuel Kant as a dry theory of knowledge, which denied the true nature of living reality. Coming into contact with Theosophy later, Steiner recognized that the movement had value in bringing forward the idea that scientific and practical truth about the invisible worlds could be perceived directly by those who developed their clairvoyant faculties. Although he did not necessarily agree with everything Blavatsky and her followers put forward, he felt their impulse was generally helpful in progressing the spiritual evolution of humankind.

In time Steiner was appointed by Annie Besant, then-leader of the movement, as General Secretary of the German Theosophical Society. But their paths were to separate when Besant proposed to announce that she had found the reincarnation of Jesus Christ, and that his name was Jiddu Krishnamurti. Steiner could not accept this notion, and when he refused the role of the reincarnated John the Baptist, Besant expelled him and the whole German branch of the Theosophical Society. More than a thousand Theosophical Society diplomas were rescinded and, while 14 German lodges kept their loyalty to Besant, the remainder were to follow

Steiner and become the bedrock of the Anthroposophical Society (see pages 146–151).

Leadbeater and Besant's plan to promote Krishnamurti as the Coming World Teacher of the 20th Century was formalized in 1911 with the founding of an organization called the Order of the Star, which was to oversee the young guru's life and works. Originally discovered in Adyar, India, in 1909 when he was just 14, Krishnamurti had been taken under Besant's wing and given an education that blended English and Indian elements. In 1929, however, after a series of spiritual experiences, he decided to reject the role of Christ-like avatar and follow a 'pathless path', which he hoped would contribute to people's liberation from suffering. He attracted many of his own students. The Order of the Star was dissolved, its assets handed back to those who had given them and the Theosophical Society was left in a state of disarray, from which it would never fully recover.

Right *Annie Besant, one-time leader of the Theosophical Society, claimed to have discovered the reincarnation of Jesus.*

Anthroposophy and the legacy of Rudolf Steiner

It is impossible to speak of Anthroposophy without fully acknowledging that it is the legacy of the mystic and spiritual philosopher Rudolf Steiner. One of a number of important spiritual teachers who flourished at the start of the 20th century, Steiner, and the organizations and movements that he helped to found, continues to have a profound influence on many aspects of contemporary life.

From food production and healthcare to schooling and the structure of communities, the marks that Steiner left on Western thought seem indelible. Born at Kraljevec on the border between Croatia and Hungary on 25 February 1861, Rudolf Steiner was the son of a relatively humble railway official. As a child with a strong academic mind, he received a sophisticated education, which he completed by writing a doctoral thesis in philosophy. On leaving college he was asked to edit the scientific writings of the great German writer and philosopher Johann Wolfgang von Goethe, who was to serve as an important inspiration in Steiner's life. Despite his strong intellectual mind, though, Steiner had also been keenly aware throughout his childhood that he was possessed of clairvoyant abilities.

STEINER'S CLAIRVOYANT PERCEPTIONS

As Steiner grew up in an educated, academic and intellectual culture, he began to see that the human search for knowledge through science and religion was limited by people's perceptions. Since people were not immediately aware of the reality of the world of spirit, they were unable to perceive the truth about their place in the world and the nature and purpose of their lives. If people were to understand reality – and even scientific truth – they would need to combine their intellect with a developed clairvoyant sense. For Steiner, this 'clairvoyance' was a different experience from what he witnessed within the Spiritualist movement. For him, the discarnate realm of the recently deceased was an 'astral' world of discarded shells. His perceptions went beyond the astral realms to deeper truths, and to the world of the Akashic Record – or the Akasha Chronicle – as Steiner preferred to call this record of all events and experiences, which could be 'read' or directly perceived by a trained and purely motivated clairvoyant.

Throughout his life Steiner continued to have profound and regular experiences of the spirit world. When the father of an early girlfriend died, Steiner had the experience of following the man into the spirit world and seeing how he was received and was able to progress spiritually. The man had been a

Above *Johann Wolfgang von Goethe, a German writer whose work covered many disciplines. His theory of colour influenced Rudolf Steiner.*

Right *Having been expelled from the Theosophical Society, Rudolf Steiner developed his own ideas of a 'spiritual science' that led him to set up the Anthroposohpical Society.*

scientific, sceptical person, but Steiner was able to see how these rational beliefs were not a hindrance in the spiritual world he now inhabited; the man's attributes of kindness and the search for truth were well able to transfer into this new phase of his evolution and development.

STEINER AND THE THEOSOPHICAL SOCIETY

When Steiner agreed to become the first General Secretary of the newly formed German section of the Theosophical Society (see page 145), there were those around him who were surprised by his apparent rejection of academia and serious intellectual thought, in favour of an apparently pseudo-religious movement that appeared to lack rigour. In fact Steiner never regarded Theosophy as the exact answer to all the world's ills, but felt that it offered a platform from which he could express his own ideas and experiences about the spirit world. His relationship with Annie Besant, Henry Steel Olcott and the remaining hierarchy of the Theosophical Society had been cemented during a visit to London in 1902, after which the Theosophists decided that Steiner merited serious consideration as someone who could take a leadership role. On his return to Germany, Steiner continued to lecture on the need for Theosophy to interact with the sciences, in order that the relationship between religion and intellectual knowledge of the world's phenomena was maintained. This was to continue to be one of the guiding themes of his life and work.

One aspect of the Theosophical Society that Steiner disagreed with was its stress on the importance of the oriental strands of spirituality. Despite its claim to be a respecter of all religions and a promoter of the brotherhood of man, Buddhism and Hinduism lay at the root of Theosophy, and the masters who had communicated through Madame Blavatsky were, by their traditions, orientalists. Blavatsky and Besant both had an anti-Christian leaning, which sometimes appeared in more overt ways than at others. In stark contrast, Steiner was throughout his life dedicated to Christianity – or, more accurately, an appreciation and understanding of the Christ impulse and its role in human spiritual evolution. In his lectures he often referred to the Mystery of Golgotha, which sometimes related to the entire life of Jesus Christ and at others only to the phase between his baptism by John, when Jesus took on the avatar role of 'the Christ', and his ascension following the crucifixion.

Left *The second Goetheanum in Dornach, Switzerland, was built after the first Goetheanum burned down. Although in a different style, it was also designed by Rudolf Steiner, using the same guiding principles.*

It was Steiner's belief that, with the correct training, all sincere seekers of Truth could perceive the spiritual worlds directly. As a spiritual teacher, his output of writing and speaking was both extensive and broad; his published works run into hundreds and covered subjects as diverse as architecture, education, farming, medicine, clairvoyance, dance and movement, social renewal, community, reincarnation and karma, the angelic realms and art. Steiner could justifiably be said to have been the Renaissance man of the 20th century. Indeed, the desire for a rebirth of the soul was exactly what he wished for. What is remarkable is that, in many of the fields he sought to influence with Spiritual Science, he left an enduring legacy.

PRACTICAL LEGACIES

Steiner's architectural achievements in the building of two Goetheanum buildings (see pages 150–151) have been acknowledged as influential and important in their own right, as well as forming the inspiration for many

With this apparent conflict with his own spiritual ideals, why would Steiner choose to become so involved with Theosophy? The answer lies in what both Steiner and Theosophy regarded as the potential enemy of humankind: unfettered scientific materialism. The 18th and 19th centuries had seen a significant rise in the social and political position of science and scientists, some of whom had been elevated to the level of gods in their own right.

STEINER'S IDEAS ON SPIRITUAL SCIENCE

From 1904 until 1912 Steiner was leader of the German section of the Theosophical Society, during which time he publicly developed his ideas on 'Spiritual Science'. When Annie Besant planned to launch her young Indian protégé Krishnamurti on the world as the new avatar (see page 145), she offered Steiner a role in the unfolding events: he could play John the Baptist to Krishnamurti's orientalized Christ figure. Steiner was in some sense appalled by what he perceived as a form of esoteric arrogance and finally decided to pursue

fully his own inner impulse and form the Anthroposophical movement.

Rudolf Steiner defined the purpose of Anthroposophy in his 1924 publication *Anthroposophical Leading Thoughts:*

Anthroposophy is a path of knowledge, to guide the spiritual in the human being to the spiritual in the universe ... Anthroposophists are those who experience, as an essential need of life, certain questions on the nature of the human being and the universe, just as one experiences hunger and thirst.

SPIRITUAL LEGACY

While Rudolf Steiner may have felt that he was failing to influence early 20th-century Europeans away from the evils of German nationalism, his impact on modern life has been surprisingly widespread. There are those who see

him as the most profound exponent of the Western mystery tradition; as a true Rosicrucian, and the closest anyone came to living on Earth in the 20th century according to the Christ impulse.

buildings that have been created by other Anthroposophical architects and by those who follow a more organic approach to the buildings we occupy.

Following a lecture in 1919 at a German factory in Stuttgart owned by Emil Molt, the first 'Waldorf' school was established. During Steiner's lifetime many more Waldorf schools were founded across Europe, following his principles and understandings about the spiritual and creative life of the individual child. Activities included art (drawing on Goethe's ideas about colour) and Eurythmy (a form of dance developed by Steiner himself). Today there are nearly a thousand independent Waldorf schools around the world.

Steiner also started communities based around the special needs of handicapped people. These Camphill communities (named after the first such community) are now also spread throughout the world. And he was involved, although more discreetly and outside his work within Anthroposophy, in the renewal of the Christian community in Germany, seeking to bring a new active impulse to traditional worship.

His work on the growing of food played an important role in the development of the organic farming movement, which has expanded so much in the last 20 years. Steiner's 'biodynamic' farming methods were based on complex ideas about the spiritual and earthly forces that act on both plants and animals as they grow. Although Steiner developed his methods through his 'super-sensory' abilities, such perceptions are not required by farmers in order to be successful; the methods are simplified and require planting of specific crops according to the phases of the moon, as well as the application of particular homeopathic preparations on the soil. Crops grown under these methods are labelled commercially under the name Demeter.

Medicine was another area of research that Steiner pursued through Spiritual Science, and the brand name Weleda is now one of the best known in the field of homeopathic medicine. And in the area of social responsibility there are now banks (mostly known by the name Triodos) that invest in projects and organizations meeting criteria that are broadly in harmony with Anthroposophical ideas.

Steiner also started communities based around the special needs of handicapped people. These Camphill communities (named after the first such community) are now spread throughout the world.

Right *Steiner used his spiritual understandings as the basis for many creative pursuits including a dance form called Eurythmy, seen here.*

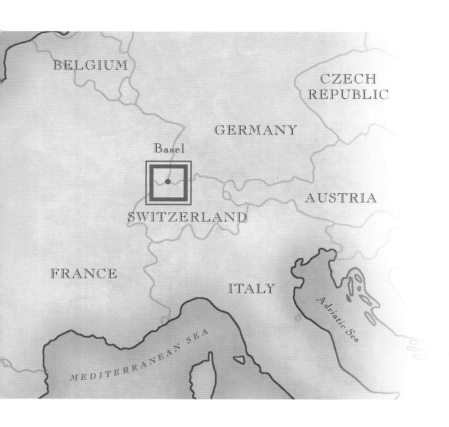

The first Goetheanum

On the evening of 20 September 1913, on a hill outside Basel in Switzerland and overlooking France and Germany, a ceremony took place that Rudolf Steiner and many of his followers felt was an event of global significance. With the shadow of world war approaching, and increasing spiritual darkness descending, Steiner undertook the solemn ritual of laying the foundation stone for a building that soon became known as the Goetheanum.

The 'stone', actually composed of a double pentagonal dodecahedron of soldered copper, represented 'the striving human soul immersed as a microcosm in the macrocosm'. As a storm howled around those present, and makeshift torches formed from vine stakes gave light to the proceedings, Steiner called on the spiritual hierarchies to protect the building that would stand as an inspiration to those seeking the truths of spiritual consciousness. So important did he view the building of this 'organic' structure that he regarded its completion as part of the 'mission of Earth itself'.

A LIVING STRUCTURE

The Goetheanum was not simply to house events, like an assembly hall or theatre. It was envisaged as a living, organic structure that would be expressive of natural forms. True, it would be made of dead matter, but through the consciousness of the building process and those involved in it, it could in some way 'resurrect' the substance and give it new life. Steiner tried to sum up some of these ideas:

If one is able to realize how the human body on the one hand is an instrument for thinking and on the other for willing, and that both these faculties are held together by the power of feeling; if one understands the whole human structure, the formation of the head, limbs and trunk, with the heart system at centre, then one is able to construct organic forms oneself also. The Goetheanum is such an organic form.

TWO INTERSECTING DOMES

Although Steiner worked with architects in the creation of the Goetheanum, the conceptual and design work were all his. Even before he had spoken to the experts, he made models of the building's interior and exterior, based on his own clairvoyant views of natural forms and their underlying etheric patterns.

Perhaps the most challenging aspect of the Goetheanum was the construction of the two intersecting domes that formed its dominant outline. When Steiner first showed his models to architects, he was told that such a structure was impossible. The larger dome was, in fact, bigger than St Peter's Basilica in Rome, and the challenge of bringing together two asymmetric domes without the supporting circular bands or hidden chains that had been used in classical times seemed beyond the scope of any expert. Eventually, however, Steiner found a Norwegian structural engineer who believed there was a solution. It hinged on using a single-tension ring that embraced both domes, and required extra supports in the manner of buttressing.

Major work on the Goetheanum started in 1914 and drew in many of the members of the Anthroposophical Society. It was Steiner's preference that those who constructed the building had an interest in the function and true meaning of the Goetheanum. This meant that many volunteers – both skilled and unskilled – were involved in aspects of the great project and found themselves working alongside Steiner himself.

SPACE, LIGHT AND COLOUR

Beneath the domes an auditorium space was created, on each side of which were seven pillars, each made from a different timber: ash, birch, cherry, elm, hornbeam, oak and maple. Each pillar was topped with a carved capital, which expressed a natural form relating to Goethe's description of plant metamorphosis.

Colour played an important part in the interior, and Steiner drew on Goethe's ideas that particular colours expressed specific 'moral' qualities. Once the building was completed in 1919 it hosted performances of music, dance and Steiner's mystery plays.

But this beacon for Anthroposophy was not to last long. On New Year's Eve 1922 the Goetheanum was consumed by a fire set deliberately. Typically resilient, Steiner worked on designing a replacement. In 1924 work started on the second Goetheanum – a more modern work of concrete, which is still the headquarters of the Anthroposophical movement today. Steiner, who died on 30 March 1925, never saw its completion.

① ROTUNDAS

The main building was formed of two interlocking rotundas. Two wings, one facing north and the other south, extended from the building at the junction of the rotundas, creating a sense of equilibrium between the harmony of the domes and the more dynamic wings.

② DOMES

Each rotunda was crowned by a dome covered in Norwegian 'Vossian' slate, which was chosen by Steiner to reflect the light of the Jura landscape.

③ ROUNDED FORM

Steiner had the building constructed using rounded forms, which he thought were spiritually expressive unlike the traditional architectural conventions of right-angles.

④ WINDOWS

The windows, which allowed coloured light to flood into the auditorium, were made of specially engraved glass in a sequence of green, blue, violet and pink. The engravings were carried out by artists working under Steiner's supervision. Some of the windows from the first Goetheanum were salvaged and incorporated into the second version of the building.

⑤ MOUNTAIN SETTING

Set in the Jura landscape, the Goetheanum rose from a hill by the village of Dornach, 9.6 km (6 miles) to the south of Basel in Switzerland. It was designed to harmonize with its surroundings: the rocky Jura mountains and the Birs river valley

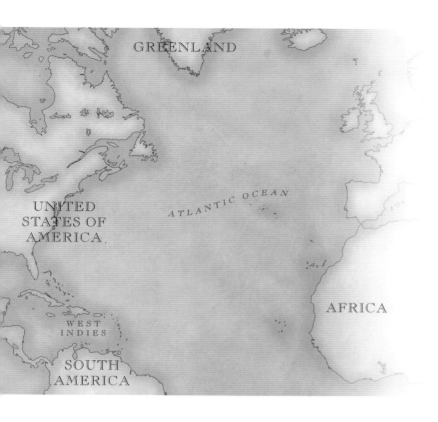

Atlanteans – the masters of wisdom

The story of Atlantis is both evocative and haunting and seems to hold echoes of the biblical Flood. The idea of a lost continent, which played host to an advanced civilization long before the rest of the world had emerged from more primitive forms of culture, is appealing. But is a belief in an alternative world history really sustainable – or a viable basis for spiritual belief systems?

For most observers, the idea of an island called Atlantis seems to have appeared first in the works of Plato, the Greek philosopher. Plato's account of Atlantis appears in his dialogues known as *The Timaeus* and *The Critias*. He describes a legendary island located 'beyond the pillars of Heracles' – that is, beyond the straits of Gibraltar in the Atlantic Ocean. The people of Atlantis, as Plato describes them, were a powerful naval race that was able to conquer parts of western Europe and Africa more than nine thousand years before his own time. They overreached themselves when they tried to invade Athens, and soon afterwards their island stronghold sank beneath the waves 'in a single day and night of misfortune' and their civilization was no more.

Many people who read Plato's description see merely an allegory of his own political theories, set in a fictional landscape. And this may indeed have been Plato's original intention. Nevertheless, some scholars have speculated on the events that inspired Plato: were they historical occurrences, such as the Trojan War in the 12th century BCE, or

the eruption of the island of Thera in around 1630 BCE? Or were they more contemporaneous, like the destruction of Helike in 373 BCE, or the failed invasion of Sicily in around 415 BCE? Other researchers have made further speculations: was Atlantis a real place, and was Plato publishing an alternative history of the world, which had been treated as secret or esoteric knowledge? Recent developments in research have convinced many people that Atlantis was indeed a real and advanced culture, and movements have grown up around the supposed beliefs and practices of this race. In the spirit of Plato, perhaps it is still possible to ask whether this lost race existed and whether it held knowledge, both spiritual and practical, that may be useful or relevant to society today?

Right *This section of a Mayan sacred text forms part of the* Troano Codex. *Written in hieroglyphics, it describes cataclysmic events believed by some to be the destruction of Atlantis.*

The map labels: GROENLAND, ISLANDE, HYPERBORÉE, AMÉRIQUE DU NORD, ATLANTIDE?, ESPAGNE, AFRIQUE, Açores, Madère, Canaries, Mer des Sargasses, Cap Vert

MORE MODERN WRITINGS

In 1627 the famous Rosicrucian and Attorney-General to Elizabeth I of England, Sir Francis Bacon, published *The New Atlantis*, a utopian novel describing life on Bensalem, an island off the west coast of America. In the novel, one of the characters provides a telling of the history of Atlantis. In many ways similar to Plato's description, this Atlantis is located somewhere in the Americas.

This link between Atlantis and the Americas was further developed by the Meso-American scholar, the Abbé Charles Étienne Brasseur de Bourbourg. In his travels through Mexico and Guatemala in the mid to late 19th century, de Bourbourg discovered many sacred texts of the indigenous peoples. One of the most remarkable was a Mayan book known as the *Troano Codex*, in which was described a great cataclysm that occurred in Central America in the distant past. De

Bourbourg identified the timing of the event as 9937 BCE. He also met natives who maintained an oral historic tradition describing the destruction of a great continent in the Atlantic Ocean, which he took to mean Atlantis. He speculated that the civilizations of both Egypt and Central (and southern) America stemmed from the displaced peoples of Atlantis, and that the 'white God from the sea' who came to rule in Central America and became Quetzalcóatl, the Plumed Serpent, was a powerful leader from Atlantis.

In the late 19th century new information about Atlantis and its civilization appeared from a more esoteric source. In her key text *The Secret Doctrine*, published in 1888, Helena Blavatsky (the founder of Theosophy, see pages 142–145) revealed information from 'Masters of Wisdom' about the culture of Atlantis and its role as the 'fourth root race'

of humanity, following on from an 'ethereal' first root race, the 'Hyberborean' second root race and the third 'Lemurian' root race. From Blavatsky's timings, it is difficult to say exactly when the Atlanteans were supposed to have existed, but it can be inferred that it was much further back than the ten thousand or so years posited by other researchers. Nevertheless, the Atlanteans were advanced in certain ways and were the initiators of various wisdom traditions, such as Druidism and the Brahminic faith. The Atlanteans, according to Blavatsky, were succeeded by the 'Aryan' or fifth root race. This idea was picked up by Adolf Hilter when he formed the National Socialists – or Nazis – in the 1930s and distorted it to fit his murderous views on racial purity. The Nazis' adoption of the swastika – an ancient Hindu symbol – was another borrowing from esoteric and spiritual symbolism.

OTHER ATLANTEAN THEORIES

Following the example of his fellow Theosophists, a British amateur anthropologist named William Scott-Elliott claimed to have studied the history of Atlantis by a process of 'astral clairvoyance', putting forward the theory that the main 'sub-race' of the Atlanteans were the Toltecs of Central America, the builders of the great civilization at Tula that predated the Aztec and Maya civilization. In his 1896 book *The Story of Atlantis*, he also claimed that the Toltecs were responsible for the building of pyramids around the world and for the creation of Stonehenge in England. He wrote that the Toltecs had a form of jet-powered aircraft and other advanced technologies, and that they used their sophisticated practical and psychic powers benignly for many years. But when they used them for more self-interested purposes, the results were catastrophic – resulting in a great flood, followed by further disasters and a final cataclysm.

Rudolf Steiner, ex-Theosophist and founder of Anthroposophy (see pages 146–151), also wrote about the histories and civilizations of Atlantis and Lemuria, another supposed lost continent that once existed in the Pacific Ocean. Steiner claimed that his source of information was the Akashic Record, the source of all knowledge and the history of Earth's civilization, existing in the astral realms and 'readable' by clairvoyants with a clear motivation. In his book he described the process of evolution in human consciousness that took place through the development of the different 'root race' civilizations, including the actual changes in brain structure that enabled increasing levels of knowledge and power. He also maintained that the people of Atlantis had annihilated the continent through their use of destructive forces following a 'fall' in their conscience.

RECENT CLAIMS

In recent years the film actor and spiritual activist Shirley MacLaine revealed details of her former life in Atlantis in her book *The Camino – Journey of the Spirit*. The story recounts a journey to the Christian pilgrimage shrine of Santiago de Compostela in north-west Spain, during which MacLaine claimed to have had a number of revelatory experiences about her past lives in different periods. During her time in Atlantis she claims that she was originally androgynous and was involved in a spiritual-scientific experiment to create a two-gendered race, motivated to reproduce itself through an inbuilt drive to continually search for its 'original' soul partner.

Some cults claim that Atlanteans were originally superior beings from outer space, who were the first culture to bring advanced, spiritual civilization to the Earth. These ideas are closer to Erich von Däniken's UFO ideas of the 1960s, which have largely fallen out of favour, even among esotericists.

Right *The British Anthropologist William Scott-Elliot put forward a theory that the early Central American Toltec civilization was actually a sub-race of the Atlanteans. This artist's impression of Atlantis shows the jet-powered aircraft that they supposedly used.*

Above *A diver swims along the Bimini Road in the West Indies. This geological formation, which appears to be man-made, has provided what many believe to be proof the existence of Atlantis.*

CAYCE'S READINGS AND THE 'BIMINI ROAD'

Perhaps the greatest step forward in the detailed study of Atlantean culture and civilization was taken by a man known as 'The Sleeping Prophet'. Edgar Cayce was born into a devout and conventional Christian family in Virginia, in the US, and became famous in adult life for producing thousands of Akashic Record readings while in a sleeping or self-hypnotic state. In response to questions posed by members of the public and his colleagues, Cayce – in a trance state – would produce detailed information about many subjects, including reincarnation and karma, survival after death, the role of various prophets in the Earth's development and early Earth cultures. Cayce's information about Atlantis concurred with many other sources by placing the main part of the island complex in the Atlantic Ocean. He talked particularly about 'Poseida', a large island just north of Cuba. He described the culture of Atlantis as being highly advanced, with ships and aircraft powered by forms of energy derived from crystals. His readings claimed was the misuse of these large crystals led to the inundation of the islands and their eventual submersion, and he predicted that parts of Atlantis would rise in 1968 or 1969 close to Bimini in the West Indies.

In 1968 a Dr J. Manson Valentine discovered a geological formation just off North Bimini Island, which, to some eyes, appeared to be man-made. Described as the 'Bimini Road', the formation seemed to be composed of walls 76 m (250 ft) long, some 6 m (20 ft) below sea level. The walls were made up of 5 m (16 ft) square blocks weighing 25.5 tonnes (25 tons) each. The divers also discovered a stylized stone head weighing some 90 kg (200 lb). Altogether the evidence was spread across an area of 98 sq km (38 sq miles). For many, the find appeared to provide positive and simultaneous evidence of Atlantis and Cayce's accuracy. Until now, though, no one has been able to make a conclusive link with a civilization as old as 10,000 years BCE for which Cayce and others have provided the date.

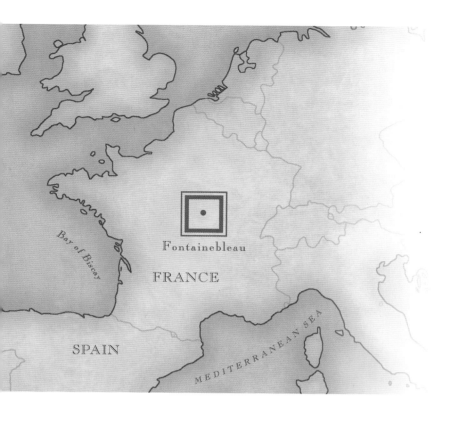

Gurdjieff and his 'Work'

George Ivanovich Gurdjieff was born in Alexandropol, Armenia, in around 1875. By the time he died in 1949 he was known throughout much of the Western world as one of the most enigmatic spiritual teachers who had ever lived. Among both pupils and observers he gained a reputation for extraordinary and mystifying behaviour; at turns he could be outrageous or harsh, hilarious or terrifying, kind or disturbing.

Above *These sacred dances were practised as part of consciousness development. Gurdjieff referred to them as 'Movements' and he also composed the music that accompanied them, together with composer Thomas de Hartmann.*

Such is the myth of impenetrability that has grown up around Gurdjieff that many people believe his true nature will never be fully understood. Nevertheless, his works live on in a number of different forms: in the books he wrote, in the records of his exchanges with pupils, and in the words of those who met him and knew him. Gurdjieff groups still meet around the world to attempt 'The Work' – the endless struggle to become more awake, by first gaining an awareness of the poverty of our functioning and our lack of real conscience. For Gurdjieff claimed that we are all deeply asleep and that the possibility of a fully conscious life could only be awakened through great effort of the will and under certain specific conditions – conditions that occur only when a more conscious teacher is present and is able to make the precise demands that will help the individual to transform.

His unique teachings, gleaned from extensive travels in the East during the earlier part of his life, endure among thousands of people worldwide, who continue their spiritual practice quietly, and seemingly

Right *George Ivanovich Gurdjieff was known for his sometimes mystifying behaviour but his legacy is as one of the most important spiritual teachers of the twentieth century. His teachings, known as 'The Work' continue to be practised in different forms all over the world.*

without the desire or need for attention. Gurdjieff's impact on European spiritual culture, present now for almost a hundred years, continues to resonate profoundly through the lives of many.

EARLY LIFE

Many people will know of George Ivanovich Gurdjieff from the Peter Brook film *Meetings with Remarkable Men.* First released in 1979, this adaptation of the Armenian mystic's own book tells the story of Gurdjieff's experiences as a child and young adult, during the time when he was discovering and forming the teaching that would later become known as 'The Work'. The story of his search – along with a group of fellow 'Seekers after Truth' – is the key to understanding the teachings that lie at the heart of Gurdjieff's unique 'way'. Often referred to as 'The Fourth Way', his teachings are neither religion nor philosophy; nor are they the original 'three ways' of spiritual progression. The first is the way of the fakir who struggles to gain mastery over his body. The second is the way of the monk who seeks to develop his emotions into higher feelings of devotion to the Divine. The third is the way of the yogi, whose intention is to overcome the limitations of the mind, through learning and mental contemplational exercises. The fourth way is different: it is not limited to the development of simply one aspect of functioning. It also represents a discipline that can be attempted by people in normal life and whose 'material' for the development of their consciousness is their everyday experience and their continuous efforts to transform themselves through specific 'consciousness' exercises.

Allied to this study of waking consciousness, 'The Work' also offered an experience of sacred dances known as the 'Movements'. Gurdjieff claimed to be, among other things, a teacher and master of dance, and in his travels he came across at least one monastery in the Caucasus where sacred dances were performed by the monks. These dances are not ordinary in any sense that we would understand; neither is their purpose for those who undertake them. Together with a European composer named Thomas de Hartmann, Gurdjieff put together music for a great variety of separate Movement Forms. Each one is normally performed by a group of up to 36 aspirants in a grid of rows and columns, and involves the complex coordination of very difficult and unusual gestures and movements of the head and limbs. The point of the exercise, though, is not simply the learning of a set of movements, for each participant is (while he or she is moving) asked to maintain a consciousness of body sensations in, for instance, the right foot or left forearm. On top of that, in some of the movements participants are also required to continue a verbal chant, which might be a non-sequential number sequence that challenges the intellect, such as 1-4-2-8-5-7, or a prayer, such as 'Lord have mercy on me. Christ have mercy on me'.

BALANCING OUR 'CENTRES'

What is the point of such movement exercises, beyond a simple test of concentration and coordination? The answer bears on Gurdjieff's conception of what we are and how our potential is limited by our inability to understand the real problem of our lives: the fact that we are asleep to our real natures. Gurdjieff said that the human is a three-brained being – by which he meant that human beings have a number of different brains or 'centres', the three main centres being the intellectual thinking centre, the emotional centre and the 'moving' or body centre. We are all, through conditioning and genetic make-up, biased most strongly towards one of these centres and weaker (to a greater or lesser degree) to the other two. We may be clever intellectually, for instance, with a reasonable sensitivity to our emotional world, but have a weaker grasp of our physical functioning, and so on.

The study, exercises and activities in the Gurdjieff system, including the 'Movements', make demands on all three of the 'centres' in an attempt to initiate greater understanding of our functioning – or lack of it. Through increased balance in the centres, Gurdjieff said, we increase the possibility of receiving more refined, higher energies that can help us to evolve. Without these efforts we become increasingly unbalanced, fossilized and lose the potential for 'essence' (or soul) progress. Those who have taken part in these demanding exercises have reported being stretched to the point where their normal personality seems to have dissolved, even if only momentarily, permitting a quite new experience of the 'essence' to take place.

When Gurdjieff opened his school at the Prieuré des Basses Loges in Fontainebleau-Avon close to Paris in 1922, it was named The Institute for the Harmonious Development of Man.

Above *The Institute for the Harmonious Development of Man, Gurdjieff's school near Paris. Pupils lived as a community, and took part in study groups and craft activities.*

If we were to live without any attempt to bring new awareness to the three centres of consciousness, we would become increasingly unbalanced and biased towards our strongest centre, losing the possibility of bringing progress to our 'essence'.

FONTAINEBLEAU

When Gurdjieff opened his school at the Prieuré des Basses Loges in Fontainebleau-Avon close to Paris in 1922, it was named The Institute for the Harmonious Development of Man. This name recognizes Gurdjieff's aim of awakening our sleeping, unbalanced, three-brained being. Adherents took part in movements, craft activities and study groups with Gurdjieff. They also lived as a community, preparing and cooking food together, building and decorating parts of the large estate and taking care of repairs. Life at the Institute was never predictable and continually tested those present to wake up to their illusions about themselves. Those working in the garden would awake to find that their plots had been dug up overnight and they must replant their work, without 'identifying' with their anger or resentment. Pupils would be asked to dig holes in the morning and fill them in again in the afternoon.

Around 1923, there were a number of public performances in France and America of 'The Struggle of the Magicians', which featured Gurdjieff's pupils demonstrating some of the dance movements. For the uninitiated public, it was a strange and perturbing experience. Gurdjieff would orchestrate events with a despotic air. Members of the audience were disturbed by the apparently omnipotent power wielded over the performers by the Master. At times Gurdjieff would clap his hands to indicate the dancers should freeze in position. For those off-balance the only option was to fall to the floor, where they would remain for the rest of the dance. Newspaper reports inevitably focused on what appeared to be the hypnotic control exerted by Mr Gurdjieff over his pupils. Questions were raised about his methods, demanding how seemingly intelligent, well-educated people – some well known in their chosen fields – could

Left *Writer Katherine Mansfield was one of the most famous visitors to the Institute. Already suffering from tuberculosis, she left her husband in London in order to gain spiritual understanding from Gurdjieff in what remained of her life.*

surrender their will to such a character and become passive in the face of such demands.

KATHERINE MANSFIELD

One of the most famous visitors to the Institute in Fontainebleau was the New Zealand-born writer Katherine Mansfield. Regarded as one of the greatest short-story writers of her generation, she arrived at the Prieuré at Fontainebleau on 16 October 1922, fearing that she might not have very long to live. She had been diagnosed with tuberculosis in October 1918 and had made the difficult and controversial decision to leave her husband, the critic and publisher

John Middleton Murry, behind in London. She knew she was risking all for the presence of a teacher whom she believed could offer the possibility of spiritually transforming her life in the short time she still had available.

In her letters to Murry she recorded her experiences of living with the community of Gurdjieff's followers. Often weak and unable to participate fully, she was confirmed in her belief that she had made the correct decision to 'work on herself' in this way while time was still available. Back in London, Murry struggled to understand his wife's decision, while appreciating that it seemed to be giving her something she sought.

> *Gurdjieff's work with his pupils was intended to establish a living teaching that could sustain itself after his death.*

A SENSE OF PURPOSE

In her tubercular state, Katherine Mansfield was treated more kindly than the rest of the community, for whom physical hardship and demanding labour were part of the cure for their spiritual sleep. For much of her stay, her accommodation was as unorthodox as everyone else's: she lived in a room above the cowshed, the warmth of the animals keeping her somewhat more comfortable than Gurdjieff's other pupils, and the breath of the cows one of the Master's remedies for her condition. A number of the people at the community took special care of her, believing Gurdjieff's assertions that she would survive her illness. Monsieur de Salzmannn (whose wife would later lead the Gurdjieff work), Mr and Mrs de Hartmann, Gurdjieff's collaborator on the Movements music and a Russian woman named Olga Ivanovna became her close friends and carers as she worked and witnessed the hardships, illuminations, sufferings and small joys that she and other spiritual seekers experienced through the harsh winter of 1922.

On New Year's Eve she wrote to Murry telling him he could come and stay at the Institute, where he would be able to see the new theatre that was being built by Gurdjieff's pupils. Arriving on 9 January 1923, Murry could see a change in his wife, an acceptance of her situation and a new calm. That day they toured the Institute together, with Murry participating in some painting at the still-unfinished theatre. The same evening, as she was ascending the stairs, Katherine Mansfield had a sudden haemorrhage and died very quickly. She was buried at the cemetery at Fontainebleau, with Gurdjieff and many of the Institute's pupils in attendance. One of her favourite Shakespeare quotations adorns her headstone: 'You, my lord fool, out of this nettle danger, we pluck the flower, safety.' Later, Murry was to acknowledge that her time with Gurdjieff and his pupils – though it had not saved her or extended her life – had brought a peace and sense of purpose to her last days.

THE LEGACY

In the early years of his teaching mission in Russia and Europe, Gurdjieff worked with a highly intelligent Russian academic named P.D. Ouspensky. Originally a mathematician and philosopher, Ouspensky had been attracted to the ideas of G.I. Gurdjieff because he believed that Mr G. had managed to discover the esoteric knowledge that he had failed to find in his own searches throughout the Middle East and the Caucasus. Ouspensky became the organ of transmission for Gurdjieff's ideas, writing them down and enshrining them in a

Above *Katherine Mansfield died following a sudden haemorrhage at the Institute. Her gravestone is testimony to the impact that the place had during the final months of her life.*

TO KNOW—TO UNDERSTAND—TO BE

The Science of the Harmonious Development of Man according to the method of G.I. GURDJIEFF.

Following a car crash in France in 1934, Gurdjieff decided to close The Institute for the Harmonious Development of Man in Fontainebleau and to concentrate on his writing. Up until his death in 1949, he was involved in the creation of his masterwork, modestly entitled *All and Everything*. It comprised three volumes: the first and most imposing was *Beelzebub's Tales to his Grandson*, an allegorical view of man's place in the Universe. It represents the most complete (and often baffling) picture of Gurdjieff's teachings in his own words. It is often said that even his most dedicated pupils find much of the book incomprehensible. It is an ongoing debate whether Gurdjieff intended to make it as hard to understand as it appears to be.

GURDJIEFF'S INFLUENCE

Gurdjieff's work with his pupils was intended to establish a living teaching that could sustain itself after his death. With this in mind, he trained a small group of people to become teachers and guides for 'The Work' after his death. The main inheritor of his mantle was Jeanne de Salzmann, who, together with a small group of teachers, continued to maintain the Master's work through three organizations; one in the UK, one in America and a third in Paris. In addition to this central strand there were various offshoots started by pupils who had decided to go their own way. These included J.G. Bennett, Maurice Nichol and Ouspensky. Many of these different groups continue to be active, some more publicly than others. While 'The Work' continued to function as an esoteric, almost secret teaching for many years after Gurdjieff's death, it is now more available to those who seek it out.

number of books. The most comprehensive was *In Search of the Miraculous*, in which the ideas of 'The Work' (including Gurdjieff's unorthodox cosmology) are most clearly expressed. Ouspensky had felt himself unable to remain with Gurdjieff as one of his pupils and broke away to establish his own groups. However, the split was not utterly bitter and, when Ouspensky asked Gurdjieff for permission to publish his own book about the teachings, *In Search of the Miraculous* Gurdjieff granted it. Ouspensky was the only one of Gurdjieff's pupils to receive this honour in the teacher's lifetime.

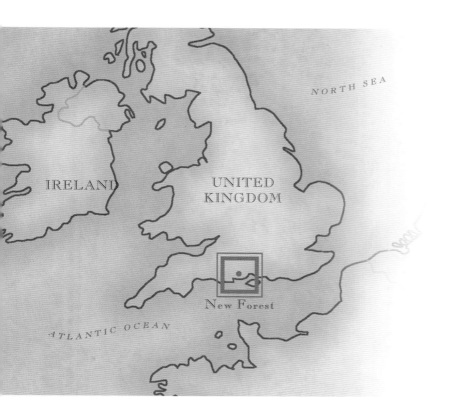

Wicca – the 'Old Religion'

Wicca is a modern religion that has its roots in the old witchcraft tradition. Its followers claim that Wicca draws on the pre-Christian Paganism of Europe and sometimes call it the 'Old Religion'. But Wicca in its modern guise appeared as late as the 1950s, when it was first popularized by a retired British civil servant named Gerald Gardner, who claimed to have been initiated by an authentic group of Wiccans.

Since Gardner's time, a number of new Wiccan traditions have evolved from his version of the religion, and each of these has distinct approaches to the ritual, practices and beliefs. Whereas Gardnerian Wicca (also known as 'lineaged' Wicca) is based on a series of initiations, there is a movement of 'eclectic' Wicca that is more liberal and does not require its adherents to believe a particular doctrine or undergo specific initiations in order to become members.

THE ORIGINS OF WICCA

It is no coincidence that Gerald Gardner first published his book *Witchcraft Today* in 1954, just three years after the repeal of the 1735 Witchcraft Act – legislation that had led to the deaths of many who practised early forms of pagan and Wiccan worship. In it, he describes how he met a group of witches known as the 'New Forest Coven' in southern England in the years before the Second World War. Once initiated into the coven, Gardner formed his own coven in north London after the war and, together with his initiates, started to spread Wicca practices.

Left *Wicca has its origins in witchcraft. Themes of nature and ritual run through most forms of Wicca, as this energy ceremony performed on a tree stump demonstrates.*

Right *Gerald Gardner was initiated into a coven and subsequently began his own group in London. He published an influential book on the subject.*

It was Gardner's contention that the witches he had met were part of an unbroken line of survival for a matriarchal pagan religion that originated in prehistoric Europe. Gardner maintained that the person by whom he was initiated in 1939 was called 'Dafo' or 'Old Dorothy', who was identified by one of Gardner's colleagues as Dorothy Clutterbuck, purportedly one of the leading members of the New Forest Coven. It has also been established that other influences went into the materials that Gardner presented as his reconstructed Wicca. He is known to have met Aleister Crowley, the occultist and leader of the 'Order of the Golden Dawn', and some Wiccan rituals appear to have been taken from Crowley's 1919 book *Blue Equinox*.

The idea of early matriarchal religions in primitive European culture attracted much interest in the first years of the 20th century. A variety of important writers, psychologists and anthropologists had taken an interest in this folklore-based tradition. Carl Jung had re-discovered important female archetypes, Robert Graves had written his hugely influential *The White Goddess* and Joseph Campbell had published '*The Hero with a Thousand Faces*. These works all confirmed the importance of the Goddess tradition. Perhaps, although important, these works were too acacdemic for some tastes and it was left to Gardner to ride the wave of popularity that a post-war Wicca managed to attract.

RITUALS

Whatever Wicca's exact origins, there is no doubt that it has flourished over the past 50 years: sometimes as a monotheistic goddess religion; sometimes as a duotheistic god–goddess faith; as a polytheistic Celtic-rooted faith; and as a pantheistic, New Age fairy-lore practice. In essence, though, Wicca is a magical religion and its rituals reflect its belief in magic. Typically a coven (often comprising 13 people) will assemble in a specially prepared and purified magic circle.

Prayers are given to the god and goddess, and the guardians of the four directions – North, South, East and West – are welcomed, before spells may be worked. Often an altar is present in the circle, on which various tools of ritual are placed. These might include a besom broom, a chalice, a wand and special knives, as well as candles, crystals, a pentacle and a *Book of Shadows*, the source of ritual lore for the coven in question. Sometimes these rituals are performed 'skyclad' or naked – a practice that has attracted the attention of the more sensationalist media. In general, though, eclectic Wiccans dress more normally for their ritual occasions.

The focus of the ritual falls on the eight 'Sabbats' and the full moons. The eight Sabbats are made up of the four main Celtic fire festivals of Imbolc, Beltane, Lughnasadh, and Samhain and the four lesser festivals of the summer solstice (Litha), the autumn equinox (Mabon), the winter solstice (Yule) and the spring equinox (Ostara).

WICCAN MORALITY

The Wiccan Rede is a phrase that sums up the ethical philosophy of Wiccans: 'An it harm none, do what ye will' ('So long as it harms no one, do what you want'). The concept of a 'rede' comes from Middle English and means advice or counsel. In this way it is different from a specific commandment and, even in longer forms, the Rede does not discuss which actions lead to harm, but leaves the individual to make their own judgements.

It does, though, bear some similarity to the idea found in most religions of a 'Golden Rule' that embodies the concept of 'ethical reciprocity'. In Christianity, for instance, this is expressed by the phrase 'Do unto others as you would have them do unto you', which is found in the Gospels of Matthew and Luke. In virtually all religions some similar formulation can be found, expressing this desire for mutual respect – not just between members of a particular faith group, but among humanity as a whole.

Not all traditional Wiccans hold the Rede as their guiding principle: some followers of Gardner choose as their touchstone the words of the *Charge of the Goddess* instead. Written by Doreen Valiente (a student of Gardner's), the opening paragraph entreats

the reader to listen to the female principle as it has expressed itself throughout human history: 'Listen to the words of the Great Mother, she who of old was also called among men Artemis, Astarte, Athene, Dione, Melusine, Aphrodite, Cerridwen, Dana, Arianrhod, Isis, Bride, and by many other names.' In particular, when it comes to ethical issues, there is one phrase that stands out: 'Keep your highest ideal, strive ever towards it; let naught stop you or turn you aside, for mine is the secret door which opens upon the door of youth.'. The *Charge of the Goddess* also refers to eight virtues that many Wiccans seek to develop through their spiritual practice. These are mirth, reverence, honour, humility, strength, beauty, power and compassion.

Some followers of Gardner's Wicca also refer to a group of 161 laws, which are known as the Ardanes and are believed to have been set down by Gardner himself. Even Doreen Valiente – one of Gardner's original priestesses – has acknowledged that these were probably created by Gardner, using archaic language, in an effort to address conflicts within the Bricket Wood coven that he established in north London.

ARADIA

A more controversial literary source for the Wiccan follower is a book called *Aradia*, subtitled 'The Gospel of the Witches'. It was first published in July 1899 and claims to be a translation of an Italian text called the *Vangelo*, which was given to the American author and folklorist Charles Godfrey Leland by a young Italian 'witch' from Florence known as 'Maddalena Talenti'. The book purports to portray an Italian pagan-witchcraft tradition and contains information about its origins, beliefs, spells and rituals. The 'Aradia' of the title is a goddess whom the book claims came to planet Earth – and in particular to Italy – to teach witchcraft to the poor peasant community who were being oppressed by the Catholic Church.

While there are many in the general Wiccan community who doubt the trustworthiness of *Aradia's* origins, the book

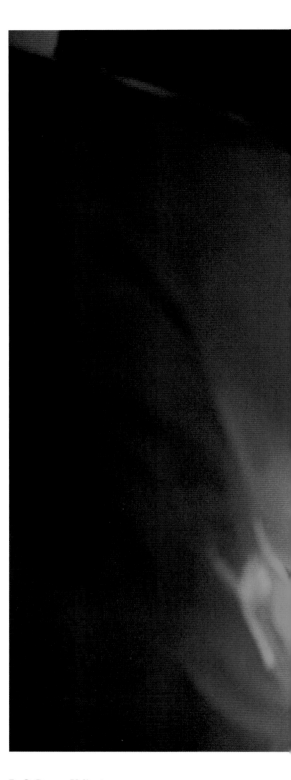

Left *Doreen Valiente with a ceremonial broomstick. She wrote* Charge of the Goddess, *which many Wiccans adopted as the guiding principles of their faith.*

gained popularity when Gardnerian Wicca chose to include part of the first chapter in its liturgy. Since that time the book has been widely available, even though it continues to generate controversy, not least because of the presence of a sun god named Lucifer and because of Leland's own assertion in the appendix of the book that 'They [the witches] adored forbidden deities and practised forbidden deeds, inspired as much by rebellion against Society as by their own passions.' This may also be the reasoning behind 'skyclad' ceremonies, which the participants perform naked.

Above *Modern Wiccan rituals include objects such as a cauldron and broomsticks, and participants often dress in robes. These practices have traditionally been linked with witchcraft.*

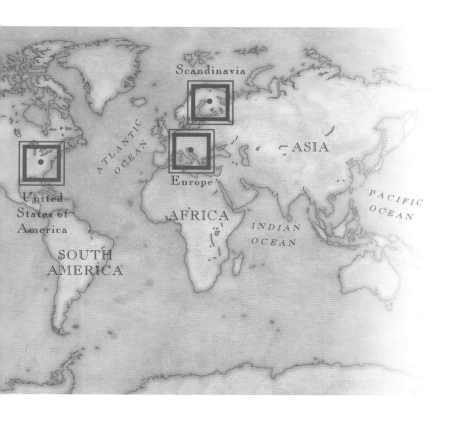

Paganism and Neo-Paganism

Although the term 'pagan' has an ancient lineage, pagan traditions today essentially revolve around nature worship and include some Druidic, Wiccan, Celtic, Fairy-faith, Goddess and shamanistic organizations. While there are many individual structures, Paganism and Neo-Paganism are movements that embody a wide variety of beliefs, and today there are also syncretisms such as 'Christian Wicca' and 'Judaeo-Paganism'.

Paganism is a confusing term for any religious movement, for it has been used by those of the Abrahamic monotheistic faiths of Christianity, Judaism and Islam to label polytheistic faiths in a pejorative way. Using their definition of pagan as any belief system that worships more than one form of divinity, even the Dharmic religions (Hinduism, Buddhism, Jainism) and Native religions in America, Australia and Japan (Shinto) would be included in the judgement. However, since the later part of the 20th century, there have been many who proudly call themselves pagans and identify with Celtic polytheistic beliefs and different forms of nature worship. Some would also lay claim to being involved in modern shamanism, pantheism or animism. Others would prefer the term 'Neo-Pagan' to describe their philosophy and worship.

THE ORIGINS OF PAGANISM

In Latin the word *paganus* literally means 'country dweller' or 'villager', and carries with it implications of peasantry and simple superstitions. When Christianity came to Britain there were many people practising various forms of folk worship, who may have been resistant to joining the new religion. It is certainly true that Christianity spread more rapidly within major cities throughout the Roman empire than in rural areas, where folk practices continued unnoticed. There is a further meaning of the word *paganus* in classical Latin: civilian or non-militant. This effectively designates pagans as those who have not joined the army of Christian soldiers.

Throughout most of the past two thousand years the term 'pagan' (both as noun and adjective) has been one of insult or accusation. The Christian writer G.K. Chesterton, eager to expose the failings in pagan thought, wrote: 'The pagan set out, with admirable sense, to enjoy himself. By the end of his civilization he had discovered that a man cannot enjoy himself and continue to enjoy anything else.' Christians have been accused by members of the Islamic faith of being pagans because of their belief in a threefold Trinity. Even within Christianity, Protestants have called Catholics pagans, due to their veneration of saints as personifications of divine qualities.

Against this background, the Neo-Pagan has picked up the wand of earlier faiths and proclaimed that Paganism is a rich and important strand in world spirituality, which has been neglected and suppressed by major religions, which have often used political and military force to erase its tradition. Paganism is re-emerging from a long, dark shadow and is no longer afraid to show its face.

HISTORY AND DEVELOPMENT

Some scholars maintain that Neo-Paganism began in the Renaissance with the reintroduction of classicism and a renewal of interest in Graeco-Roman polytheism. This was supported by literary works such as *Theologica mythologica* in 1532 and by a move towards an Arcadian style of painting in the 17th century, with artists like Nicholas Poussin. In the 18th century the reappearance of Old Norse literature and Germanic poetry led to a renewed interest in Gemanic and Scandinavian Paganism. In Germany this coincided with the Völkisch movement, which was eventually linked to nationalism. In Great Britain new forms of Druidism arose and the later part of the

19th century saw the appearance of the Hermetic Order of the Golden Dawn and, in 1904, the Ordo Templi Orientis, which sought to integrate other traditions such as the Kabbalah and ancient Egyptian beliefs.

Through the 1920s and 1930s anthropologist and Egyptologist Margaret Murray posited the idea that a pre-Christian pagan religion based around the Horned God – a form of witchcraft – had managed to survive oppression in an unbroken series of underground expressions. Although her theories were heavily criticized, they appeared to answer a thirst in British society for a form of nature religion. When Gerald Gardner joined a coven influenced by the writings of Murray, it was the start of a movement that became Wicca (see pages 162–165), an important aspect of Neo-Paganism.

Whereas the British revival continued as an independent esoteric stream, the new Germanic Paganism was absorbed into the occult ideas of the rising Nazi Party and its aim of national identity. During the Second World War, J.R.R. Tolkein, author of *The Lord of the Rings*, wrote of the abuses being perpetrated against German mythology by the Nazis and of their adoption of Neo-Pagan ideas: a 1941 letter describes Hitler's corruption of 'that noble northern spirit, a supreme contribution to Europe, which I have ever loved and tried to present in its true light'. Nevertheless pagan ideas were soon tainted, along with many other occult ideas that the Nazis sought to appropriate.

The abuses of the name of Neo-Paganism led to its decline following the Second World War, and it was not until the 1960s and 1970s that Neo-Pagan concepts – perhaps in tandem with ideas about the New Age, feminism and increasing acceptance of alternative culture – enabled the pagan movement to spread its wings in a number of new forms, including Wicca, Dianic Wicca and Reconstructionist Paganism. Now, with 30 or 40 years of free development, the Neo-Pagan movement has diversified and includes a huge variety of organizations that express specific aspects of the pagan belief system. But what are the common features that unite this disparate movement?

RITUALS AND BELIEFS

Most Neo-Pagans revere the Earth in some way, often as an expression of the Goddess, Mother Earth or 'Gaia', the Greek goddess of the Earth. As practical expressions of their faith, many practitioners are involved in action – and even activism – that is aligned to their commitment. Whether through the support of organizations that protect rainforests, seek to reduce pollution or promote organic farming, or through more direct action in the form of radical protest, Neo-Pagans are often in the vanguard when it comes to 'saving the planet'. A number of Neo-Pagans are involved in causes that espouse the better treatment of animals: veganism and vegetarianism are common among practitioners. Historically, though, many pagan traditions would have included animal sacrifice in their rituals.

Many of Neo-Paganism's 'outer' expressions may be founded on their belief system that the Earth is a living entity, an expression of the Divine, and deserves the respect of a human race that depends on the Earth's resources for its continuance. Others base their actions on mystical experiences of connection to particular energies and divinities, to which they have been exposed during specific rituals.

In Paganism, the Divine can be visualized in a number of ways. In the female world there are many goddesses who equate with the Earth: as well as Gaia, there are the Egyptian goddess Isis (see pages 48–51), the Roman goddess Diana, the Greek goddesses Artemis (see pages 52–55), Athena and Aphrodite (see pages 56–59), the Celtic Cerridwen and Bride, and many more. In the male world the gods who are evoked are the Green Man, the Horned God, the Celtic Cernunnos and the Greek Pan. Many Neo-Pagans say that one of the aspects of their faith they most cherish is its sense of respect and the equal value that it places on both genders – perhaps a veiled criticism of the orthodoxy of mainstream religions such as Christianity and Islam.

There are natural forces that can also be evoked: the elements of Fire, Earth, Air and Water and other manifestations of nature, such as certain trees and species of animals, have aspects that can be imbued through a magical process of connection and absorption. Other magical rites that are used by Neo-Pagans include the casting of spells for a range of purposes. While some critics might question the use of spells as having 'dark' motivations, pagans and those involved in witchcraft distinguish between white and black rites and look at the motivation of the practitioner. Those involved in white witchcraft follow the Wiccan Rede or advice (see page 164), which tells adherents that their first duty is to do harm to none.

Most rituals are based around the four main festivals of Imbolc (the first signs of spring), Beltane (the full growth of nature), Lughnasadh (a festival of harvest) and Samhain (the descent into winter and darkness). These are interleaved with the other four key events that make up the 'Eight Sabbats': the summer and winter solstices and spring and autumn equinoxes. The main festivals are usually celebrated on a full moon.

Neo-Pagans also have their own ceremonies and rituals for births, namings, weddings and funerals, which are in keeping with their belief systems: weddings, for instance, are called 'hand-fastings' and involve the partners entering a circle of supportive celebrants where, under the guidance of a priest and priestess, they make their mutual promises.

Left *Hand-fasting is a Neo-Pagan ceremony of marriage that can be temporary or permanent. Different groups use different traditions. This photograph was taken at a ceremony at the Avebury Stone Circle.*

Right *This relief on the Cauldron of Gundestrup shows the horned Celtic god Cernunnos. Pagan groups often evoke this deity, but male and female divinities are given equal reverence.*

THE EXTENT OF NEO-PAGANISM

For a movement that exists in such a diverse and multi-aspected form, it is hard to say exactly how many practitioners are involved in Neo-Paganism. Recent estimates say that there are as many as one million Neo-Pagans worldwide, with around 250,000 in the UK and a further 300,000 in the United States. An organization called the 'Covenant of the Goddess' conducted research in 1999 into the numbers of self-declared Neo-Pagans in the US and Canada and came to a figure of more than 750,000 adherents. It seems clear that Neo-Paganism is flourishing at a time when nature seems to be more threatened than ever before, and when spiritually-based respect for the planet's environment may be essential for our survival.

Index

Acknowledgements

PICTURE ACKNOWLEDGEMENTS

Akg-images 34, 49, 93, 95, 96, 100, 101, 105, 146, 147, 149, 169, British Library 6, 13, Hervé Champollion 79, Hilbich 77. 10-11, 12, 15 above, 18, 45, 58, Joseph Martin 56, Nimatallah 57, Jean-Louis Nou 62, Schutze/Rodemann 8/9, Bildarchiv Steffens 21, Irmgard Wagner 67; **Alamy** Edward Parker 29, Aliki Sapountzi/Aliki Image Library 113, Mehdi Chebil 120, Robert Harding Picture Library 114, David Hoffman Photo Library 168; Norma Joseph 126, The London Art Archive 128, Mary Evans Picture Library 140, Bildarchiv Monheim GmbH 148, The Print Collector 134, Hitendra Sinkar photograph 124, Chris Howes/Wild Places Photography 27, Maciej Wojtkowiak 69; **Ancient Art and Architecture Collection** S Coyne 19, Interfoto 121, R Sheridan 37, 89, 109 right; **The Art Archive** Topkapi Library Istanbul/Gianni Dagli Orti 115; **The Beinecke Rare Book and Manuscript Library, Yale University** 99; **The Bridgeman Art Library** British Museum, London, 48, 87, Private Collection/Archives Charmet 65, 97, Bibliothèque Nationale, Paris, 142, © The Trustees of the Chester Beatty Library, Dublin, Private Collection/photo © Christie's Images 70, Musée Condé, Chantilly/Giraudon 167 top, Egyptian National Museum, Cairo 84, National Museum, Aleppo/Giraudon 46, National Archaeological Museum, Athens 88, Private Collection/Ann & Bury Peerless Picture Library 118, India Office Library, London,123, Private Collection 112, 167 bottom, The Stapleton Collection 30; **Corbis** 61, 138, The Art Archive 53, 122, Yann Arthus-Bertrand 52, Bettmann 35, 145, 153, Blue Lantern Studio 111, Michael Cartier/Cordaiy Photo Library Ltd 28, Floris Leeuwenberg/The Cover Story 162, Gianni Dagli Orti 33, Andrew Fox 135, Gianni Giansanti 75, Michele Falzone/JAI 127, Catherine Cabrol/Kipa 129, Chris Knapton 132/133, Massimo Listri 22, 25, Araldo de Luca 26, Kevin Schafer 80/81, The Stapleton Collection 104, Rebecca McEntee/Sygma 165, Frederic Soltan/Sygma 63, Werner Forman 23, Roger Wood 15 bottom; **Getty Images** 31, Hulton Archive 157, 159, Jane Sweeney 44, Nico Tondini 40/41, Roger Viollet 119; **Gilgamesh Publishing** 158; **Institute for Antiquity and Christianity, Claremont, California** 98 all; **photo compliments of Linda Lappin, author of Katherine's Wish (Wordcraft of Oregon, 2008)** 160; **Mary Evans Picture Library** 83, 136, 152, Illustrated London News 141; **National Geographic Society** 155; **Scala, Florence** 47, 73, 74, BPK, Bildagentur für Kunst, Kultur und Geschichte, Berlin 20, 76, HIP 24, C M Dixon/HIP 42, Ann Ronan/HIP 85, 94, courtesy Ministero per I Beni e le Attivita Culturali 43, 59, The Metropolitan Museum of Art/Art Resource 60; **Topfoto.co.uk** 36, 161, 163, 164, HIP 78, Fortean 110, 139, Charles Walker 109 left, 143, 137; Private Collection 156; **World Religions** 66, 125.

Executive Editor Sandra Rigby
Senior Editor Lisa John
Executive Art Editor Sally Bond
Designer Elizabeth Healey
Illustrator Chuck Carter
Picture Researcher Claire Gouldstone
Senior Production Controller Simone Nauerth/Hannah Burke